G(UNDE?   URE

*The Policy Process in a
Post-Parliamentary Democracy*

Government and Administration Series
Edited by F. F. RIDLEY, *Professor of Political Theory and Institutions, University of Liverpool*

Implementation in a Bureaucracy
The Execution Process Volume 1
ANDREW DUNSIRE

Control in a Bureaucracy
The Execution Process Volume 2
ANDREW DUNSIRE

Public Administration and the Law
GAVIN DREWRY

The Government of Education
KEITH FENWICK and PETER MCBRIDE

Management in Local Government
ROYSTON GREENWOOD, C. R. HININGS, STEWART RANSON, KIERON WALSH

Policy Analysis
W. I. JENKINS

Government and Administration in Europe
edited by F. F. RIDLEY

Administration and the State
BRIAN C. SMITH and G. D. WOOD

The Politics of the Firm
LEONARD TIVEY

GOVERNING UNDER PRESSURE

The Policy Process in a Post-Parliamentary Democracy

J. J. Richardson
A. G. Jordan

MARTIN ROBERTSON

First published in 1979
and reprinted in 1981 by
Martin Robertson & Company Ltd.,
108 Cowley Road, Oxford OX4 1JF.

British Library Cataloguing in Publication Data
Richardson, J. J.
  Governing under pressure.
  − (Government and administration series)
  1. Great Britain − Politics and government −
  1964-
  I. Title   II. Jordan, A. G.   III. Series
  354.41   JN318
  ISBN 0-85520-237-8 (case)
  ISBN 0-85520-314-5 (paper)

Typeset by Santype International Ltd., Salisbury
Printed and bound by The Pitman Press, Bath

Contents

Preface   vii

SECTION I: THE POLICY FRAMEWORK

CHAPTER 1   Group Theory and Incrementalism.   3

CHAPTER 2   Central Policy-Making.   25

CHAPTER 3   The Policy Machinery.   41

SECTION II: THE POLICY PROCESS

CHAPTER 4   The Emergence of Issues and Policies.   77

CHAPTER 5   The Processing of Issues.   97

CHAPTER 6   Legislation, Decisions and the Role of Groups.   118

CHAPTER 7   Groups and the Implementation Process.   137

SECTION III: ASSESSMENT

CHAPTER 8   Pressure Groups and the Political System:
             Broader Comparative Perspectives.   157

CHAPTER 9   Costs, Benefits and Development of the
             Group System.   171

Notes and References   193

Select Bibliography   204

Index   211

Preface

This book is an attempt to describe how policies are made in contemporary Britain. The familiar framework for studying policies – examining legislative behaviour, political parties, elections – inadequately explains how key issues are managed. We see the current policy style as the balancing of group pressures. It may once have been legitimate to see the role of groups as simply articulating demands to be 'processed' in the legislative/governmental machine. Now the groups are intimately involved in decision and implementation processes. A symbiotic relationship between groups and government has developed. We of course recognise that there is not *one* policy style in any political system. Different styles will be evident at different times and in different policy areas, but we have tried to describe what we see as the dominant style of policy-making in the UK.

We have been influenced by many writers, not all of whom might recognise or welcome their ideas in our formulation. We have, however, been particularly influenced in our understanding of the pressure group and policy systems by the teaching and various works of S. E. Finer, by J. E. S. Hayward, whose writing on 'humdrum' and 'herioc' policy styles has raised fundamental questions about the way in which societies should formulate public policies, and by L. A. Gunn (who over the years has generously supplied his many papers on the nature of the policy process), whose analysis of the policy process in terms of a series of sub-processes has certainly influenced the structure of this book.

These names imply something else about our book – namely that it is an attempt to produce an account of both the pressure group system and the policy system. We recognise that trying to ride two horses at once is possibly an unwise task to attempt, but we have done so because of our belief that the group system has such a profound influence upon the nature of the policy system – the two are but different sides of the same coin. We acknowledge that this means that we have attempted to cover a wide area in what is intended as a reasonably brief introductory account. One of the strengths, we hope, of the following is that there are signposts to much material that is under used in other accounts of British policy making.

The text of the book was completed in 1978. By early 1979 the Government was under considerable pressure by a succession of major strikes. It might seem that these developments weaken our central proposition that decision-making is governed by the acceptance of 'rules of the game'. Yet there is in fact little in our account that we would wish to change. For one thing we have suggested that the area of pay negotiation is more intractable than other areas: the problem is to imbue that process with the atmosphere found in other areas. For another the pressure under which the trade union leadership finds itself is the predicted 'cost' of close involvement with the Government in earlier pay rounds. In any case, despite the crisis atmosphere we see a surprising degree of acceptance of what is or is not 'legitimate': certain kinds of 'picketing' have been limited. And, finally, how will this (or any other) Government resolve matters but by the further integration of these groups? There is in fact – despite the party rhetoric – very little disagreement between the political parties, as they both want to sit down with the CBI/TUC to work something out, and the problem is not, perhaps, with union leaders but their members. If unions and their leaders did not exist the Government would have to invent them to mediate between themselves and the public.

We wish to record our thanks to the many practitioners in several policy areas who have supplied information for the examples of group activity and policy-making cited throughout the book. We would like to thank our wives for their tolerance during the writing of this book and those who coped with our handwriting as they typed the manuscript – Pam Cotterill at Keele and Miss Findlay and Mrs Janice Gordon and others at Aberdeen. Finally we would like to thank Joan Stringer for checking the proofs.

J. J. Richardson, University of Keele
A. G. Jordan, University of Aberdeen

SECTION I:

The Policy Framework

CHAPTER 1

Group Theory and Incrementalism

GROUP THEORY

> This need to consult and persuade, to secure the support of groups who have the power to block its actions, limits policy options open to government. [Lord Croham, 1978; formerly Head of the Home Civil Service]

> All phenomena of government are phenomena of groups pressing one another, forming one another and pushing out new groups and group representatives (the organs or agencies of government) to mediate the adjustments. [A. F. Bentley, 1908[1]]

The latter quotation, taken from the most famous of the 'group theorists', Arthur Bentley, illustrates one of the two closely related themes running through this book – namely that the interplay of group pressures is the dominating feature of the policy process in Western democracies. (The other theme is that the policy process is essentially 'incremental' rather than 'rational'.) This is not, of course, to deny the importance of other factors, for example, ideology, reason and individual initiative in the policy process. But a proper understanding of the ways in which issues arrive on the political agenda (or indeed the way in which they are kept off it), the way in which policies are decided, their actual content, and subsequent implementation, can only be reached by reference to the group system.

At its purest, Bentleyism sees the group approach to the study of politics as the near perfect answer to the struggle by political scientists for *the* theory of politics. To Bentley, 'when the groups are adequately stated, everything is stated. When I say everything I mean everything. The complete description will mean the complete science, in the study of social phenomena, as in any other field.'[2] An important consequence of Bentley's approach is that policy-making is

3

characterised as a process by which an equilibrium is reached between the competing groups in society. This is not to suggest that
the group system always produces a *stable* equilibrium.

The phenomenon of compromise with powerful sectional groups,
often seen as a factor supporting the stability of political systems, can
also be seen as a factor either leading to their destruction or having
a most damaging effect on the outputs of the political system – which
in turn tends to threaten the system's stability. In fact these two
views are not necessarily in conflict. For example, Sweden and
Holland might be seen as examples of countries in which the primacy
of the group process in determining policy outcomes was well
established and recognised as having contributed to the economic
and social 'success' of those two countries for most of the period
since World War II. On the other hand, it might be argued that a
point has been reached in both those systems where the primacy of
group influence threatens the continuance of that success by preventing the introduction and implementation of essential restructuring economic policies.

Group theorists such as Bentley or Earl Latham see all policies,
however derived, as essentially a compromise between the conflicting
interests of competing groups. Public policy is seen by Latham as
the equilibrium reached in the group struggle at any point in time
and as representing '... a balance which the contending factions of
groups constantly try to weigh in their favor'.[3] Thus we might see
the wages/prices/taxation policies of the post-1974 Labour Government in Britain as the balance struck between a number of competing
interests. For example, the Trades Union Congress (TUC) has played
a crucial role in determining the nature of successive incomes policies
and in a very real sense the policies adopted by the Labour
Government have been those that the TUC and other groups in
society had either determined or were prepared to accept.[4]

Incomes policies are in fact a good example of the importance of
groups in the process not only of formulating and selecting public
policies but also of implementing public policies. For it is in the
implementation process that group influence may be at its most
effective. Increasingly, Western governments are finding difficulties
in the application of policies or decisions arrived at in a perfectly
"constitutional' manner. Perhaps the most notable British example
in the 1970s was the failure of the 1970–74 Conservative Government to achieve the successful implementation of its industrial

relations policies (preceded by the failure of the previous Labour Government to carry its own policy). This was almost entirely due to the powerful resistance of the trade union movement. The Conservatives in opposition in 1977 stated that they (a) would not attempt to reintroduce their previous industrial relations policies and (b) would not try to force an abandonment of the 'closed shop' even though they found it to be abhorrent. The reason for this important policy shift was that the Conservative leaders saw little or no prospect of being able to implement their ideas, whatever majority they achieved in a general election. The Labour Government at the same time saw no point in introducing a statutory incomes policy for the very same reason and even looked to the TUC as the guardian of the twelve-month rule for a decision on the admissibility of particular wage claims.

It is important to remember, however, that though trade union power is seen as the prime example of group power in the 1970s the difficulties over implementation are by no means confined to this category of organised pressure group. Whilst it is true that producer groups (i.e. employers and employees) are generally the most effective groups, other, newer groups have begun to impinge upon the policy process with increasing effect. Nuclear energy policy is an important area that has seen this development in a number of democracies – notably the USA, Japan, West Germany, France, Switzerland, Sweden, Austria and, to a far lesser extent, the UK. In varying degrees their governments have come up against serious difficulties in implementing their nuclear energy policies, largely because new groups have emerged in order to challenge existing decisions. Such difficulties can be seen as symptomatic of a much wider phenomenon of the emergence of a vast number of groups broadly characterised as 'environmental'. As a result, all Western governments have found the policy process more difficult to manage in areas such as airport and transport planning, urban renewal and redevelopment.

By more difficult we mean that governments were faced with new groups, often well organised and with considerable media support, having different values and beliefs and making quite new demands that conflicted with those traditionally made by established groups. In a survey of environmental groups in West Germay, commissioned by the Federal Office for the Environment, groups are reported as viewing themselves as spokesmen for interests that previously had no chance against powerful political and economic pressure groups. Governments had, therefore, to strike a balance between a more complex matrix of competing interests than hitherto. This made some options politically impossible (such as the building of a third London airport), delayed the introduction of some, or changed the choice available in a given situation.

The environmentalists illustrate the argument that the allocation of values that societies make (effectively the policies they adopt) is a reflection of the strength of particular groups at any one time.[5] Although the group theorists see public policies as statements of the balance of power between societal groups, they do not see the existing configuration of group interests as in any way fixed. Groups come and go, and those that stay may be powerful at one time or in one policy area and powerless at others. A small but significant UK example is the discussions in the early 1970s about amending the regulations governing the weight and dimension of lorries on British roads. Traditionally this issue, being highly technical, had been settled through discussions between the then Ministry of Transport and the various transport pressure groups directly involved. But once the environment had become a political issue, groups such as the Civic Trust became involved and through parliamentary and public pressure managed to secure 'consultation rights' with the new Department of the Environment. This provided a counterweight to the influence of the established transport groups. New groups had thus forced their way into that particular segment of transport policy to the disadvantage of those already 'in residence'. It is, therefore, important to bear in mind that the group 'map' in any given policy area is subject to change, as is indeed that for society as a whole.

The debate over increased child benefits in the UK in the mid 1970s is an example from another policy area of group conflict. The essence of the scheme was the removal of tax allowances for children to permit increased cash benefits to mothers. The scheme would have been of most aid to the lower paid who would lose little or no tax relief (as non-payers) and would benefit from the increased payments. In introducing his Child Benefit Bill in 1975, the Secretary of State had claimed that the Bill was supported by everyone including the trade unions. In fact, in the subsequent Cabinet-level discussions about implementation in 1976 it was realised that the Chancellor's task of minimising pay increases would be made more difficult if tax relief was removed. The Prime Minister put the issue to the TUC and six selected union leaders met privately with members of the Cabinet. Cabinet minutes for the next day stated: 'on being informed of the reduction in take-home pay, which the child benefits scheme would involve, the TUC representatives had reacted immediately and violently against its implementation, irrespective of the level of benefits which would accompany the reduction in take-home pay.' Thus, although the Act appeared to have few opponents, the eventual gradual implementation was the result of conflict between the Department of Health and Social Security (DHSS), the Treasury, the poverty lobby and the trade unions. This brief presentation of the dispute necessarily simplifies – for example, the poverty lobby's umbrella organisation, the Child Benefits Now Campaign, had several trade unions in its nineteen member organisations – but it does illustrate how the final policy choice reflects group pressures.[6]

Thus, an important factor in the government's selection of a policy option is the 'package' of interests associated with that option. The need to weigh the balance of group pressures in any given situation is neatly reflected by Mr Stan Orme, Minister for Social Security, who is quoted as saying, 'If you think your group is specially deserving, it is incumbent on you to say which groups are less deserving'.[7]

Much of what we have written so far has indicated that the vital role that groups play in the policy process makes governing more difficult. As Finer suggests, there is evidence that groups are becoming more intransigent in that they are less willing to accept even parliamentary decisions.[8] Or, as King argues, the number of acts of non-compliance with which modern governments are faced, in Britain at least, is increasing and is helping to cause governmental 'overload'.[9]

Such analyses should, however, be seen as neutral observations of the way in which political systems operate. We are not intending to convince the reader that pressure groups are either 'bad' or 'good', although it is important to note that group theorists have been criticised for taking an excessively benign view of the activity and influence of pressure groups in society. However, critics of the group theorists are in danger of rejecting the group approach as an *explanation* of the workings of the policy process because they have moral objections to the group system itself. For example, Odegard asks if the vogue for group theory reflects 'an escape from freedom and a nostalgia for neo-medieval corporate society'. He legitimately asks us whether or not Bentley's view of the process of government is 'substantially different from that described by Thrasymachus, Machiavelli and Hobbes? Does it in effect defend the principle that Might is Right?'[10] Those of us who generally accept the thesis put forward by Bentley and his followers would answer that if we examine the policy process from start to finish, then it is normally the case that the strongest and mightiest win. But we are not saying that we necessarily like or approve of this. Like W. J. M. Mackenzie, we may feel uneasy about the group system as it operates and may subscribe to the view that '... if great problems are to be handled at all it must be by a government prepared to use its majority'.[11]

However, there are many examples of group activity that would receive general approval in a moral sense and many cases of group activity that, for example, make the job of governing much easier. This is even true for the implementation stage, since it is not always the case that group activity makes implementation more difficult. Groups may even take over the implementation function as they may be more effective as policy delivery agencies than the government itself. This is particularly true in the area of social welfare where voluntary organisations, as well as regularly applying pressure on the government, also act as agencies for delivering policies to 'clients' because the government lacks the manpower or the knowhow, or is held in suspicion by the citizens it is trying to help. In other circumstances, a group may be more effective at implementing a policy because it is able to coordinate many separate and autonomous public official agencies in order to solve a particular problem. It is also undeniable that many policies, now widely accepted, would never have got on the political agenda had it not been for the activities of pressure groups.

The group theorists have in fact tried to produce a theoretical defence of the group system and the way it operates. Following Bentley, David Truman has argued that '... the behaviors that constitute the process of government cannot be adequately understood apart from the groups ... which are operative at any one point in time'.[12] But his main contribution is his attempt to demonstrate that the threat to democracy, which many critics have seen in the group system, has been exaggerated. He believes that there are at least two safeguards acting as a brake on excessive group influence.

The safeguards are (1) overlapping membership and (2) potential interest groups.

The essence of the concept of overlapping membership is that any one individual has a number of interests and is therefore likely to be a member of several groups. When he is participating in any one group he will always be aware of his other, possibly conflicting, interests and this will lead him to oppose any 'excessive' behaviour on the part of the group. The example given to illustrate the argument is that of members of a Parent–Teacher Association who, in considering policies of the Association, will be aware of the fact that some members will be Catholics, some will be members of the local chamber of commerce and others of the local taxpayers league. Thus Truman argues that 'it is the competing claims of other groups *within* a given interest group that threaten its cohesion and force it to reconcile its claims with those of other groups active in the political scene'.[13] Clearly such situations do arise and they do modify group activity, but it should be noted that the phenomenon may be more important in certain categories of groups than in others.

In certain types of groups, the central interest of members of that group may be quite sufficient to override all other interests and affiliations the members might have. For example, many would argue that the balance between producers (employers and employees) and consumers in modern industrial societies has become weighted too heavily in favour of the producers. The rise in the USA of groups such as Common Cause and Ralph Nader's Public Citizen group, who aim to protect the interests of American consumers, are an attempt to redress this imbalance. The fact that all producers are also consumers has not effectively inhibited them from pressing what are often seen as 'excessive' demands. Their interests as producers far outweigh their other interests and associational memberships.

We would, therefore, lay far less stress upon overlapping membership as a constraint on group activity than does Truman. Indeed, it is important to note that overlapping membership can equally be argued to *strengthen* group pressure in particular circumstances. In Britain, Transport 2000 is a group consisting of railway unions and environmentalists in which the combined efforts of the two groups are more effective than their individual efforts. In this case overlapping membership increases group influence rather than reduces it. Similarly, the Wing Airport Resistance Association was able to benefit from the fact that many of its members were also members of long-established groups in the area, and in many of its campaigns Friends of the Lake District utilises the contacts its members have through their membership of other pressure groups.

On the other hand, divisions *within* groups may well result in the adoption of a more moderate objective and style by the group leaders. Normally these divisions have nothing to do with overlapping membership but reflect the differing interests and opinions of the members. The wider the 'interests' a group seeks to represent, the more difficult it becomes for the group to adopt any clearly defined policy objectives. A typical example of this phenomenon is the Confederation of British Industry (CBI), where tensions exist between large and small firms. The same is true in the National Farmers' Union regarding small and large farmers. (In the USA this conflict of interests is reflected by the fact that there are several different organisations representing farming interests.) The National Union of Mineworkers in Britain is habitually split by the differing ideologies of the 'moderates' and the 'militants' and by differing objectives from one coalfield to another.

So, while we de-emphasise the importance of overlapping membership as such, it is important to note the considerable importance of internal group politics in determining group behaviour as a whole. Many instances of group activity can therefore be fully understood only by reference to the group leaders' need to maintain internal cohesion rather than their desire to influence public policies. In some cases leaders may well adopt tactics that they consider to be quite counter-productive in terms of achieving desired public policies but that are forced upon them by the need to demonstrate to their own membership that the leaders are active – 'doing something' – on their members' behalf.

Truman's second category of 'restraint' – the phenomenon of potential groups – is in reality a much more effective moderating influence on group behaviour than the phenomenon of overlapping membership. As indicated earlier, observers such as Latham have described public policies as the outcomes of the group struggle. Truman argues that any mutual interest or shared attitude is a *potential* group. If existing organised groups behave in such a way as to seriously threaten the interests of these potential groups, then new organised pressure groups will emerge. Countless examples abound. In particular, the emergence of numerous environmental groups in all Western democracies (and indeed in some totalitarian states) referred to on page 5 indicates a potential interest being transferred into active organised form in order to challenge the influence of long-established groups. We are all familiar with the emergence of 'defence' groups when a local beauty spot or cherished local building is threatened by a new development.

In fact this phenomenon has been so widespread internationally that a wide range of procedures for accommodating these new groups has had to be devised. The activity of these new groups has thus not only challenged the existing distribution of power amongst established groups but has also forced changes in the policy-making process itself. Indeed, many environmental groups have seen changes in the processes by which decisions are reached by governments and other public authorities as a primary objective, so that they stand a greater chance of ultimately changing the policies themselves. They have seen existing procedures as favouring established groups. One might argue that 'environmentalists' remained unorganised as long as physical and technical developments were not too damaging (or because 'the environmentalists' were preoccupied with other policy issues). When those interests pressing scientific and other developments went 'too far' (according to the perceptions of those members of society who were 'interested' in the environment), then people were moved to organise themselves into pressure groups in order to halt, reverse or change developments. A very simple example of this was the 'battle of the elms' in Stockholm. A stand of elms in one of Stockholm's famous city centre squares was threatened by a proposed new underground station. This development prompted the formation of a group to fight the decision (as it turned out, successfully). The National Coal Board's plan to mine coal in the Vale of Belvoir in England likewise prompted the formation of a pressure group to defend the Vale. Similarly, the very success of the Abortion Law Reform Association in Britain in the 1960s prompted the formation of a counter group, the Society for the Protection of the Unborn Child.

Truman sees the mere *threat* of the transformation from potential to organised group as a guarantee that such interests will be taken into account. This is certainly true in the environmental field where developers are now much more cautious and constrained because they are aware that if they are *too* successful they will soon be faced with a vociferous and troublesome preservationist group. Even the trade unions ultimately face this threat, despite their tremendous advantages in an integrated and technological society, as some electricity power workers discovered in 1977 when public hostility was vented on the strikers and their families. A more common response to trade union power in the UK has been for an increasing number of existing groups to adopt trade union type tactics in order to achieve their policy objectives. If tactics hitherto seen as illegitimate are used with success, then other groups will soon adopt them too. Another development is the drift of white collar workers into the TUC. Once the TUC was seen to be very influential in settling pay, prices and taxation policies in the UK, in that a 'social contract' agreed between the Government and the TUC was applied to everyone, whether or not his union was affiliated to the TUC, then the white collar groups also decided to become the 'ins' on the principle that 'if you can't beat them then join them.' The long-term consequence of this trend, of course, is possibly to undermine the effectiveness of the TUC because it will find it increasingly difficult to represent manual and non-manual, skilled and unskilled workers at the same time.

So the unions, it might be argued, will suffer the same fate as the employers. Just as activity by employers forced workers to organise in order to defend themselves, so the activity of trade unions, if it did become 'excessive', will either activate potential groups in society or lead existing groups to behave in such a way as to negate the success of the unions. Truman, in emphasising the importance of potential groups, introduces another concept, that of the 'rules of the game'. As an example of what he means by this, he cites '... the value generally attached to the dignity of the individual human being, loosely expressed in terms of fair dealing, or more explicitly verbalized in formulations such as the Bill of Rights'.[14] If existing organised groups violate these rules of the game, this will both cause tensions within the group itself and cause it to lose status with the community at large. The firemen's union in Britain in 1977 had to make a fine and difficult calculation when going on strike against the Government's pay policy as to whether the extra deaths that might result from the strike would alienate public opinion and thus strengthen the hand of the Government in the battle.

In discussing the various restraining mechanisms on 'excessive' group activity, we have so far not stressed what is perhaps the most important restraint of all. This is the fact that in developed societies most long-term interests are already organised. If a group of citizens have a common interest and see governmental action as either threatening or promising benefits, they are likely to become organised into a pressure group. So any given policy area in a developed society will already be populated by a range of groups, each trying to manipulate that policy area to its advantage. In other words, some *competition* will normally exist. This can take a number of forms. For example, there may be several groups competing for the same membership (as in US agriculture).

More important as a restraining mechanism is the direct opposition of one group by another. Abortion reform is a case in point. In terms of Britain's membership of the EEC, the pro-membership groups were opposed by the anti-EEC groups and indeed both were financed by the state during the EEC referendum. As the TUC presses for its own policies regarding the use of North Sea oil revenues, so the CBI presents a set of counter proposals.

So as a group turns one corner, it is met by another group going in the opposite direction. The result of the ensuing crash depends upon the circumstances of the time and the strengths of the two groups. Sometimes one wins, sometimes the other wins, and sometimes the result is that no policy change is possible at all. The status quo is maintained because to depart from it will disturb the position of one of the groups. This situation has typified the rather half-hearted attempts to coordinate transport in the UK. Rail unions have tended to favour coordination of transport because they see it as a means of increasing transport of goods and passengers by rail. On the other hand, unions representing lorry drivers, though not attacking the concept of coordination, have never been willing to support coordination policies because such policies might reduce earnings in road transport. They are supported in this view by their fellow producers – the road haulage owners. So transport coordination remains a case of the irresistible force meeting the immovable object and no policy change results.

Group competition, of course, is by no means a case of perfect competition. Just as in economics, 'perfect competition' rarely exists except in theory. In practice, we have at best an oligopolistic situation and at worst a monopolistic situation.[15] In other words, groups attempt to manipulate the market in their favour. But they rarely succeed in achieving total control of the market (in our case total control of a particular policy area) for very long, for the reasons outlined above. More importantly, just as monopolistic firms are ultimately faced by governmental action in the form of anti-trust laws and anti-trust agencies, so monopolistic pressure groups are also faced by the government. This is not to suggest that, because we have governments, monopolistic groups are controlled effectively, just as anti-trust laws do not always effectively control monpolies and restrictive practices. But it does mean that usually the monopoly group is at least faced with some kind of contest, if only because the government generally feels it necessary to represent a rather wider membership than any given group or set of groups.

On the other hand, groups do try to capture or colonise the government of the day (a phenomenon discussed in more detail in chapter 5). Even when the government has not been captured, for that particular policy issue, the contest may be unequal. As Finer argues, the government has certain strengths and weaknesses, and groups have certain strengths and weaknesses.[16] The government has a monopoly of force, it has greater legitimacy, because it has been elected, and it can often manipulate a broader spectrum of events than can groups.

In our advanced technological and integrated society, groups have come to possess very considerable sanctions that they can use against the government. So in a sense the struggle between the government on the one hand and groups on the other becomes more equally balanced as societies develop. As Anthony King suggests in discussing the miners' strike of 1974, '... government had ceased to be the authoritative allocator of values for society and had become merely one participant, albeit a powerful one, in a complex process of bargaining...' He concludes that the state in the UK and possibly other Western countries, will become '... merely one among a number of contenders for wealth, power and influence, the others including large companies, trade unions and their members, foreign companies, foreign governments, international organizations'.[17]

It will be appreciated that if we generally accept these descriptions of political life in the 1970s then there are important implications for the meaning of the term 'pressure group'. If we see the policy process as increasingly a struggle between competing groups and between groups and the government, then it becomes difficult to make a clear theoretical distinction between the government on the one hand and groups on the other. Indeed Finer seems to be implying that the distinction to be drawn is through a 'checklist' of differing strengths and weaknesses, which does not necessarily mean that the government is always 'on top'. This view is rather similar to that of Latham, who considers that the apparatus of the state exhibits many of the characteristics of groups outside the structure of government. He concedes that governmental institutions are often in a privileged position vis-à-vis non-governmental groups but argues that what he calls 'governmental groups' are distinguished from what we normally regard as pressure groups 'only in the characteristic of officiality. The designation "official" is the sign manifest that the bearer is authorized by social understanding to exercise against all groups and individuals certain powers which they may not exercise against him.'[18] So to Latham the only real difference between the institutions of government and private pressure groups is the 'officiality' of the former.

The view of governmental institutions as themselves pressure groups will be discussed in chapter 2, where are deal with the way in which Whitehall departments in the UK compete with each other because of their differing policy objectives arising from their differing interests. In other words, it is possible to detect departmental pluralism within governments and agencies. Bureaucracies should be seen as having their own interests, just as members of the British Medical Association have their interests, which they will pursue with whatever means are available to them.[19] In this sense there is no distinction in principle to be made between *internal* government 'demands' arising because a particular department is pressing its own interest and external 'pressure group demands' from bodies such as the National Farmers' Union. We need look no further for the proof of this view than the well-documented reports of the Treasury attempting to impose its policies on (a) other government departments, (b) the Cabinet and (c) groups outside government.

The view of government as just another group, even if it is an accurate description of how the policy process actually operates, is a disturbing conclusion. But it has also raised theoretical objections from critics of the group theory approach. Odegard, for example, argues that this very broad definition of group leads us to a meaningless statement: '... when Congress and the Courts and the President and all other institutions and aggregations... are defined as interest groups, the term becomes synonymous not merely with politics but with human life itself.'[20] (In fact it may, as Eckstein suggests, be wrong to describe the group approach as a *theory* at all in that it may not be an *explanation* of the political process.[21] However, by adopting the group approach, our attention is drawn to the real forces at work in the political process.) But some group theorists, though denying that their view of the political process leads to a meaningless statement, certainly would not deny that human life *is* characterised by the interplay of group forces. Gumplowicz, an early group theorist writing at the end of the last century, claimed that the social process thoughout history 'has consisted in the relations and reciprocal actions between heterogeneous social groups'.[22] Similarly, Marxists will readily recognise the principles behind the group theory approach. Rather interestingly, writers discussing the pressure group system in the Soviet Union implicitly accept Latham's definition of pressure group. Most of the 'groups' described are official or semi-official agencies.

But is it necessary to accept Latham's very wide and, to some, sloppy, definition of a group in order to be an advocate of the group theory approach? In fact not. Throughout the rest of the book we shall continue to use 'pressure group' in the commonly accepted sense of the word: any group that '... articulates a demand that the authorities in the political system or sub-systems, should make an authoritative allocation',[23] or, to quote Finer's pioneering definition of what he chooses to term 'the lobby', 'The sum of organizations in so far as they are occupied at any point in time trying to influence the policy of public bodies in their chosen direction, though (unlike political parties) never themselves prepared to undertake the direct government of the country'.[24]

Even this conventional definition of pressure group should be regarded as fairly broad. For example, though in using the term 'pressure group' or 'lobby' we tend to think of associations of individuals or associations of organisations, we should also note that organisations such as companies are acting as pressure groups all the time. Thus the Ford Motor Company is in constant touch with the British government and the number of meetings each year between Ford and the government runs into thousands: as a major motor manufacturer it has regular dealings with the Department of Transport and the Department of the Environment; as a supplier of vehicles it has dealings with various government departments; as a major employer it is in regular contact with the Department of Employment; and as a major industrial company it is in close touch with the Department of Energy. In other words, the Ford Motor Company is as much a pressure group as the British Medical Association or the Abortion Law Reform Association.

A common distinction between a political party and a pressure group is that a political party is interested in assuming governmental responsibilities over a wide range of issues, whereas a pressure group seeks to further a far narrower range of issues and does not wish to become the government. Empirically there are problems with this distinction. Is the Scottish National Party really interested in forming a separate government or is it merely furthering particular interests in the UK context? Or, if one accepts that its intentions are governmental, is its actual role that of a pressure group?

With our broad interpretation of the 'pressure group' term, we would argue that parties themselves are a forum for group struggles – and no profound satisfactory distinction can be made between party and group. For example, within the Conservative party in the late 1970s there were definite strands of opinion about matters such as pay policy and industrial relations. On devolution, a group of over forty Tory backbenchers formed the unofficial Union Flag group, which attempted to make the party leadership far less ambiguous on devolution. During discussion of the committee stage of the Scotland and Wales Bill, the Union Flag group put down 338 amendments while the backbench put down only forty-five – and Conservative devolutionists put down ten. In the run-up to the 1979 election, the Labour party equivocated on whether or not to make anti-blood sports one of the main items on the manifesto. This 'to-ing' and 'fro-ing' can easily be interpreted as the shifting fortunes of various groups within the party.

As a further definitional exercise we shall be accepting the conventional distinction between *sectional* and *promotional* groups. *Sectional* pressure groups seek to protect the interests of a particular section of society, while *promotional* groups seek to promote causes arising from a given set of attitudes.[25] Furthermore, we do accept the general thesis of Bentley, Latham, *et al.*, that the governmental *process* is fairly accurately characterised by the group process model. Thus, as this book is essentially processual in its approach, we shall be viewing the government (and various official agencies) as a 'group actor' in the same sense that we view the CBI and TUC as group actors in the policy process. In doing so, we make no claim to be the inventors of this approach. Others have already trodden the path.

For example, Stein Rokkan, in discussing numerical democracy and corporate pluralism in Norway, has observed that the Norwegian government can 'rarely, if ever, force through decisions on the basis of its electoral power but has to temper its policies in complex consultations and bargains with the major interest organisations'.[26]

POLICY-MAKING MODELS

If, as we have argued, groups play a central role in the various stages of the policy process, then what are the implications of this for the *style* of policy-making that political systems exhibit? Many theories of policy-making have been developed, but they have been conventionally grouped under two main headings: 'incremental' and 'rational'. Discussion of these models tends to present them as alternatives, and Herbert Simon (of the rational school) and Charles Lindblom (of the incremental) are usually regarded as the extremes on some theoretical continuum. In contrast, we choose to emphasise the remarkable agreement between both approaches on the description of how policies are actually made. The 'rationalists' might wish to change the policy-making process, but their description of existing practices is at times very near to that offered by Lindblom, Wildavsky and other incrementalists. The second theme of this chapter is then that policy-making in Britain can be described as 'incremental'.

Earlier we noted that with group theory there is a tendency for recognition of the explanatory value of the theory to be confused with uncritical approval of its consequences. So it is with incrementalism. A distinction between its descriptive and normative aspects must be made. Other parallels can be drawn between the group and incremental approaches. In their original sources they share what often appears as a deliberately provocative style of exposition. This common feature can probably be accounted for by their similar purposes. Each was developed as a debunking exercise to counter a ruling orthodoxy. Group theory was developed to question a legalistic and institutional tradition in political sciences; incrementalism was developed as an alternative to what Lindblom refers to as 'conventional' decision-making theory.

Rational model

Our brief account of rational policy-making models is primarily to provide a contrast with what we see as the more useful descriptive incremental model.[27] There is, however, a second reason for examining models of rationality. While rational models may have had little or no impact on how policies have actually been made, the concept of rationality has actively influenced a whole range of attempts, particularly in the USA and UK, to improve the quality of the policy-making system. Policy-makers have become aware of the weaknesses of the policy machinery and have therefore looked for ways of improving the processes and institutions of policy-making. We discuss some of these attempts in chapter 2, but it is important to note that there may be a fundamental conflict between a system that stresses the accommodation of group demands and a system of policy-making that stresses rationality in some objective sense.

The concept of rationality adopted by policy-makers in various governmental reforms was based on an intuitive and simple commonsense view of rationality rather than on the more refined concept of rationality as devised by, for example, Herbert Simon. Thus, if one looks at the rationality implied in experiments such as Programme Budgeting or Corporate Management, one can discern that the (implicit) rational approach is along the lines of the 'so-called rational' scheme, which was described by the incrementalist Lindblom as follows:

So-called rational model
1. Faced with a given problem
2. a rational man first clarifies his goals, values, or objectives and then ranks or otherwise organizes them in his mind;
3. he then lists all important possible ways of – policies for – achieving his goals
4. and investigates all the important consequences that would follow from each of the alternative policies,
5. at which point he is in a position to compare consequences of each policy with goals
6. and so choose the policy with consequences most closely matching his goals.[28]

Lindblom, of course, rejected this pattern as being impractical: he is unconvinced that it is possible to perform operations such as clarifying goals, values and objectives and ranking them, or listing all important ways of achieving goals. However Lindblom's so-called 'rationality' model is akin to the means–end model whose weaknesses were earlier identified by Simon.[29] The means–end model also involves selecting appropriate means to each desired end. For Simon, such a conception of decision-making has limitations, and accordingly he claims that many arguments of 'the ends justify the means' type are futile because the means employed involve value questions. He makes his point by arguing that the *means* involved in enforcing Prohibition in the United States involved questions of personal liberty, proper police methods, etc. and these value questions soon overshadowed the 'ultimate' objective of temperance. Accordingly, Simon is essentially in sympathy with Lindblom in rejecting Lindblom's form of commonsense 'so-called rationality' outlined above. For example, he discusses the triangle of limits. By this he means that rationality, in practice, is bounded by the individual's unconscious skills, habits and reflexes; he is limited by his values and conceptions of purpose and by the extent of his knowledge and information. Simon, rejecting the means–end distinction, constructs a preferred model of rational behaviour in decision-making. This rests instead on consideration of available alternatives and their consequences. In this approach the task of decision-making is seen to involve three principle steps.

Behaviour Alternatives Model (BAM)
1. The listing of *all* the alternative strategies;
2. The determination of all the consequences that follow upon each of these strategies;
3. The comparative evaluation of these sets of consequences.[30]

Where Simon does differ from Lindblom and his colleagues is that he views the rationality implied in the Behaviour Alternatives Model as something worth pursuing – whereas Lindblom would argue that to engage in even such a limited exercise is to indulge in dangerous pseudo-rationality. We would add that to attempt something like BAM is in effect to challenge the group system. It may be possible, but it will lead to a lot of conflict. But again one must stress that Simon was very much aware of the gulf between the ideal of BAM and the necessary limitations of actual behaviour. For example, Simon has no sooner described BAM than he goes on to qualify it as follows; 'It is obviously impossible for the individual to know *all* his alternatives or *all* their consequences, and this impossibility is a very important departure of actual behavior from the model of objective rationality.'

As an observer of how decisions are made, Simon recognises the utility of the *satisficing* idea – that decision makers examine options until something satisfactory (probably less than the optimum) is discovered. If nothing satisfactory is found, the level of aspiration will be reduced until eventually what is desired matches what is available in policy terms. Simon, the observer, is much closer to Lindblom than he is often portrayed.[31]

Incrementalism – Charles Lindblom

As hinted above, the main difference between Simon and Lindblom lies in their attitude to the practices they observe. For Lindblom, 'muddling through' or 'incrementalism' are processes to be commended and not condemned. Lindblom has aided his many interpreters by conveniently contrasting the main features of his 'incremental' or Successive Limited Comparison (SLC) approaches with his version of 'conventional' rationality. (It is perhaps worth stressing that the 'conventional' rationality against which Lindblom reacts is not the rationality advocated by Simon. On the contrary, it is closer to the means–end formulation also criticised by Simon.)

Rational comprehensive model	*Successive limited comparison model*
– clarification of values or objectives distinct from and usually prerequisite to empirical analysis of alternative policies.	– selection of value goals and empirical analysis of the needed action are not distinct from one another but are closely entwined.
– policy formulation is therefore approached through means–end analysis; first the ends are isolated, then the means to achieve them are sought.	– since means and ends are not distinct, means–end analysis is often inappropriate or limited.
– the test of a good policy is that it can be shown to be the more appropriate means to desired ends.	– the test of a good policy is typically that various analysts find themselves agreeing on a policy (without their agreeing that it is the most appropriate means to an agreed objective).

| – analysis is comprehensive; every relevant factor is taken into account. | – analysis is drastically limited;
 (a) important possible outcomes are neglected;
 (b) important potential policies are neglected;
 (c) important affected values are neglected; |
| – theory is often heavily relied upon. | – a succession of comparisons greatly reduces or eliminates reliance on theory.[32] |

Lindblom argues that only a narrow range of possibilities is in practice seriously considered. The process of policy-making is one of selecting between the (comparatively) few alternatives that suggest themselves. In comparing these limited numbers of alternatives one does not dwell overlong on values or goals; instead one starts from the problem and considers a manageable range of alternatives. In choosing which option to adopt, one has reference to values, but (as in Simon's Behaviour Alternatives Model) the choice of policy instrument is combined with the ranking of values. In this approach there is a tendency for policy innovations to be small-scale extensions of past efforts with an expectation that there will be a constant return to the problem to make further extensions and to reconsider the problem in the light of new data, etc. In other words, successive limited comparisons – hence the SLC acronym.

The SLC concept leads on to another, which has even more direct connection with our interest in the role of groups in the policy process – that of Partisan Mutual Adjustment (PMA).[33] One of the ideas underpinning SLC is that *policy-making involves achieving agreement between groups*. This is one of the reasons for avoiding a preliminary insistence on clarification of values or objectives – the probability of harmony at that stage is low. There is more chance of agreement on a specific proposal than there is of agreement on objectives. For example, the 'devolution' cause in Britain was supported by groups with very different – even incompatible – motivations and intentions. Some groups saw devolution as a step towards independence; others saw it as a means of *preventing* independence. The best policy is one that gains agreement. This emphasis on accommodation between groups explains why decision-making takes the form of comparison between pragmatic available alternatives. There is also an economy of effort principle at work.

If agreement is sought it is unrealistic to consider too radical proposals as they are unlikely to have wide enough attractions for the
various interests. This encourages only relatively minor changes to
be put on the agenda. Discussion among varieties of minor incre-
ment is thus the realistic scope of consideration. Such limited
alternatives also have two other benefits (other than realism).

The first of these is that consideration of a number of specific
options is an intellectually manageable operation. It is possible to
give reasonable attention to restricted options, but if the whole range
of alternatives and the whole package of past agreements is open (as
the conventional rationalists would prefer) then the scope is too
demanding: the task is impossible. Thus there is an economy of effort
involved in looking at the margins, where one reasonably expects
the end-choice will come from. But, further, one looks at only the
margins because, it is argued, one can only sensibly consider a
relatively few possibilities. The third ingredient in this series of
mutually reinforcing points is that what has been agreed in the
past – what is the base – is not itself an arbitrary position but
represents a negotiated balance. Current negotiations presumably
involve similar interests, conflicts over values, preferences and
demands, and accordingly it is likely that any current agreement
will differ only marginally from the previous position, unless of
course the balance of group power has shifted. This is an extension
of the first point, but whereas that claimed agreement was almost
certain to be only marginally different from what went before, and
therefore there was little profit in looking at too radical options,
this extension suggests that what was agreed before was probably
a tolerably close approximation of the most satisfactory solution that
is obtainable.

Lindblom describes how policy is evolved in this system as
follows:

> In the United States, for example, no part of government
> attempts a comprehensive overview of policy on income dis-
> tribution. A policy nonetheless evolves, and one responding
> to a wide variety of interests. A process of mutual adjustment
> among farm groups, labor unions, municipalities and school
> boards, tax authorities and government agencies with responsi-
> bilities in the fields of housing, health, highways, national parks,
> fire and police accomplishes a distribution of income in which
> particular income problems neglected at one point in the deci-
> sion processes become central in another point.[34]

Lindblom is not always content to sound so close to Truman, Bentley and the others we have considered in the earlier part of this chapter. For example, in *The Intelligence of Democracy*, in which the concept of PMA is most fully developed, Lindblom takes pains to distinguish his position from that of Bentley, Truman, Latham, Herring, *et al.*[35] The 'fit' between incrementalism and group theory is then inexact, but in some ways the amendments Lindblom would make to group theory suit our preferred version of group theory. For example, he considers Latham is too conservative in presenting the legislature as a 'referee' of the group struggle. He claims: 'In fact, however, governmental participants in mutual adjustment often play no less an entrepreneurial or activating role than do private group leaders.'[36] In other areas Lindblom is considering possibilities neglected by group theorists – e.g. that rationality might best be produced by the interaction of groups. But while the group and the incremental theories are not wholly in harmony (and nor are individual versions of the same 'schools'), we feel confident that they are sufficiently in sympathy in broad terms to be twin starting points for an understanding of how policies are determined. In our view, Lindblom's model of the policy process most accurately describes what actually happens. This is because groups are closely integrated in the process and this in turn usually leads to an incremental style of policy-making.

CHAPTER 2

Central Policy-Making

INTRODUCTION

As indicated in chapter 1, we see advantages in using the term 'pressure group' fairly broadly. For example, we see 'official' organisations and agencies (such as government departments, nationalised industries, etc.) as behaving in almost exactly the same way as more conventional 'external' pressure groups such as the CBI. Central government departments, whilst often being the target of external pressure groups, are also playing pressure group roles themselves. By concentrating on the policy process, we begin to see just how much political activity is that of 'pressure groups' in this broad sense. In this chapter, we draw attention to the internal divisions within government itself and stress the degree to which 'government' is plural and not singular. Policies are the outcome of departmental conflict within government as well as the result of pressures on the government from outside. The process of departmental conflict and its resolution is yet another factor leading to incremental policy adjustments. It is therefore important to understand the nature of the central bureaucracy and its role in the policy process. In recent years studies have substantially altered our image of how the centre operates.[1] Discussion of how pressure groups relate to the centre appears to have been slow to acknowledge this more sophisticated understanding of how decisions are made there.

TRADITIONAL CRITICISMS OF CENTRAL POLICY-MAKING

It is sometimes claimed that changes in the machinery of government that have taken place have not really been an attempt to destroy one game and replace it by another with a different set of rules.[2] We argue, however, that it is more useful to view the many changes of the 1960s and 1970s as precisely such an attempt. Indeed, one of the permanent secretaries behind the changes in machinery and methods has described them as a 'revolution'.[3] The revolution may be flawed, even failed, but it was attempted.

The deficiencies in the old rules have been repeatedly described since World War I. The starting point is usually an implicit or explicit concept of the Cabinet. This holds that the Cabinet exists to act as a jury sitting to assess policy options – on the basis of shared political attitudes and priorities. Such a view was held by Barbara Castle before experience as a Cabinet minister persuaded her otherwise.[4] Before joining the Labour Cabinet in 1964 she believed that 'cabinets were groups of politicians who met together and said, these are the policies we are elected on, now what will be our political priorities? And they would reach certain political decisions and then would refer those decisions to an official committee to work out the administrative implications of what they had decided.' After entering the Cabinet she soon realised the naivety of this view; '... I suddenly found I wasn't in a political caucus at all. I was faced by departmental enemies.'

The main criticism of the system of central policy-making is therefore that policy is made through a process of departmental pluralism. Crossman describes one of many similar Cabinet meetings as follows: 'We come briefed by our Departments to fight for our departmental budgets, not as Cabinet Ministers with a Cabinet view. Even Tony Crosland – I suppose because his education estimates were at stake – displayed a completely defeatist departmentalism.'[5] Crossman also describes how the Cabinet (non) reaction to the likely Soviet intervention in Czechoslovakia was determined by departmental interests:

> ... all the departmental Ministers intervene on the side of prudence. The Board of Trade, of course, is concerned to get the ban on strategic materials reduced and to see that there are no upsets in our improved trade relations with the USSR. Wedgy Benn is almost entirely concerned with the sale of computers to Russians. All my colleagues have their departmental interests in economic relations with Russia and that takes the edge off any conviction that we are in any sense prepared to stand by the Czechs.[6]

Departments are characteristically in *competition* in policy-making. There are battles over administrative territory (for example, local government, the Department of Education and the Manpower Services Commission were all involved in 1977 in a struggle over control of the Youth Opportunities Programme), but more importantly departments are in conflict over obtaining resources. At Cabinet level, those ministers with departmental responsibilities appear to view their pre-eminent task as the representation of that department (and often its associated clientele). Even Margaret Thatcher, who began her tenure in 1970 as Minister for Education with a reputation for favouring spending cuts, was one year later citing increased spending as an index of success. 'I have', she said, 'done everything possible to show my confidence in the future of higher education. In my monthly battles with the Treasury, I managed to get another £76 million for student grants and last week announced the biggest ever development programme for further education and polytechnics.'[7] A final example might be to contrast the attitude of Peter (now Lord) Thorneycroft, who resigned as Chancellor in 1958 because his Cabinet colleagues insisted on what he regarded as excessive government expenditure. Two years later he returned to the Government as Minister of Aviation and he became an advocate of Concorde. He later explained his enthusiasm in these terms:

> Was I an enthusiast? That's a good question. You're put at the head of a great Ministry and you do get caught up with the thrill. You are the one hope your chaps have, and you have all the skills of argument. Part of your duty is to put the case for the thing. There are plenty of people to put the opposite case. And in the end you do tend to become sold on it yourself.[8]

At the very minimum, ministers tend not to be impartial in judging between the claims of departments for resources. Increased allocation for his (or her) department indicates political power and abilities, establishes a personal reputation and impresses client groups. Partly, departmental pluralism derives from the adopting by ministers of this advocacy role and it has been a recurring theme in prescriptions to improve the Cabinet that those Cabinet ministers allocating resources should (as far as possible) not be representing particular departmental interests. The best-known example of this idea was that of L. S. Amery who advocated a 'policy cabinet' consisting of six or seven ministers free from departmental duties.

Departmental pluralism is seen as emerging not only because ministers consciously choose and prefer the advocate role, but also because under pressure of work they can do no more than deal with their own department. For example, in the 1950s Harold Macmillan used to deal with his housing files during Cabinet discussion of topics such as Europe.[9] Again, Crossman provides innumerable illustrations. Thus he reports that in November 1964 it was a journalist who warned him that the Government was heading straight for devaluation.[10] Crossman says that this made him come out of his departmental seclusion for the first time since he had been appointed. He also relates how for once he decided to participate in a discussion on Vietnam – but to do so in an informed fashion meant that he had to neglect his departmental red boxes for a weekend.[11]

Some would argue that there is something sinister in the way that ministers adopt the departmental view. It has been claimed that in the 1960s every Foreign Office minister, without exception, endorsed the departmental strategy on European entry, even though two at least – Michael Stewart and George Thomson – took office resolutely opposed to it. Each of the ministers primarily concerned with relations with the EEC – Edward Heath, Michael Stewart, George Thomson, above all George Brown – swiftly accepted that the departmental tactics (of isolating France and relying on the 'friendly five', and particularly Germany) were shrewd and correct.[12] Similarly, Treasury ministers are often accused of having adopted Treasury orthodoxy. The phenomenon, though, is probably not one of departmental brainwashing of their minister, but that minister and department working together begin to share priorities and expectations. Working full time on the problem of, say, the Health Service it is difficult not to believe that the needs there are more pressing than in, say, motorway construction or agriculture. Ministers adapt themselves to the departmental line not necessarily because that is their easiest option, but because the evidence that convinced the department will look very similar to a minister viewing the case from the same perspective. There is also a question of time. Ministers cannot master all the policy issues covered by a department; their personal impact can be effective on only a few issues, and otherwise they must act as spokesman.

The second source of departmental pluralism is then the overloading of ministers who find it difficult enough to absorb and articulate departmental problems without concerning themselves in other areas. This has led to recommendations to simplify the departmental structure. The argument has been made on several occasions that the pattern of departments had evolved in piecemeal fashion as a series of ad hoc responses to crises and that a simpler pattern would lead to fewer viewpoints needing representation in the Cabinet and less interdepartmental coordination. Each major problem would have one (and only one) department. This would allow the Cabinet time to stand back and examine alternative policies.

The traditional criticism of the centre of government is therefore that policy is made through the competition of departments and ministers rather than through the imposition of consistent priorities by a team of political leaders. The 'rational' allocation of priorities is frustrated because departmental boundaries do not correspond to problem boundaries and this defective structure produces time-consuming negotiations that prevent rational analysis. The image of clashing departmental interests is not unique to Britain. It is the starting point for many discussions of policy-making in the United States, but it is perhaps the more novel in Britain where the conventional wisdom has been of a socially and organisationally homogeneous Civil Service. The situation is perhaps akin to the 'discovery' of British pressure groups in the 1950s.

DEPARTMENTS AND THEIR PARTNERS

The rest of this chapter deals with the responses to the situation we have described. It was felt that there had to be a better way of policy-making than making messy trade-offs. From the Report of the Plowden Committee in 1961 (Cmnd. 1432) onwards, a series of experiments took place. These can usefully be regarded as an attempt to replace an essentially incrementalist system with a rationalist style of policy-making. But the above description in this chapter also seeks to provide the background for a different theme. The evidence would seem sufficient to sustain the generalisation that departments themselves are competing groups. There is competition for administrative territory, competition with the Treasury for resources, competition for legislative time and priority. Understanding the divided nature of the centre and the manner in which policy is handled permits the crucial understanding that pressure groups can be – and we would go as far as to say often are – allies of departments. Ministers and their associated pressure groups often conflict over details of policy, but generally they share a commitment to greater resources for that policy area. This simplification needs qualification, but the starting point for a description of the relationship between ministers, departments and pressure groups is to appreciate their common concerns.

For example, a press release from the Country Landowners' Association (CLA) in May 1976 congratulated the Minister of Agriculture on persuading his Cabinet colleagues not to accept the Layfield Committee's reasoning in favour of the rating of agricultural land and buildings. In other words, the Minister was not the target of CLA pressure, but was a spokesman for their interests. The language used by Lord Boyle (former Education Minister) is revealing: 'The most important single role [of the Department of Education and Science] is fighting for resources'; 'The Ministry of Education wants to be *the* sponsoring Department'; 'The Department has to fight for more resources for the educational priority area'.[13] This importance of the minister as spokesman was shown by the concern of the president of the British Legion when the Minister of Pensions was succeeded by a Minister of Pensions and National Insurance. When they had had their 'own' minister, he acted as an advocate for them with government. It was feared that the new minister would be 'trammelled by responsibility for vast numbers of other people who are not ex-Service people', and that 'his single minded advocacy' would no longer be at the Legion's disposal.[14]

A more recent example comes from Crossman, while he was Secretary of State for Health and Social Services. The doctors had been adopting what he thought was an aggressive style about which he complained, telling them that he could not be their sponsor and look after them if without warning they slapped down an ultimatum. How could he possibly represent them if they behaved in this way?[15] Examples are indeed difficult to avoid! One Saturday afternoon in early 1978, in an interview on the BBC sports programme 'Grandstand', the Minister for Sport used the occasion to plead for more public pressure on him for increased spending on sport. He explained that the reason the Arts Council received disproportionately more than the Sports Council was because its minister was the subject of articulate and informed pressure. He could use this type of overt public concern in arguments over spending.

Public failure to recognise this reality of ministers and pressure groups in partnership often means that ministers are unfairly abused. For example, during the politicking over the Water Act 1973, Peter Walker, as Secretary of State at the DOE, was attacked in the press for being indecisive in failing to come to a decision over the future of land drainage. In reality he himself had come to a decision very early in the process – but he was unable to get agreement within Whitehall. It was *because* he was decisive and stuck to his decision that no quick and easy compromise formula emerged. Had he been less radical and more incremental in style he would have been able to get a policy through much quicker. Similarly, in the negotiations over police salaries in phase III (1977/78) of pay policy, the Home Secretary was seen as rigid and inflexible in failing to satisfy police demands. Again, the (leaked) fact appears to have been that within the Cabinet committee he was arguing for a 25 per cent increase for the police, but was unable to get the agreement of colleagues unless 'their' groups received similar increases. Ministers thus have the frustration of being attacked by groups for being unsympathetic and criticised by colleagues for too strongly presenting the claims of the same groups.

This pattern of ministers and client groups in competition with other such partnerships is a long way from the situation in the centre envisaged by Barbara Castle (above) before going into office. The experiments at the centre in the past fifteen years are uniformly inspired by the idea that this pattern should be replaced by one where politicians, acting together, could assess, evaluate and decide between options. Some of these attempts to move away from departmental pluralism and incrementalism to a more 'rational' system are described below.

PUBLIC EXPENDITURE SURVEY AND OTHER ATTEMPTS AT RATIONALISM

The development of the Public Expenditure Survey was the first of the contemporary responses to the traditional criticisms of the centre. This innovation was a response to the view that in the late 1950s public expenditure had got out of control.[16] Before World

War II the Treasury's task was relatively simple as deflationary economics were the current orthodoxy. But during and after the war with the acceptance of Keynesian thinking there was no automatic ceiling on spending – it was no longer accepted that it could be financed only by conscious, deliberate and unpopular raising of taxes. Ministers were no longer imbued with the idea that spending was a 'bad thing'; on the contrary, while ministers might see the merit of economy in general, particular proposals always seemed to have merit. Thus in the 50s the ministers with spending responsibilities tended to gang up on the chancellor. At first sight one might expect them to curb each other on the ground that the less obtained by one would mean the more for the rest, but in fact the practice was to attempt to obtain an increase for a colleague, which then set a precedent for an increase in one's own budget. This practice is illustrated by Crossman's account of how Cabinet sat silently while the Home Secretary, Roy Jenkins, attempted to evade a Public Expenditure Survey cut of £600,000 on his budget. This was because each of the others would thereby have 'an enormously strengthened case for remitting his PESC cut too ... It's all a question of grabbing what you can get for yourself'.[17] This demonstrates the kind of thinking that made the Public Expenditure Survey Committee (PESC) system necessary. Spending ministers did not think the £600,000 to the Home Office meant less money for the rest of them. If Jenkins could break out of his financial limits, so might they.

We are told that pre-PESC chancellors repeatedly lost out to this spending caucus and this led to the forecasting of the 'scissors' scenario by Treasury officials. As Heclo and Wildavsky put it, 'with post Korean defence cut-backs finite and civil expenditure growing faster than GNP it was only a question of time before total public expenditure devoured the entire national output'.[18] The remedy fitting this diagnosis was provided by the Plowden Committee of 1961. Their report made the central point that 'decisions involving substantial future expenditure should always be taken in the light of public expenditure as a whole, over a period of years, and in relation to the prospective resources'. Out of the Plowden proposals came the PESC system. This meant that a committee of officials (PESC) estimated the future cost of what was already committed to departments by existing policy. At the same time the Treasury produced its forecast of economic prospects – whether the economy would develop sufficiently to afford existing policy and whether new policy commitments could be made. This allowed Cabinet-level decisions on how to cut commitments to keep within estimates of growth or how to share out the extra resources provided by growth. This PESC machinery therefore provided a mechanism that allowed the Chancellor to remind his colleagues about the implications of any proposal for overall spending levels. Instead of individual spending decisions being made 'on their merits', they had to be reconciled with overall resource availability. As well as this control/financial ceiling idea, PESC was also about choice. The hope was that the Cabinet would act collectively in making judgements on the opportunities that were revealed by the PESC projections.

The PESC system was, however, beset by difficulties.[19] Periodic financial cuts vitiated against planning, departments 'loaded' spending in the early years of the five-year cycles, etc. It also turned out to be a politically sensitive (rather than a technical) exercise, as departments attempted to argue that 'existing policy' entitled them to more than the Treasury might allow. Another difficulty was that the figures in the first two years of the PESC programme had to be taken as fixed. Thus the Tories on coming into office in 1970 intending to cut spending found that, 'short of making decisions which would be economically and socially wasteful and disruptive, what could be achieved in the short term ... was circumscribed by the scale of existing [PESC] commitments'.[20] This 'new law of public expenditure, that each Government in its first two years has the public expenditure bequeathed by its predecessor',[21] led to complaints by ministers such as Crossman.

Above all, PESC had the problem of failing to change the attitude of spending ministers. It was all very well for PESC to provide the opportunity for ministers to get together to decide on the pruning of the budget or the sharing of the cake, but there is little evidence that they adopted this new cooperative spirit. Experiments have been tried. In the early 1960s the Tories had the Ministerial Action Group on Public Expenditure (MAGPIE), but this was unsuccessful – as was Labour's similarly 'neutral' Committee of Non-Spending Ministers in the late 1960s.[22] The failures stemmed from a lack of suitable 'neutral', but senior, ministers to man the Committees and accordingly a reluctance by spending ministers to accept the verdict. There were inevitably appeals back to full Cabinet – where if defeat was still forthcoming the minister in question could be seen to be 'fighting his corner'.

Heclo and Wildavsky's interviews among civil servants and ministers found a common refrain: 'The spending minister who does not put up a fight loses authority forever.' They offer a cautionary tale of one well-meaning minister who was disposed to cooperate in helping the government control expenditure. When the Chancellor proposed a substantial cut in his departmental funds the minister accepted a cut of half the initial proposal. No one outside this private arrangement knew that the Chancellor had initially asked for a larger cut: all that was visible was a minister failing to object to the Chancellor's cut. The minister himself described the result as follows; 'So when I went to the Cabinet and did not fight, I looked bad. It made me very unpopular because word leaked out and some people informed journalists that I did not fight and this gets around to the ... lobby.' Heclo and Wildavsky sum up;

> ... the man had crippled his reputation. Department officials considered him weak. His Cabinet colleagues believed that they could easily run over him. *The interests affected no longer wanted him to deal with their subject. Other interests who wanted a strong minister to look after their affairs would be upset if he came to an office affecting them* [our emphasis].[23]

PESC thus did not produce rational choices by the Cabinet between competing policies. Indeed, and ironically, it is seen as producing the opposite effect. Instead of the collegiate Cabinet deciding which of various options was the 'best buy' with the available spare resources or the most justified cut to meet the resources limit, ministers made sure that their department received its *fair share* of resources. Previously, the outcome of who got what was rather unclear, but the openness of the PESC figures made it plain who had lost out. If there was an overall 5 per cent increase available, each minister demanded that his budget got its 5 per cent boost. Thus incrementalism was entrenched not weakened.

PESC has been presented here – in its origins if not in its execution – as the first of the rationalist alternatives. But we would not wish to push this point too far. Some commentators have discussed PESC as a form of a Planning–Programming–Budgeting–System (PPBS), but this seems unjustified. In fact, PPBS has been considered in several Whitehall departments. Again we see the government machine groping for an alternative policy-making system to the pluralist, incrementalist model. PPBS has been described by the Department of Education and Science as a formal system for establishing: (i) what a department is aiming to achieve – what its objectives are – in the areas of policy for which it is responsible; (ii) which activities are contributing to these objectives; (iii) what resources or inputs are being devoted to these activities; (iv) what is actually being achieved, or what the outputs are.[24]

This process of deciding what is necessary and guaging the various activities of the department in terms of how cost effective they are in contributing towards it, is a fairly well-developed manifestation of rationality – of the commonsense type we have earlier defined. But PESC was not so well developed, and arguably it could be as accurately described as a pragmatic response to a crisis in public expenditure control as a form of rationalist decision-making. With PESC there was no attempt to define overall goals, no attempt to develop options within a department's submission to Cabinet, no attempt to weigh one option against another in quantitative fashion. PPBS (or Output Budgeting) is manifestly a more highly formalised system than PESC. PPBS attempts are unambiguously a rationalist response to the existing incrementalist process. Other 'rationalistic' developments, such as a managerial water industry, a management-orientated Health Service, corporate management in local government, the use of cost–benefit analysis, departmental restructuring to give more managerial autonomy (departmental agencies, etc.), all seem to be identifiably to do with getting away from incrementalism – but only to a limited extent was their connection with rationalist theory made explicit.

Of course, in Britain the introduction of PPBS is no easy matter to document. At various times different departments have developed different forms and under different labels. Defence and Education have probably been to the fore, but the Forestry Commission has attempted to build a financial control model and the former Ministry of Technology built a computerised model of the energy sector of the economy. Various tools were developed in different parts of Whitehall. But these efforts were piecemeal and department-centred. The most significant attempt to produce a genuinely alternative policy-making system was the 1970 Conservative White Paper on the Reorganisation of Central Government (Cmnd. 4506).

THE 1970 WHITE PAPER AND THE RATIONALIST SYSTEM

We can return to the earlier discussion of traditional criticisms of
the centre because finally, in 1970, these strictures had some effect.
The choice between rational allocation and bargained allocation was
put neatly by Anthony Crosland, speaking of his experiences as
Secretary of State for Education and Science.[25] He suggested that a
minister gets resources by 'an endless tactical battle which requires
determination, cunning and occasional unscrupulousness'. This very
much echoes and confirms the picture of departmental bargaining
and conflict that we have outlined. Crosland rather scornfully goes
on, 'in an ideal world it would all no doubt be settled by some
omniscient central unit, but this is the way it happens in our crude
democratic world'. The critics were essentially seeking this 'omniscient central unit', rejected as impractical by Crosland. While many see
little chance of a revival of the 'policy cabinet' idea, we believe the
first of the two major intellectual sources of the 1970 White Paper
can be seen as groping towards this. It suggested very familiar
remedies: fewer departments, hence fewer Cabinet ministers; less
inter-departmental negotiation; a smaller range of options brought
up to Cabinet for adjudication by the Cabinet team.

The White Paper, however, also owed something to another strand
of reformist thought, and advocated quantitative aids to decision-
making – a 'best value for money' approach in selecting between
options. The policy-making system implicit in the White Paper is
then a mixture of policy Cabinet and PPBS. Of course, the irony was
that Britain's rationalist system was to be introduced only in-
crementally. The commitment was inescapably to the rationalistic
school but the style was meekly incremental. Thus the Government
recognised that the task of producing a strategic definition of
objectives was a new and formidable one and decided that it could
only be approached gradually! The proposed Central Policy
Review Staff (CPRS) was to remedy the fact that governments 'may
pay too little attention to the difficult, but critical task of evaluating
as objectively as possible the alternative policy options and priorities
open to them'.

Linked to the creation of the CPRS was the innovation of Programme Analysis and Review (PAR). If PESC was mainly concerned
with the overall departmental budgets, the idea of PAR was to look
at the relative value of individual projects. Unlike PAR, PESC did not

'... call for the explicit statements of the objectives of expenditure in a way that would enable a Minister's plan to be tested against general government strategy'. PESC was involved in totals and did not necessarily involve itself in the effectiveness of how these departmental budgets were utilised. In theory, there was central evaluation – but only between options when cuts were needed or increases possible. There was no evaluation of expenditure below 'the base'. PAR was intended to supply this capacity. In principle (in the language of the time) it was intended that a rolling programme of in-depth studies of ongoing projects should be carried out. Over three or so years all major policy areas would be tested for effectiveness and alternative methods of fulfilling the same task considered. Consequently, one can see the CPRS as a central marshalling organisation for these specific PAR studies. It was 'a capability at the centre for assessment of policies and projects in relation to strategic objectives' (para. 16).

All this adds up to an alternative system, which in fact presented a real challenge to vested interests both within and outside Whitehall. With hindsight it is certain that the Government (or at least the Prime Minister, Mr Heath) had failed to appreciate just how big a challenge this was to the traditional and deeply entrenched pluralist system. Policies had hitherto been determined by a process of bargaining and adjustment between competing groups (both Whitehall 'groups' and traditional 'pressure groups') and Heath was trying to sweep this aside in favour of a more rational objective process. Indeed, the White Paper made great use of the concept of aims. There was a very clear implication that policies had definite specifiable *objectives*. Policies were supposed to solve problems in society. In fact the past had shown that quite often problem-solving was a rather minor function of public policies. More often than not policies were designed to get an issue off the agenda (see chapter 4) or to ratify an agreement between competing interests, i.e. to *minimise conflict*. But through the vehicle of PAR studies, ministers collectively were to be given the opportunity of appraising, against objective criteria, the main governmental programme. Sir Richard Clarke, who was a leading senior civil servant closely associated with the changes, wrote: 'PAR and PESC are designed to become the basis of a new system of formulating and carrying out the government's policy. *This should not be regarded as an addition to the conventional system: for if it survives it must ultimately replace the traditional system . . .'* (our emphasis).[26] Writing in 1971, Clarke admits that at the time the system was 'transitional' and that it would be two to five years before the new procedures were fully operational. Clarke does, however, spell out in clearer fashion than the White Paper how the new system was intended to function. For example, in his description he explains the importance of the creation of giant departments:

> We start with nine operating departments – FCO, Defence, DTI, DOE, DHSS, DES, Home Office, MAFF, Employment. It is important to recognise that operation could not be effectively carried out with 20 departments. The essence of PAR is that a large number of individuals (Cabinet Ministers and the officials in the centre) must understand the programmes of all departments and relate them to each other and compare them. This may be just possible with nine returns – though six would be much better. It becomes utterly impossible when one gets into higher figures for no one can comprehend so many programmes.[27]

He describes how PAR reports would eventually be annual, with specific areas selected by the CPRS for examination in depth. After examination at the centre by the Treasury, CPRS and sometimes the Civil Service Dept. (CSD), each PAR would be considered by Cabinet or a special Cabinet committee (but one involving nearly everybody in a Cabinet of sixteen to seventeen people). He points out that '. . . the spending Ministers must see all other spending programmes and the taxation programme in order to carry out their dual role as departmental Minister and Cabinet Minister. If departmental ministers are allowed to escape from collective responsibility for the whole they will obviously believe as departmental Ministers and not as Cabinet Ministers.'[28]

Clarke was, of course, talking in 1971 about what he envisaged in five or so years but writing in 1978, we are now further from, not nearer to, the system he advocated. For one thing we have experienced a wave of departmental proliferation. The Department of Trade and Industry has been split into the Department of Prices and Consumer Protection, Department of Trade, Department of Industry and the Department of Energy. The Department of the Environment has become the Department of the Environment and the Department of Transport.

This in itself would have caused a proliferation of PARs – which by Clarke's own admission would have made the system unmanageable. But in any case comprehensive departmental PARs quickly proved unworkable,[29] and instead the PARs became analysis of particular areas of departmental work. These specific exercises might have been useful but they were hardly systematic – which was Clarke's essential requirement. Furthermore, as Heclo and Wildavsky describe, PARs became just another weapon in the Whitehall battle for resources.[30] Departments used the PAR studies merely as opportunities to lay claim to extra resources.

In short then, although developments continue, there is no longer any serious contention that a comprehensive pattern of resource allocation through comparison of costed alternatives is to be developed across Whitehall. We are then back to the old rules. Our discussion of the rationalistic experiments confirms the existence and tenacity of the old pluralist habits and practices. The old system acts as a gyroscope. Any deviation is soon automatically corrected either by pressure from outside groups or by pressure from within the Whitehall system itself.

The implication of this discussion is that many of the important decisions in British political life are not really open to change at (for example) general elections. The enduring competition between alliances of departments and groups remains even if the complexion of the government changes. Examination of how public expenditure is allocated between departments reveals a remarkably constant pattern – despite the claims of the parties to have very distinctive priorities. The quasi-stalemate of competing departments means that little change has been possible. The former Head of the Home Civil Service and former Permanent Secretary of the Treasury, Lord Armstrong, has stated that 'the highest figures [for alteration of a department's budget] I have ever heard anybody put on it is about $2\frac{1}{2}\%$ ... of total public spending'.[31] This may have changed in the successive crises of recent years; we may have given an exaggerated impression by discussing (in the main) departmental budgets rather than what departments do with budgets; but there seems little doubt that in British policy-making we have a strong incrementalist bias.

THE BRITISH POLICY-MAKING STYLE

In discussing how decisions are made between departments we have said relatively little about pressure groups. But in fact there is a connection between how decisions are taken within Whitehall and how pressure groups relate to the overall pattern of policy-making. The style of Whitehall policy-making and the accommodation of group pressures are closely related. An incremental Whitehall style makes it easy to accommodate group pressures. Equally, a strong group system leads Whitehall into an incremental style. With the expectation of minimal change, with the tendency to leave each policy sector to those most intimately concerned, with the tendency to compromise, it seems to have been easy to accommodate the concession of veto power in policy-making to interested groups. Lindblom's 'partisan mutual adjustment' is as apt a description as 'incrementalist'.

Jack Hayward has characterised the British system of policy-making as 'humdrum'. There seems much evidence for his diagnosis:

> Firstly, there are no explicit, over-riding medium or long term objectives. Secondly, unplanned decision-making is incremental. Thirdly, humdrum or unplanned decisions are arrived at by a continuous process of mutual adjustment between a plurality of autonomous policy makers operating in the context of a highly fragmented multiple flow of influence. Not only is plenty of scope offered to interest group spokesmen to shape the outcome by participation in the advocacy process. The aim is to secure through bargaining at least passive acceptance of the decision by the interests affected.[32]

We think this 'humdrum' characterisation is accurate, but we see it as perhaps more inevitable than does Hayward. Incrementalism reflects the realities of the world we live in. Pressure groups exist and White Papers will not make them go away. They have power resting on effective sanctions and that power has to be bargained with in all political systems. Government departments have self-interest and power too, and that has to be fitted into the policy system. There are certain policy-making demands that necessarily follow from making policy in advanced industrial societies. Each country develops its own machinery for securing accommodation and consensus. In the next chapter we describe the main elements of the British version of this machinery.

CHAPTER 3

The Policy Machinery

INTRODUCTION

This chapter is a reaction to what appears to us as the still wide-spread view that British policy-making is a process played out between the electorate, Parliament and Cabinet. In 1977 a survey on the political awareness of 15 and 16 year olds revealed that about half of those interviewed thought that the House of Commons made all the important decisions in the running of the country. Writers on Parliament often become seduced by this concept of parliamentary government and fail to discuss the impact of party.[1] Even most recent 'revisionist' interpretations emphasising the influence of the Civil Service and pressure groups tend to treat them as interesting and important – but as adjuncts to an accepted, recognised system. Our own focus is on the government–Civil Service–pressure group network. In part this different focus results from our wider definition of policy. Parliament is certainly important in topics of high political 'sex-appeal' – for example, the discussion of the Dock Work Regulation Bill of 1975. But it can be argued that such topics receive such parliamentary attention precisely because Parliament was unable to influence the central political issues of the day. At that time an 'industrial strategy' was being worked out by government and trade unions; the International Monetary Fund was imposing conditions on economic policy, etc. Many 'key' parliamentary issues are in fact symbolic gestures to satisfy the government's parliamentary majority who are effectively ignored in more central matters. Even with these issues one cannot credit Parliament with *initiating* them. They usually have extra-parliamentary origins.

An issue is not necessarily important just because it receives much party political attention – sometimes even the reverse. And many unambiguously important policy decisions are made outside the parliamentary framework. For example, the decision to let the pound float upwards in late 1977 was not even taken in full Cabinet, but in Cabinet committee. Similarly, the important decisions on vetting pay settlements in 1977/78 were taken in Cabinet committee. Certainly our framework of government–Civil Service–pressure groups handles 'lower grade' policy decisions. Decisions on, say, the specific level of Rate Support Grant to local government and the detail of legislation such as the Community Land Act are worked out in this 'alternative machinery'. However, we are also claiming that many, if not most, decisions of the first order are also settled (insofar as they ever are settled) in this network.

In rejecting 'parliamentary government' as a description of our system, can we go on and likewise reject 'party government'? That theory suggests that democracy consists of allowing citizens to choose between competing parties and competing party programmes. The parliamentary majority of the elected government allows it to push through its legislation – so encouraging Lord Hailsham to describe the system as 'elected dictatorship'. This view, hardly accords with much of the evidence. For example, does it readily account for the stability in resource allocation between departments? In defence for example, despite the rhetoric of the parties, the reality of their financial commitment has shown little difference between them. Defence's share of Gross Domestic Product declined quite sharply in the years of adjustment (with a Conservative Government) immediately after the Korean War, but since 1955 the decline has been gradual and largely irrespective of the party complexion of government. In real terms the commitment of resources has been remarkably stable[2] – indeed, despite the popular image of contraction, real spending was higher in 1974 than in 1955. A department's share of GDP can change (e.g. Defence's from 9.1 per cent in 1955 to 5.7 per cent in 1976), but only very slowly. As one Heclo and Wildavsky respondent put it, 98 per cent of the expenditures are committed: 'All we did is mess about at the margins.'[3]

The 'adversary politics'/party competition notions suggest that in Britain competitive two-party politics have been developed to such a point that success in the competition is all that matters and that the opposition has seen its function merely as the negation of government.[4] On election, a new government feels obliged automatically to undo the work of its predecessor. But again the evidence seems against this notion of mindless alternatives. Major investment proposals such as Concorde, third London airport, Channel tunnel and AGR nuclear reactors have originated within ministries and their client groups. Which proceeded and which were cut had little to do with party norms and the area for choice for an incoming government is in fact rather narrow. The public cannot be said to have clear-cut and consistent policy choices from the parties and positions well-defined in opposition have grown less so in government. As one Conservative MP put it: 'In Government the choices are frighteningly few'.[5] This is not to say that parties never find themselves following their manifesto. For example, Richard Crossman as Minister of Housing and Local Government in 1966 pointed out how the Government felt obliged to legislate to introduce a Land Commission as promised in the manifesto, but he felt that a more modest measure would have been preferable.[6] When Labour regained office in 1974 they felt obliged to introduce legislation on the extension of protected tenancies to furnished accommodation even though it may have been anticipated (correctly) within the Department that the effect would be to limit the supply.

Despite such examples, the main feature of the British system is that ongoing problems and constraints force successive governments into very similar policy positions. Problems are handled similarly irrespective of what government is in power. Agreement will be sought within the community of groups involved in, say, local government, and all in that community will have an interest in more resources. Our argument in this chapter is summed up in Table 3.1, which posits strong boundaries between subject matters and indistinct, merged relationships between departments and relevant groups within individual policy areas.

Of course, not all groups are involved in all aspects of even an area as narrowly defined as 'education'. On, say, curriculum development the National Foundation for Educational Research (NFER) might be more central than the Association of Metropolitan Authorities (AMA), but on, say, levels of staffing the AMA will be more central and the NFER more maginal. And while groups such as the British Road Federation are very much part of the Department of Transport's clientele, groups such as Transport 2000 – who are generally less well disposed to the Department – have a different relationship. The central point is that policy-making is fragmented into sub-systems, and that the main boundaries are between sub-

TABLE 3.1 *Examples of policy communities*

Policy area:	Education	Transport	Local government
Department:	Department of Education and Science	Department of Transport	Department of the Environment
Client groups	National Union of Teachers, Association of University Teachers, Association of Metropolitan Authorities, National Foundation for Educational Research, Association of Teachers in Technical Institutions, Council of Local Education Authorities, etc.	Automobile Association, British Road Federation, Society of Motor Manufacturers & Trades, National Council on Inland Transport, Freight Transport Association, Road Haulage Association, Transport 2000, etc.	Association of Metropolitan Authorities, Association of County Councils, National Association of Local Government Officers, National Association of Ratepayers Action Groups, etc.

systems rather than between the component units of the sub-system. There is a breaking down of conceptual distinctions between government, agencies and pressure groups; an interpenetration of department and client group, an osmosis in personnel terms with ex-civil servants appearing in groups (and less so, vice versa).[7]

In attempting to answer the question 'How are policies made?', we see a process where government very publicly and frequently demonstrates that it cannot make up its mind – e.g. its attitude to nuclear power. As one civil servant put it privately, while issues tend to be discussed in terms of the merits of the case, 'the substance of the discussion concerns putting together a coalition of those interests whose cause will be advanced by a particular decision... The departmental view cuts little ice nowadays unless supported by politically more powerful voices from outside. So officials too must canvass and negotiate – not to frustrate or outmanoeuvre their masters, but to produce advice that is relevant in modern government.'

CONSENSUS AND CONSULTATION

The dominant values in British policy-making are consensual. This is to say not that conflicts do not exist, but that there are limits to conflict. Beer has drawn attention to the paradox of a govern-mental system apparently designed for effective action and yet very reluctant to act without first consulting and agreeing policies with all interested parties.[8] One explanation for this put forward by Beer is the *increasing specificity of the essential governmental decision*. He convincingly argues that if the role of government is to promulgate general rules, then it can do so without consultation, and a legislature can act in such a sphere. But with decisions that are specific, technical, complex, managerial, then awareness of particular circumstances is all important. In such cases, the affected parties need to be contacted and their agreement sought. There is an instinctive reaction to consult. For example, a study of mature recruits into the British Civil Service in the early 1970s indicated that the most frequently mentioned problem of adaptation to the Civil Service was handling the 'process of *consultation*'. One respon-dent commented: 'One is honour bound to discuss issues both inside and outside the Ministry, which is jolly difficult. On the outside there is a reluctance to consult, because this indicates an inability to make decisions.'[9]

An excellent example of what consensus and consultation mean in practice is contained in a study, based on the experience of an under-secretary, of the introduction of Value Added Tax (VAT) into Britain in 1973.[10] Once the Conservatives had made a policy decision to introduce VAT, the process of consultation began. The Customs and Excise Department received the views of over 800 different trade and professional organisations and held meetings with over 300 of them. Indeed meetings became so frequent that the Department lost count of them! A number of generalisations can be made from the VAT case.

1. In one sense *consultation can be essentially a process of exclusion*. This may at first seem a contradiction, but in the VAT case there was such widespread interest that it became very difficult to 'consult' and to process all the views. In any case, consultation means consultation with organised *groups*, not with the general public.

2. As a result, although 400 associations were 'recognised' by the Department to the extent of receiving consultation papers, there was a much smaller group of principal groups. Consultation beyond these groups was more a matter of disseminating information than of receiving views.

3. The invitations to the Department from trade and professional

bodies to talk about VAT at meetings, annual conferences, luncheons, etc. were of great importance. This 'whistle stop tour' by civil servants engaged in drafting legislation is a feature of many policy areas. This helps break down Civil Service anonymity and once it is obvious that the civil servant (rather than the politician) is in day-to-day charge of detailed legislation it reinforces Civil Service/pressure group contact.

4. The representative bodies gave valuable technical assistance. The fact that the civil servant is very often breaking unfamiliar ground and requires guidance is, of course, akin to Beer's point on the *specificity* of decisions.

5. Consultation on the VAT case raised the general matter of parliamentary involvement. Johnstone describes how on several occasions MPs attempted to ensure that copies of discussion papers should be available for their consideration, but these efforts were rebuffed by ministers with a series of arguments such as: 'a number have become obsolescent or obsolete and it would be misleading to give them a wider circulation'; 'Papers prepared as a basis for discussion with interested bodies on forthcoming legislation are normally concerned with specific and often technical or procedural problems. Outside the framework of such discussions these papers could be misleading and it is not therefore the practice to make them available to Hon Members.'; 'If we are to have the simplest VAT in Europe... it is essential that the Customs and Excise, in its discussions with trade and industry, shall not be hamstrung in any way. I hope the House will agree with that attitude'. Members of Parliament felt, with every justification, that they were excluded from the detailed matters of policy-making. Parliament, as usual, played an insignificant role in the policy process.

Consultation in the VAT exercise was about the technicalities of introducing and operating a policy that had already been decided. There was no serious prospect of VAT not appearing in some shape approximating to the final version.

The case of the reorganisation of the water industry in England and Wales between 1968 and 1974 again involved the paraphernalia of consultation – questionnaires to groups, oral and written evidence, consultation papers, innumerable meetings, concessions and compromise – but it differed in that there was some doubt about the *outcomes*. Again, the process was labelled consultative, but this time there was real dispute and uncertainty over the final nature of the reorganised industry. In this dispute the political parties were more or less marginal. Parliamentary discussion tended to degenerate into a debate on the merits of a nationalised versus a non-nationalised industry, yet this was an inappropriate distinction as in any case the non-nationalised industry was so heavily limited by governmental restrictions. The real change that was under discussion from 1968 onwards was about how to manage the water system.

The real (as opposed to the political) debate ran on across the change in governments in 1970. The impetus to reform was organisational. The different functions of the pre-reorganised industry were administered by separate organisations: water supply was in the hands of 198 separate water supply undertakings; sewerage and sewage disposal were dealt with by more than 1300 county borough and county district councils and twenty-four joint sewerage boards; water conservation had been the responsibility of twenty-nine river authorities. This complex system was replaced in 1974 by one based upon ten Regional Water Authorities. The boundaries of these authorities were hydrologically determined and reflected natural water sheds and not local government or other administrative boundaries. Within these limits each multi-purpose authority was made responsible for all water activities. Thus, following the 1973 Act, functions were administered within large, managerially orientated, integrated organisations instead of small-scale, uncoordinated units. This change was as radical a policy switch as can be cited in post-war Britain.

The reform was largely the initiative of the Ministry of Housing and Local Government (later DOE). Its reasons were various but included a desire to avoid having to adjudicate in local disputes in the industry. The Ministry also felt that water tended to be neglected in local authorities and so favoured the setting up of a self-financing water industry where *management* would have a higher priority and status. This solution also reflects the fashion of the time – 'the managerial revolution'. (It is worth noting that within the Ministry there was a difference of opinion between the water and local government divisions. The latter was less keen to remove water from 'its clients'.)

The problem for the Ministry of Housing and Local Government was how to sell its new policy to the groups involved in the existing organisations. The professional associations such as the Institution of Water Engineers, the Institute of Water Pollution Control, were in favour of the change, representing as it did a move to give greater authority to their members. But the main groups involved, such as the Association of Municipal Corporations, the County Councils' Associations and the Rural District Councils Associations, were against the change as the implication was that they were not performing adequately in relation to water. The National Farmers' Union and the Country Landowners' Association were also concerned that their particular interest – land drainage – could be harmed by being lost in an organisation with many other water responsibilities.

So this 'consultation' was about the policy outcome. Over 100 groups submitted written evidence to the Central Advisory Water Committee, and almost half gave oral evidence. Despite its lack of party politicisation, this was a well-delineated dispute with the DOE on the one side and the Ministry of Agriculture, Fisheries and Food and the bulk of interested groups on the other. Perhaps the conflict went beyond what is normally indicated by consultation, but, of course, 'consultation' is very often used as a synonym for negotiation. (It was after 'consultations' with the TUC that the Labour Government in 1969 let lapse the White Paper *In Place of Strife*.)

TRIPARTITE CONSULTATIONS?

We are here sketching in only a few of the main types of consultative processes that might be seen as supplementing Parliament's scrutiny role on legislation. VAT was a case of consultation on detail – and it might be argued that these details were too specialised to require parliamentary attention. In the second (water) type of consultation, the policy area might be seen as inappropriate for party politicisation and therefore unlikely to provoke parliamentary interest. We believe that the two categories cover such a broad range of policies and at sufficiently important levels as to undermine any idea of 'parliamentary government'. These matters are just too major to be considered as some kind of delegation by a Parliament busy on more *important* matters. In any case, the third kind of 'consultation' that we look at challenges the myth of Parliament more directly. Tripartism appears to be founded on the opposite premise that major policies are too important to be left to Parliament. Direct discussion between the government, TUC and CBI have supplemented, if not supplanted, parliamentary discussion in key policy areas. This participation also extends to the implementation of policies. For example, the CBI and TUC have been granted formal participation in some of the major executive agencies created in recent years (see Table 3.2).

TABLE 3.2 *Group representation in executive agencies*

	Manpower Services Commission	*Health and Safety Commission*	*Arbitration and Conciliation Service*
The Secretary of State appoints:	1 chairman 3 members after consulting orgs. representing employers 3 members after consulting orgs. representing employees 2 members after consulting orgs. representing local authorities	1 chairman 3 members after consulting orgs. representing employers 3 members after consulting orgs. representing employees Up to 3 members after consulting orgs. representing local authorities and other bodies	1 chairman 3 members after consulting orgs. representing employers 3 members after consulting orgs. representing workers 3 other members, if he thinks fit, including 2 further members representing (1 each) orgs. representing employers and workers
	1 member after consulting orgs. concerned with education		

Other legislation makes the consultation with the CBI/TUC less explicit, but with much the same result. For example, the Scottish Development Agency Act (1975) states that the members of the agency shall be appointed from any persons who appear to the Secretary of State to have a wide experience of, and to have shown capacity in, industry, banking, accounting or finance, environmental matters, local government or the representation of workers. This 'proportionality' extends to many other bodies operating in vital economic sectors (see Table 3.3).

The most spectacular and commented upon institutional manifestation of tripartism is, of course, the National Economic Develop-

TABLE 3.3 *Trade union appointments on public corporations*

	Number of salaried appointments made since June 1975	Number of salaried appointments given to trade unionists
British Shipbuilders	9	3
National Enterprise Board	13	4
Post Office	24	8
British Aerospace	12	2

Source: Hansard, 10 February 1978.

ment Office (NEDO), set up in 1962. In November 1977, the Council of NEDO consisted of seven government ministers, six CBI representatives, six from the TUC, two from nationalised industries, the chairmen of the Manpower Services Commission and the National Enterprise Board, the director general of NEDO, and two independents – viz. Lord Roll, chairman of J. G. Warburg and Co. Ltd., and Michael Shanks, chairman of the National Consumer Council.

There is some controversy over the meaning of tripartism, but our use of the term is illustrated by Edward Heath's claim at the Conservative party conference in 1972. He said that he had made 'an offer to employers and unions to share fully with the Government the benefits and obligations involved in running the country'.[11] In other words, policy emerges from discussions of three 'partners'; the government is merely one of three participants. Arthur Bentley, writing over sixty years earlier, would not have dissented from that!

Tripartism needs to be distinguished from the general involvement of the CBI and the TUC in governmental decision-making. The TUC has representation on around 100 governmental or quasi-governmental bodies – such as the Coal Consumers Council, Export Credit Guarantees Advisory Council, Metrication Board and the Potato Marketing Board. The CBI is similarly involved in a range of bodies. Contact in that form is mainly concerned with detailed, specialised matters, but tripartism in the Edward Heath sense is an attempt to solve major economic problems by direct negotiation.

This is something of fairly recent origins – since NEDO was set up. Throughout the 1950s there were statements such as that by the Prime Minister, Sir Anthony Eden, in 1956 that discussion with both sides of industry was a 'necessary process' in the working out of 'truly national solutions'. Such language might *sound* tripartite but it is unlikely that direct co-equal negotiations were envisaged. Indeed, tripartism was not initially an important feature of NEDO.[12] But with a move away from the attempt at indicative planning in the mid-1960s, NEDO became more like a tripartite institution. Thus tripartism should be seen as something more systematic, more political, more representational, than the earlier relationships between government, TUC and CBI.

A good example of tripartism is the 'industrial strategy' of 1976. This was described by the Treasury as a common approach to industrial strategy, agreed between government, management and unions. As part of this, thirty-seven Sector Working Parties were set up. They were composed of representatives involved in particular economic sectors – e.g. clothing, machine tools, mining, machinery, wool textiles, etc. This agreement certainly covered a key policy area and can be seen as a genuine attempt to formulate policy in a tripartite manner. There were, however, tensions between the 'partners', as illustrated by the threatened withdrawal by the CBI from the agreement when the Government increased employers' national insurance contributions by £1000m in July 1976. This was not seen as furthering industrial recovery.

Grant and Marsh have suggested that consensus is a necessary definitional precondition for tripartism to operate.[13] They doubt that such consensus exists and have little confidence that a genuinely tripartite system prevails. For example, they argue that in 1970–74 the Conservatives thought that they themselves represented business and were accordingly suspicious of the CBI's claims. They further argue that the 1971 Industrial Relations Act (to which the unions were bitterly opposed) was 'the real body blow to hopes of meaningful tripartism'.

Thus, if tripartism means a relationship based on consensus, or a relationship where *all* major decisions are taken, then it probably does not exist in Britain – which is Grant and Marsh's argument. But nevertheless there remains a very important predilection for handling problems in such a forum. The phenomenon is important even though it may not be as 'tidy' as the tripartite label implies. The CBI and the TUC appear to recognise that some compromise is required even if they cannot share explicit long-term goals.[14] The basis for negotiation is not consensual agreement on basic policies but a recognition that a policy is needed. The move away from the House of Commons is not the result of the 'under-pass' argument of the earlier forms of consultation – where the messy detail is 'beneath' Parliament – but because the House of Commons can no longer automatically mobilise the consent of the major groups in key policy areas. The TUC and CBI can claim more say over unemployment policies than can Parliament. Accordingly, when Michael Foot (later Leader of the House of Commons) was in opposition he argued that one of the most serious threats to the power of the Commons was the notion that you could have a meeting in Downing Street of the government, the CBI and the TUC to make an agreement that was binding without the Commons having the power to tear that bargain apart.[15]

One of the more important instances of this by-passing of Parliament took place in the Budget of 1976. This concerned the proposal by the Chancellor to cut income tax providing the TUC accepted pay restraint. Many saw this as a constitutional outrage, with *The Times* commenting that the Budget was no longer an act of government, dependent only upon Parliament, but had become a matter of negotiation between the government and an outside body representative of any one section of the community. This is hardly tripartism proper as the negotiations were bilateral, but it is significant that there are recurring attempts to settle wages formally in a CBI/TUC/ governmental council. The fashionable idea is that a 'kitty' – the amount of money available for wage increases in the coming year – should be agreed in consultations between the government, CBI and unions. It is, in reality, the PESC mentality applied to wage bargaining – anyone can have what they want but the total must not exceed the resources available.

Parliamentarians might complain that for the government to come to tell them what deal had been done with the 'partners' would be presumptuous, but even under a minority government in the late 70s there was little sign of a parliamentary contribution to the pay policy debate. In contrast, the CBI has clearly had some success over the Government's use of controversial clauses in state contracts in 1977/78. The Government had originally flatly stated that contracts would not be placed with companies who exceeded the wage increase guidelines, but the CBI won concessions on a relaxation of the responsibilities of contractors for sub-contractors, an appeals procedure against cancellation of contracts and a limitation of the clauses to one pay round and a general promise to consult the CBI. Certainly the CBI negotiations had more influence than the parliamentary storm that preceded them.

The CBI 'success' was at a price. Although the CBI director-general, Sir John Methven, saw the change in the Government's proposals as from 'thoroughly bad' to 'merely bad', the newspaper headlines were of the form 'CBI back sanctions against the rebels'. Thus the price of obtaining concessions was that the CBI had to (reluctantly) support (or at least temper criticism of) the Government even against some of its own members. One cannot really obtain concessions without some recompense. As Bruce-Gardyne and Lawson put it, 'the lobby is accorded the privilege of prior consultation; in return it is expected to help sell the bargain – a bargain struck somewhere in the no-mans land between the most the interest group will swallow and the minimum the department is prepared to have'.[16]

GROUP SUBGOVERNMENT – BEYOND CONSULTATION

Next we look at two closely related characteristics – group sub-government and clientelism. The number of groups (outside govern-ment itself) that exist and that are relevant to policy-making is unfathomable. Several sets of figures collected for particular areas of policy show the scale. It has been estimated that 4250 groups are active in Birmingham.[17] There are well over 1250 active local amenity societies in Britain, the majority formed after 1957.[18] Over 130 groups are involved in 'the environment' at national level. Even in the most esoteric policy areas the number of groups is vast. For example, the Department of Agriculture and Fisheries for Scotland maintains a list of over 170 bodies connected with the fishing industry.

The point is not only that many groups are involved in policy-making, but that policy-making is to a large extent made in 'issue communities'. Policy-making is segmented. In the VAT case the Customs and Excise Department was ready to circulate a general draft guide to 'a limited number of major representative bodies which had already shown some interest in VAT'. On devolution the Depart-ment of Education and Science consulted its 'clients' – the Arts Council, the British Film Institute, the research councils, the University Grants Commission, the Committee of Vice Chancellors and Principals, the Association of University Teachers, eighteen other groups and the teacher associations represented on the Burnham Committee. Another example of segmentation can be drawn from the policy process leading to the Water Act 1973. The Central Advisory Water Committee (CAWC) was asked by the Ministry of Housing and Local Government to examine the state of the industry, and was supplied with a list of forty-one bodies (including other government departments) with the intention that they be asked to give evidence. This is not to say that the Ministry wished to limit discussion but it was a recognition that not all groups can be consulted. Experience had suggested that forty-one was the correct 'field' for that issue. In other words, civil servants know their customers. When asked how the membership of CAWC was selected, a civil servant involved replied: 'its a small universe one is dealing with: one knows everyone who is anyone.'

Perhaps the best-documented example of policy segmentation is the education world. Writing in 1971 Kogan observed that 'Pressure groups both constrain and stimulate. The education service is not unique in this respect but it works within a particularly strong and long-lived professional constituency which might be called the old educational establishment.'[19] Thus he argues that neither Crosland nor Boyle (both former Ministers of Education) 'would have thought to move very far without consulting Sir William Alexander, Secretary to the Association of Education Committees, Sir Ronald Gould, Secretary to the National Union of Teachers and their counterparts in other local authority and teachers' organisations. Officials such as Sir William Alexander constitute a powerful – perhaps the most powerful – entity within the education service for a longer period than any Minister or Permanent Secretary and most senior officials in the Department.'[20]

Where the government moves out into a new unknown area or enters a world where no group 'universe' exists, it faces problems. Thus one of the complications in water reorganisation was that there was no natural body representing all the sewerage side of the industry and there was no convenient 'voice' for the Ministry to contact. Another example from the water saga occurred when there was an unexpected volume of protest against the implications of reorganisation in the canal network. The proposal was to leave the management of canals to each of the Regional Water Authorities through which they flowed – and to scrap the British Waterways Board, which managed the network. In February 1972, the Department of the Environment (DOE) called a major conference of interested groups – ranging from the National Trust to the Association of Pleasure Craft Operators to the Scout Association, but as canals were previously a low priority area in the Department (and had been treated as a transport rather than amenity problem) the DOE had very little idea who should be at the conference. Accordingly, the DOE was grateful for the assistance of the main pressure group – the Inland Waterways Association (IWA) – for suggestions as to who should be invited. Such assistance also helped the 'legitimisation' of the IWA.

CLIENTELISM

Clientelism is a concept related to group subgovernment, but at the same time stressing a different aspect. Group subgovernment implies that the significant policy differences are within the group sub-system, whereas clientelism notes the shared priorities within the sub-system and the fashion in which departments or agencies identify with 'their' lobby. Several examples of this were given in chapter 2 when we put forward the idea of a partnership between depart- ments and their pressure groups. The theme has been well captured by J. B. Christoph:

> The vast majority of Whitehall departments manage policies affecting identifiable clienteles, organized or elsewhere. While part of the job of civil servants is to analyse, verify, and cost the claim of such groups, and forward them to higher centres of decision, it would be unnatural if officials did not identify in some way with the interests of their clienteles, and within the overall framework of current government policy advance claims finding favor in the department.[21]

Joseph La Palombara's study of the Italian interest groups in the early 1960s revealed a similar 'clientela' system. He at least partially concedes that 'The Italian bureaucracy, the focus of attention of major aggregations of organized interests, is correctly identified as a series of feudal holdings in which those in Italy who are theoretically empowered to make the rules are strikingly at the mercy of others whom the rules are supposed to control and regulate'.[22] The clientele concept has an ambiguity: sometimes it seems to mean that the departments articulate the views of their clients (in a professional/client sense), but sometimes it means that the pressure groups control the departments. But really the latter interpretation is only a hostile version of the former. The phenomenon is widespread and in Suleiman's discussion of the relations between the French administration and interest groups it is obvious that the groups there are more involved than is often suggested. Suleiman presents quotations from civil servants that fit the clientele concept very neatly – e.g. 'some civil servants allow themselves to become lawyers for groups'.[23]

The phenomenon is particularly strong in Britain where pressure groups are powerful in terms of membership and cohesiveness. Again we can draw on our study of the Water Act 1973 for a good example of what is meant by shared priorities in the sub-system. The DOE's proposals to set up Regional Water Authorities (RWAS) happened to threaten the interests of both the Ministry of Agriculture, Fisheries and Food (MAFF) and the agricultural lobby interested in the problem of land drainage. The lobby (including the National Farmers' Union and the Country Landowners' Association) wanted to keep the control of land drainage in specialist agricultural hands and MAFF wanted to avoid losing its existing control over land drainage to the rival Department of the Environment. Consequently, a series of meetings was held between MAFF and its clients in order to plan a campaign to prevent the take-over of land drainage by the RWAS and the DOE. The meetings were certainly not examples of the groups 'pressurising' the Ministry – indeed at one meeting the Permanent Secretary of MAFF told the groups that the Ministry would need all the help it could get! The only sense in which 'pressure' was applied by the groups was the sending of formal submissions from the groups to MAFF, which appeared as demands for action from an unsympathetic ministry. In fact, this pressure was a charade and was merely intended to be used by MAFF in its battle with the DOE in order to demonstrate what 'strong pressure' MAFF was under.[24]

In other ways, too, the group/department distinction is blurred. For example, the Metropolitan Police at New Scotland Yard are neither pressure group nor government department, yet they maintain a CID Policy and Legislation Unit, which has a primary purpose of dissemination of information but also looks at forthcoming legislation and anticipates repercussions on police work. Thus the Metropolitan Police become another voice commenting upon legislation – and will inevitably be drawn into direct consultations on problems such as how to handle marches and demonstrations. Departments can in part finance groups. The provisions of the 1968 Health Services and Public Health Act allow the minister to give a voluntary organisation assistance by way of a grant or loan to enable the group to perform 'a relevant service'. This means that, for example, the Disablement Income Group is given finance to allow it to help advise the disabled on the correct rate of benefit. But, of course, enabling the group to perform that role more efficiently enables it – through the opportunity to gather factual material – to perform its policy advocacy and 'pressure' roles better.

THE DISINTEGRATION OF THE CENTRE

Writing as recently as 1967, one observer claimed that '... it is possible without too much equivocation to draw a line round the thirty major departments, together with some forty or fifty minor departments, and refer to them collectively as the central administration ... the core of British central government'.[25] Though acknowledging complications to the pattern it was felt that there was something coherent and reasonably well delineated that could be labelled 'central government'. Ten years on this image of a clear-cut 'government' is less useful.[26] There appears no reasonable means of distinguishing between 'central administration' and bodies outside that perimeter. Principles such as the right to a parliamentary vote, the responsibility of a minister, legal status of employees, do not in fact give a single and authoritative distinction between central and non-central administration or even between government and pressure groups.

A number of factors have contributed to this:

1. Within central departments there has been the development of new organisational forms – trading fund organisations and administrative departmental agencies. These are intended as being within departments (for example, the Property Services Agency within the DOE). They are staffed by civil servants, but (in theory) with considerable management autonomy. In 1976 over a quarter of the 739,000 civil servants in post were working in departmental agencies.[27]

These moves pose problems for a neat concept of the central government. Is a departmental agency such as the Royal Mint financed as a trading fund more governmental than a body such as the Training Services Division, which is ultimately financed by the Department of Employment? The notion of a Department of Employment 'group' is currently used to cover the Department of Employment, Manpower Services Commission, Training Services Division, Employment Services Agency, Health and Safety Executive. But this is less a considered, planned development indicating a coherent philosophy in these areas than a compromise covering a situation where union pressure prevented the agencies being fully hived off from the Civil Service structure. No clear governmental/non-governmental criteria appear to be available.

2. A second factor eroding the precise concept of 'government' is that any recent growth in government has been in precisely these ill-defined margins. Hood suggests 'a figure of 250–300 ... central non-Departmental bodies of a permanent nature'.[28] In the past, such bodies might have been seen as marginal cases, but the growth in their number inhibits us from continuing to treat them as exceptions to an otherwise clear pattern.

3. A 'pure' concept of government is, of course, tarnished by the continuing problem in the relationship between the government and public corporations/nationalised industries. The 'arm length' doctrine has failed to operate and there is 'seepage' between the centre and operating agencies. For example, in practice how much difference does the new status as public corporation make to the Post Office? Is there something called 'central government' that is really distinct from a broader 'public sector'?

4. There is also the development of the 'government contract sector' among private firms. These depend wholly or largely on public sector contracts and thus can be regarded as part of the public sector. Again the point is that clear lines have been eroded: a continuum takes their place. One can even extend this notion of the 'private public sector'. As a means of enforcing voluntary pay policy in 1977, the Government found it could control companies that did not depend on government contracts but depended on the threat of removal of Export Credit Guarantees, regional aid and the like.

There is still something recognisable as the centre of government – the main departments with ministerial representation in the Cabinet – but with developments of the type leading up to the Department of

Employment 'group' situation, the 'centre' has lost precision. The result of this is that in allocating resources the government finds it has demands and pressures from bodies such as the Training Services Division, the Scottish Development Agency, the Arts Council, etc. The relationship between the centre and such bodies is not dissimilar to that between the centre and other non-governmental groups (or indeed relations within the centre). The constitutional status of the groups is of little consequence. The need to aid the 'private' Chrysler Corporation in 1975/76 was as pressing as the need to help the 'public' British Leyland in 1977.

Government is involved in bargaining relationships with its own components and creations as much as with external agencies. Indeed, because creations are often highly dependent on the centre for their existence and resources, the relations can be more strained, the politicking more intense. For example, in November 1977 the Scottish press ran stories with headlines such as 'Scottish Development Agency Call for Oil Revenues'. At a press conference (and surely that itself is significant) the SDA made a public bid for more resources. The chairman, Sir William Gray, claimed that the £200 million already approved and a further £100 million that could be authorised by the Secretary of State for the first five years of agency activity would not be sufficient: 'North sea oil revenues would be a good source and we can think of no better use to which they can be put.' Thus in the UK we have developed in a similar way to the USA where, as Graham Wilson notes, '... distinguishing between pressure groups and agencies... is not easy'.[29]

THE PRAGMATIC STYLE

This 'pragmatic improvisation' where authority is shared with private and semi-private institutions and new structures are created has been described as a characteristic of both British and American practice.[30] From the most major to comparatively trivial policy areas, this improvisation demonstrates itself. Pay policy in the UK in 1977/78 – whereby the Government enforced a 'voluntary' policy through a variety of techniques (TUC/CBI cooperation, cash limits in the public sector, the threat of lost government contracts in the private sector, etc.) – is perhaps the best example of recent years, but it is difficult to find cases where it does not occur.

For example, criticism of invalid carriages was instrumental in a policy change by which the Government planned to cease providing special tricycle vehicles for the disabled who could make use of them. Instead, the Government sought to pay a mobility allowance to a wider range of the disabled – drivers and non-drivers alike. This was welcomed by some, but in turn caused discontent among those who were to lose a vehicle that would be replaced by an allowance too small to allow them to buy a replacement. The outcome of this series of controversies was that, at the suggestion of the Government, a group of prominent people drawn from the professions, from finance and industry, from voluntary bodies and from the trade unions, and chaired by Lord Goodman, set up a voluntary organisation working in collaboration with the Government to ensure that disabled people who wanted to use their mobility allowance to obtain a vehicle would get maximum value for their money in doing so. So in effect the Government was discreetly inventing a charity (Motability) to provide about 45,000 vehicles for those disabled who sign over their mobility allowance to Motability. The ingenious solution may well solve the problem very nicely – but is 'Motability' governmental or non-governmental? If in the future it asks for an increase in the mobility allowance, is it then a pressure group or a non-governmental agency bidding for funds? The classification is not made any simpler by an answer to a parliamentary question on 12 December 1977 that stated that Motability would receive 'administrative assistance' – subject to periodic review.

Similarly, a study of the National House Builders' Registration Council found that although the arrangement devised to protect the public against bad housebuilding was formally a private, commercial one, 'in reality, it extends government power over an important private-sector industry'. Although nominally the Council was independent of government – and had steered clear of receipt of government funding – subtle controls existed. The chairman and one other member are appointed by the Secretary of State for the Environment, and DOE civil servants attend meetings of the Council and its operating committees. The Council's papers, procedures and required building specifications need ministerial approval.[31]

The organisational growth in recent years appears to have been on the 'fringe'[32] – making the older idea of a recognisable centre with a few peripheral problem cases less acceptable. Thus, in the case of the DOE alone, the following bodies were listed in reply to a parliamentary question on 6 February 1978 asking how many 'new public national governmental organisations' were created between 1974 and 1978:[33]

Advisory Group on Commercial Property Development
Commission for Local Administration in England
Construction Experts Advisory Board
Construction Industry Manpower Board
Environmental Board
Housing Association's Registration Advisory Committee
Housing Corporation Advisory Committee on Co-operatives
Housing Services Advisory Group
New Towns Staff Commission
Scientific Authority for Animals
Waste Management Advisory Council (jointly with the D of I)

We begin to see the truth in Harry Hanson's prophecy in the late 1960s that 'the likelihood is that, whatever government is in power, the public and private sectors of British industry will increasingly interpenetrate, and in doing so raise political and constitutional issues equally important as and more intractable than those originally raised by the creation of public corporations...'[34]

THE PERSONNEL NETWORK

In discussing the 'disintegration of the centre' and 'the pragmatic style' we have attempted to argue that it is increasingly difficult to differentiate groups, agencies and departments – they are players in the same game. Boundaries are unclear; 'government' and 'governed' is difficult to maintain as a distinction. Matching this complex network of organisations is a complex network of personnel. Movement of individuals between Whitehall and the 'outside' produces an atmosphere of mutual confidence in negotiations. In effect, policy is now made between an internal and an external bureaucracy. So similar are both sides that transfer is relatively easy.[35] At least since the 1968 Fulton Report on the Civil Service it has been the accepted wisdom that the development of such practices in Britain would make the Civil Service more business-like, more efficient and responsive. In short, that more mobility would be a 'good thing'. A formal exchange scheme of secondments was introduced with the objective (among others) of contributing 'to the development of more effective communication and understanding between government, business and other sectors at various levels'. The movements involved since 1968 are shown in Table 3.4. These figures particularly pre-1973) are admitted by the Civil Service to be unreliable and they overstate the business/Civil Service contact because the figures include interchanges with local authorities and universities as well as with the business community. (For 1973 and subsequent years these sub-totals are given in brackets.) The CSD has explained that both the Civil Service and business sides have been unwilling to release high quality personnel for the sake of long-term gain.

TABLE 3.4   *Secondments to and from the Civil Service*

	Out of Civil Service	Into Civil Service
1968	12	19
1969	21	33
1970	12	33
1971	13	22
1972	10	14
1973	22 (10)	45 (22)
1974	15 (7)	34 (9)
1975	25 (14)	39 (15)

While these numbers are limited, the cumulative effect of the years 1968 to 1975 does mean that there must be a few hundred individuals with this experience. But the impact perhaps rests not on totals but levels. The most noteworthy case of secondment was probably that of Mr (now Sir) Campbell Adamson, who was seconded to the Department of Economic Affairs (DEA) as Deputy Under-Secretary of State between 1967 and 1969 and who then became director-general of the CBI between 1969 and 1976.

Another means whereby the barriers between the Civil Service and business communities are broken down are permanent recruitments from the other pool. In French administration there is the well-known idea of 'pantouflage' whereby civil servants move easily out of the Civil Service and into industry. Civil servants in Britain are particularly liable to 'cross' at the end of their careers. Rules exist on the acceptance of outside appointments by Crown servants, which claim that it is in the public interest that people with experience of public administration should be able to move into business and industry. It is, however, recognised that it is important to avoid any suspicion 'that serving officers might be ready to bestow favours on firms in the hope of future benefits to come'. Rules therefore exist 'to guard against the risk that a particular firm might be thought to be gaining an unfair advantage over its competitors by employing an officer who, during his service, had access to technical or other information which those competitors could legitimately regard as their own trade secrets'. Accordingly, all under-secretaries and above require official assent before accepting posts with certain relevant companies within two years of resignation or retirement from the Civil Service. Table 3.5 shows the number of cases where permission was granted during the period 1960–1975. These figures show a significant number of cases but even so they *under-state* the phenomenon in that they (a) relate only to *under-secretaries and above*, (b) cover only *companies with which the civil servant had dealings* in his Civil Service career, (c) cover only *the first two years* after the individual left the Civil Service.

TABLE 3.5   *Departure of civil servants to industry 1960–1975*

1960–63	22
1964–67	18
1968–71	40
1972–75	41

Source: condensed from *Hansard*, 4 January 1976.

In recent years there have been some quite well-publicised examples – including the appointment of the former head of the Home Civil Service, Lord Armstrong, to be chairman of the Midland Bank from 1975. His colleague, Sir Godfrey Agnew, Deputy Secretary at the Cabinet Office between 1972 and 1974, became a director of the Sun Life Assurance Society Ltd. in 1974. The Head of the Northern Ireland Civil Service, 1965–70, became a director of the Allied Irish Bank in 1970 and chairman of G. Heyn and Sons in 1971. Alex Jarratt, who was Secretary to the National Board for Prices and Incomes from 1965 to 1968 and Deputy Secretary at the Ministry of Agriculture, Fisheries and Food in 1970, became managing director of the International Publishing Corporation in 1970 and chairman and chief executive of Reed International in 1974. Sir William Nield, who was Permanent Secretary of the Cabinet Office from 1969 to 1972 and of the Northern Ireland Office from 1972 to 1973, became deputy chairman of Rolls Royce (1971) Ltd. from 1973 to 1976. Denis Haviland, formerly Deputy Secretary at the Ministry of Aviation (1959–64), became chairman and managing director of Staveley Industries Ltd. from 1965 to 1969. Sir R. Melville, ex-Permanent Secretary at the Ministry of Aviation Supply, became director of the Electronics Components Board of Westland Aircraft. Sir Edward Ashmore, who retired as Chief of Defence Staff in 1977, joined Racal Electronics – a firm involved in the military electronics market. And, of course, the most publicised example of 1977 was the BBC Television 'Master-mind', Sir David Hunt. He had served as private secretary to prime ministers Attlee and Churchill and on his retirement as an ambassa-dor had taken a post as deputy chairman and export finance adviser with a London firm of consultants. In 1978 some controversy was generated when, in connection with oil 'sanctions busting' in Rhodesia, it was discovered that an assistant secretary in the petroleum division of the Ministry of Power had moved to a senior position with British Petroleum.

No detailed figures are collected by the Civil Service (except of those who require permission), but it does appear that there are enough movements at a sufficiently influential level to qualify an image of distinct Civil Service and business cadres.

There is also, of course, recruitment into the Civil Service from those with a business background. In the late 50s and 60s, schemes were introduced to recruit administrators in mid-career with a public or private sector background. Partly these schemes were designed to fill a shortfall within the Civil Service in the number of middle managers, but they also stemmed from the general view that mobility between public and private sectors was desirable. A study of the seventy-seven entrants from the 'private sector' to Principal grade between 1961 and 1966 (there have also been a handful of appointments at higher levels) showed that only one-third of these recruits had actually had experience of private industry – others came from universities, public corporations, journalism, unions and em-ployees associations, etc.[36] Consequently, this form of recruitment has not really provided the Civil Service with much outside manage-ment expertise. Recruitment has been on a limited scale and there is little evidence that this is a major bridge between private and public sectors, but it does contribute to the overall flow.

The Conservative Government of 1970–74 experimented with a more direct infusion of business experience into Whitehall. In opposition, a team of eighteen businessmen was created to help mould the party's policy on topics such as 'hiving-off', procurement and the reorganisation of central government. A number of these men entered Whitehall on a short-term basis, and, while they had an impact on the development of new organisational forms, there seems little evidence of a major lasting change (or at least of changes that would not have happened in any case because of the mood within the service at that time).

Given the growth of the public sector, it is not surprising that movements between the public and private sectors are now fairly commonplace. For anything other to be the case would mean that sectors had little in common and involved discrete professionalisms: this is plainly not the case. Discussion of movement has been dominated by the notion that policy would be better made if each side were better informed of the practices and problems of the other, but before long British opinion might follow American and begin to question the advisability of what has been called the 'revolving door' between sectors. It can have dangers of partiality as well as benefits of communication.

We have observed that civil servants have experience of industry through secondment and that they not infrequently assume important positions in industry, especially on retirement. Even more relevant for our discussion is the practice that seems to be developing for ex-civil servants to appear manning representative associations and 'peak organisations'. If it is useful for an organisation like the Midland Bank to have the ex-Head of the Home Civil Service leading their fight against nationalisation in 1977/78, trade associations and other interest groups can also benefit from the experience of ex-civil servants, who know the man in the right position and how to feed a point of view into the governmental machine. For example, Tom Caulcott, currently secretary of the Association of Metropolitan Authorities (AMA), was previously Principal Finance Officer for Local Government Financial Policy at the DOE. In the words of the AMA journal, 'his Whitehall post made him in effect the Government's chief financial adviser in the Rate Support Grant negotiations with the local authority associations'.[37] The change meant a 'move to the opposite side of the table'. The AMA similarly recruited as their education officer an under-secretary formerly in charge of the teachers' branch at the Department of Education and Science.

Richard Crossman records moves (ultimately not pursued) towards another such appointment – and hints at the difficulties. Clifford Jarrett, Permanent Secretary at the Department of Health and Social Security, sought permission to take up a post as president of the Corporation of Society of Pensions Consultants on his retirement. He had received permission from the Head of the Home Civil Service but Crossman felt,

> Well here we are in the middle of a battle royal with the whole of the pensions interests, including the pension consultants, and he has been talking with them about this forthcoming job. I am sure there is nothing dishonest about it ... but in the following three years all the important decisions will be taken about its [the Superannuation Bill] application and he will be there to look after their interests... I really don't want to have him by as Permanent Secretary if he is negotiating with the enemy about crossing the line as soon as he leaves the Department.[38]

Other examples include: Chris Hall (perhaps a case of a different type), who moved from his post as Chief Information Officer at the Ministry of Transport to become in 1969 secretary of the Ramblers' Association and in 1973 director of the Council for the Protection of Rural England. James Douglas was Assistant Secretary, Ministry of Housing and Local Government from 1964 and Secretary of the Royal Commission on local Government from 1966 to 1969; he eventually became secretary-general of the Country Landowners' Association. E. P. James, who was in the Foreign and Commonwealth Office from 1961 to 1974, became executive director of the Institute of Directors from 1975 to 1976 and deputy director-general at the CBI in 1976. Sir William Godfrey, ex-Deputy Secretary at the Cabinet Office, is consultant at the Council of Engineering Institutions. Denis Haviland, ex-Deputy Secretary at the Ministry of Aviation, is a consultant member of the Council of the British Institute of Management. T. F. Brenchley, who was seconded from the Diplomatic Service as Deputy Secretary at the Cabinet Office in 1975, is now deputy secretary-general at the Arab–British Chamber of Commerce. Sir Geoffrey Farlonge, ex-ambassador, has been treasurer at the Arab–British Centre since 1977. R. C. C. Hunt, Assistant Under-Secretary of State at the Foreign and Commonwealth Office until 1973, became director of the British National Committee, International Chamber of Commerce from 1973 to 1976. R. C. Kent, Deputy Under-Secretary of State at the Ministry of Defence, became director (administration) of the Institution of Civil Engineers in 1977. The present director- general of the NFU – George Cattell – served in the Department of Employment and Productivity between 1968 and 1970. Sir Eugene Melville, who was at one time UK permanent representative at the United Nations, is now director-general of the British Property Federation. In his study of the Rent Act, 1957, M. J. Barnett notes the weight given by the Ministry of Housing to the memoranda prepared by H. Symson, who had moved from the Ministry in 1955 to the directorship of a landlords' pressure group.[39] Sir William Peterson was Deputy Secretary at the DEA from 1964 to 1968, moved to become clerk and director general of the Greater London Council between 1968 and 1972 and then returned to Whitehall as Permanent Secretary at the Home Office (1972–77). Other groups such as the Scottish Seed Potato Promotion Association and the Scottish Fishermens Organisation have also recruited from the Civil Service.

Such appointments will not be made by all pressure groups. They are only appropriate where a certain working relationship has been evolved (or is anticipated) with the relevant ministry. These close relationships are enjoyed by the major sectional groups and 're-spectable' established promotional groups such as the Council for Environmental Conservation or the Civic Trust. Where detailed policy is made by negotiations between competing bureaucracies, then the character of the work is likely to be similar on both sides. And a recruit from the other side is likely to have useful contacts. As one of these ex-civil servants put it to us:

> You may wonder whether former Civil Servants are useful to pressure groups. Undoubtedly they are. They know how the machine works. They know that the cry, 'go to the man at the top' is fallacious, and that it is often better to speak to the chap who drafts the letter rather than the chap who signs it. Further they know who the former chap is. No Civil Servant can be useful to his Minister unless he has some political antennae and these antennae are useful to the pressure group.

Such moves 'around the table' may be important but they are probably outnumbered by moves from central 'main-stream' departments to the extensive penumbra of government we noted when discussing the disintegration of the centre. It is not difficult to discover examples. Jack Beddoe, Under-Secretary at the DOE in charge of the Water Act 1973, became chief executive of one of the new Regional Water Authorities created by the Act. Michael Casey, Under-Secretary at the Department of Industry, became chief executive of British Shipbuilders. Alan Blackshaw, Under-Secretary at the Department of Energy, became director-general of the Offshore Supplies Office – a position he himself described as 'at the interface between the public and private sector enterprise'. Geoffrey Cokerhill moved from his post as Secretary at the Department of Education and Science (DES) to become secretary to the University Grants Committee. Such moves all help break any neat categorisation about where the public service agencies end and private groups begin.

Ex-civil servants also appear in perhaps less politically sensitive posts on their retirement. Again, examples are not difficult to discover. It is merely a matter of thinking of recently retired senior civil servants, and it appears that almost without exception they are involved in some charity, government arbitration body, commission or the like. Dame Evelyn Sharp retired as Permanent Secretary of the Ministry of Housing and Local Government (MHLG) and became a member of the Independent Broadcasting Authority from 1966 to 1973. Sir Philip Allen, Permanent Under-Secretary of State at the Home Office, became chairman of the Occupational Pensions Board in 1973. Sir Mathew Stevenson, Permanent Secretary at MHLG from 1966 to 1970, became deputy chairman of the Mersey Docks and Harbours Board from 1970 to 1971 and a member of the British Steel Corporation between 1971 and 1976. Sir Edward Compton, Comptroller and Auditor General from 1958 to 1966 and 'Ombudsman' from 1967 to 1971, has since been chairman of the English Local Government Boundary Commission. Sir Arnold France, Permanent Secretary at the Ministry of Health from 1964 to 1968 and Chairman of the Board of Inland Revenue from 1968 to 1973, has since been the chairman of the Central Board of Finance of the Church of England. Sir George Godber, Chief Medical Officer at the DHSS, DES and Home Office, became chairman of the Health Education Council. Sir Clifford Jarrett, Permanent Under-Secretary of State at the DHSS from 1964 to 1970, has been chairman of the Tobacco Research Council since 1971. Sir Robert Marshall, who was second Permanent Secretary at the DOE until 1978, and was in charge of water policy, retired only to become chairman of the National Water Council. Likewise, in 1978, the ex-Permanent Secretary at the Scottish Office was appointed chairman of the North of Scotland Hydro Electric Board.

The above is, then, a brief account of the export/import of personnel from and to Whitehall. Judged against a Civil Service of 745,000 staff, these might be insignificant, but against the 750 under-secretaries and above, the numbers are more noteworthy. The effect of missionary, outward movements by civil servants, accompanying the colonisation of the private sector by government, is matched by the integration of outsiders in the machine. In an extreme example the government can recruit its erstwhile opponents. In 1972 John Humphries, chairman of the Inland Waterways Association (IWA) was appointed as special adviser to the relevant minister. This was in the middle of a campaign by the IWA against the implications for canals of the Government's water reorganisation plans. There was some ill feeling in the Association that this was a 'nobbling' attempt to reduce criticism. An American observer has commented that if the late Martin Luther King Jr had lived in London rather than Montgomery, Alabama, he would not have been a moving force behind a revolution on race relations. He would have been chairman of the Community Relations Commission.[40]

More typically, representatives of outside interests are integrated into the Whitehall system by participation on commissions or royal commissions inquiring into some area or other. Thus, W. C. Anderson, general secretary of NALGO to 1973, served on the Fulton Committee (1966–68), the National Insurance Advisory Committee (1970–76), the Industrial Injuries Advisory Council (1970–74), the Royal Commission on Civil Liability and Compensation of Civil Injury (1973), etc. Tom Jackson, general secretary of the Union of Post Office Workers, has been HM Government Director, British Petroleum Co. Ltd. since 1975, and has served on the Press Council since 1973 and on the 'Annan' Committee on Broadcasting (1974–77) and was a governor of the BBC (1968–73). James Jack, general secretary of the Scottish TUC has been a member of the Scottish Postal Board since 1972, of the Board of the Crown Agents since 1975, of the Scottish Development Agency since 1975, etc. In July 1977, the Secretary of State for Employment estimated that the thirty members of the TUC General Council held 180 state appointments between them.

And, of course, on the employers' side the picture is similar. Sir Michael Clapham, past president of the CBI, was a member of the Industrial Reorganisation Corporation (1968–71), of the Standing Advisory Committee on Pay of Higher Civil Service (1968–71) and of the Review Body of Doctors' and Dentists' Remuneration (1968–70). Lord Plowden is chairman of the CBI Companies Committee and has been chairman of the Atomic Energy Authority (1954–59), chairman of committees of enquiry on Treasury Control of Public Expenditure (1959–61), the Organisation of Representational Services Overseas (1963–64), the Aircraft Industry (1964–65), the Structure of Electricity Supply Industry in England and Wales (1974), etc.

COMMITTEES

The final feature of the British policy machinery that we wish to cover is the vast range of committees. Several problems prevent a full account. One is that a variety of types of committee exist – and not all committees in fact perform their ostensible role. The simplest kind of committee is probably the type set up to investigate a particular issue or incident. Generally, they will be referred to as departmental committees – but royal commissions can perform similar tasks.[41] For no very clear-cut reasons, they will appear under the name of working party, steering group or whatever. These ad hoc inquiries generally have terms of reference of the type given to the Committee on Motorway Service Areas in 1978: '*To consider and report on* [our emphasis] how far the present facilities and services available at motorway service areas meet the needs of motorway users having particular regard to price, quality, variety and effective competition; and on what further provision should be made for the convenience of travellers, bearing in mind road safety and any other relevant matters.' The members of this committee had relevant experience and expertise but were not *directly* involved in the problem area. Although they were not representing interested parties, insofar as the committee received evidence, heard witnesses, etc., it was 'group' views that it obtained.

Indeed, there was astonishment when a similarly independent committee on the registration of builders in effect rejected the views of all interested groups.[42] Very often, however, the membership reflects the various groups involved in the issue. Thus the 'steering committee' set up to consider the feasibility of an experiment in the tape-recording of police interrogations was more directly composed of representative spokesmen: for example, it included representatives of the Home Office, the Bar Council, the Law Society, the Justice Clerk's Society, the Association of Chief Police Officers and a member of the Probation Service. Such 'representative' committees are probably more likely to engage in bargaining between the various points of view and be less involved in the establishing of matters of fact – but it is difficult to generalise, and each example requires careful scrutiny.

It has been calculated that between 1945 and 1969 a mean of sixty-four of these ad hoc committees were sitting each year.[43] As well as ad hoc committees there are also permanent advisory bodies – created on an even more lavish scale. Members of Parliament have periodically attempted to discover exactly how many exist. In 1958, Marcus Lipton, MP, discovered that there were about 850 advisory bodies of a central or national character. In 1965, Mr Paul Dean, MP, secured a list of permanent standing advisory committees advising Her Majesty's Government on various aspects of policy. Around 250 committees were listed – ranging from the Law Reform Committee, through the Advisory Committee on Dairy Sterilisers, the University Grants Committee, to the Mobile Radio Committee. And while that was no doubt a precise answer to the exact wording of the question, different answers at a later date imply a far greater total of advisory committees (perhaps doing other than 'advising on policy'). Thus, in 1976, an answer to one of a series of questions from David Knox, MP, revealed that the Lord Chancellor was aided by 250 advisory committees on Justices of the Peace in England and Wales (excluding Lancashire) [*sic*] and 78 advisory committees on General Commissioners of Income Tax. These 328 advisory committees were only some of the bodies advising one minister, and hence the present total is much larger than implied by the answer to Mr Dean's question in 1965. It cannot be pretended that these advisory bodies are all relevant to the commanding heights of the polity. For example, a parliamentary question in 1978 discovered that the Hill Farming Advisory Committee, which reports to the Secretary of State for Scotland, had met only twice in the previous five years and no date had been fixed for a future meeting. But whereas individual examples are perhaps of limited importance, the overall pattern might be more relevant in a discussion of groups in the policy-making system than impressive-sounding institutions such as NEDO. There can be few subjects without some advisory committee where the government (through civil servants) can discuss problems with interested parties.

An advisory committee can be given the right not only to advise the government on matters referred to it but also to make representations on any question within its field of work on which it thought it right to express an opinion. However, two committees that have been examined closely have been found to be employed responding to governmental invitations and not volunteering advice. In his study of the Plowden Committee on Primary Education, Maurice Kogan reports that the Secretary of State for Education and Science was required by Section 4 of the Education Act, 1944, to appoint Central Advisory Councils (CACs) for Education for both England and Wales.[44] The Act stated that the CAC will 'advise the Secretary of State upon such matters connected with educational theory and practice as they think fit, and upon any question referred to them by him' (Section 4(1)). Although initially the CAC reports were based on terms of reference created by the Council for itself, 'it was soon thought preferable by everybody concerned that the Department should take the initiative'. More generally, Kogan has observed that Central Advisory Committees in education 'have had functions somewhat different from those conveyed by their formal designations. . . The Department . . . use them as both a jury against which departmental policies could be tested ... and as a centre for negotiations'.[45]

Our own study of the Central Advisory Water Committee (CAWC) came to similar conclusions.[46] Despite its statutory basis under the 1945 Water Act, it was allowed to lapse periodically by the Ministry until a specific inquiry was needed. (Thus there may not be a major difference between ad hoc and permanent advisory bodies.) Despite the fact that members were appointed as individuals, in practice they represented their 'parent' groups. This meant that some members also sat on the committees of bodies preparing evidence for submission to CAWC. Thus, this network of advisory committees serves as a means to involve a wide range of groups in particular policy decisions. Of course, not all committees are set up to obtain a decision – some are set up to delay; others are set up in an attempt by the department to educate its clients about the difficulties it faces. On the whole, however, they are an important channel of access for groups.

As well as 'advice', committees/boards are also involved in executive action. One of the best-documented examples is the work of agricultural marketing boards. Marketing boards have in the past been set up for hops, milk, bacon, pigs, potatoes, tomatoes and cucumber, wool and eggs. The boards consist of a mixture of ministerial appointees and representatives elected by producers, and have an 'impressive range of independent "governmental" powers.'[47]

These executive boards are not too dissimilar to the 'independent' National Housebuilders' Registration Council described earlier (p. 60). It can also be difficult to distinguish an executive board from an advisory committee. Without looking in detail at particular cases, it is impossible to state whether, say, the 'Advisory Committee on Tip Safety' or the 'Advisory Committee on Investment Grants' or the 'Advisory Committee for Mineral Processing and Metals Extraction' are giving general advice to the minister or taking *de facto* decisions.

The attempts in more recent years by MPs to discover the extent of this phenomenon of boards and committees have met with little success. One might naively expect a central register to be maintained, but in accordance with our earlier emphasis on 'departmentalism', it is found that individual departments are responsible for their own committees. When it comes to answering parliamentary questions, some departments give a full answer but others reply that there are too many to list, others answer privately and yet others answer using their own definition of committee, board and council or whatever. So the attempts by e.g. Mr Speed in 1969, Mr Sharples in 1970, Mr Knox in 1976, Mr Dykes in 1977, have produced a very patchy response – but sufficient information to confirm that such committees are a major British characteristic. The Secretary of State for Education and Science alone appoints 667 places on 67 separate bodies – and that in total does not include what the Department termed minor appointments, which would be costly to identify.[48]

PARLIAMENTARY GOVERNMENT, PARTY GOVERNMENT OR POLICY COMMUNITIES?

In describing the tendency for boundaries between government and groups to become less distinct through a whole range of pragmatic developments, we see policies being made (and administered) between a myriad of interconnecting, interpenetrating organisations. It is the relationships involved in committees, the *policy community* of departments and groups, the practices of co-option and the consensual style, that perhaps better account for policy outcomes than do examinations of party stances, of manifestoes or of parliamentary influence. The process we describe is obscure – though not necessarily thereby sinister – and is a long way from the clear-cut and traditional principles of parliamentary and party government. Though a confusing system, partly because of its obscurity and partly because it has not been rationally 'planned', it does have some unwritten rules, which we shall discuss in chapter 5.

SECTION II:

The Policy Process

CHAPTER 4

The Emergence of Issues and Policies

INTRODUCTION

Great emphasis is placed by political scientists on the ways in which political issues get resolved. How was the decision reached? Why did that particular piece of legislation take the form it did? What groups were active during the legislative process and with what success? Such questions are, of course, of vital importance. But we need to ask a prior series of questions. How do issues arrive on the political agenda? Who decides that some problem or other requires governmental action? (We use the term action rather than legislation deliberately – in chapter 7 we shall discuss the extent to which much of modern government is concerned with making decisions and taking action rather than with the process of legislation itself.) Why do seemingly important issues get delayed on their way to the political agenda or never arrive at all? Such questions have been relatively ignored in the past. In other words, we have been more concerned with the political debate as enacted before our eyes than with explaining the ways in which societies decide what to have political debates about. For example, why did the environment become a political issue in most Western democracies in the mid to late 1960s? No doubt there was plenty of pollution before then. Lakes were being poisoned, the air was being contaminated by all sorts of emission, the countryside was being despoiled. Yet it was only in 1970 that Britain set up a Department of the *Environment* (the first nation to do so in fact). Similarly, why did worker 'participation' become an issue (again in most Western democracies) in the 1970s when 'the problem' had clearly existed long before that? No doubt in ten years' time we shall be able to look at the then big political issues and will be puzzled that they were not issues now

(1978). In other words, are there important *problems* that ought to command the attention of our political leaders and institutions of government right *now* that are being ignored? If there are such problems (and we would all be able to produce our own pet list), why are they being ignored? Is it something to do with lack of information and poor information flows, or are powerful groups (or individuals) in society deliberately supressing discussion of such problems in their own interests? Given the limitations of time and resources, particularly financial, that all governments are subject to, it is of central interest to know how and why these scarce resources are concentrated upon some problems but not others. Indeed, we need to know much more about differences in what governments in different political systems actually *do*.

Rose has attempted to classify the activities of the modern state but has found that '... there is no common pattern of resource mobilization and social services in contemporary industrial nations'.[1] Activities that in one political system may be regarded as without dispute the concern of the state, in others may be regarded as essentially private or market activities and of no particular concern of the state. Political systems face different problems and are subject to differing pressures (either through the ballot box or more usually through the activity of pressure groups) and so it is not surprising that governments are faced with quite different 'agendas for action'. On the other hand, there is a very strong tendency for states never to abandon their activities.[2] This proposition, as Rose suggests, is really a proposition about the power of groups entrenched in government. Once a policy or programme has been adopted, the groups who benefit, be they bureaucrats or 'outside' groups, will fight to the limit in order to retain their benefits. Put simply, it is always more difficult to take away benefits from groups than to refuse to grant those benefits in the first place. So just as groups play an important role in getting issues onto the agenda and in keeping them off it, they also play a crucial role in preventing the *removal* of issues and policies from the political agenda.

A GENERAL THEORY?

As we have indicated, the *emergence* of issues, as opposed to the processing of issues that have already emerged, has been relatively neglected as an area of study. Some writers have, however, recognised that getting issues onto the political agenda, and keeping them off it, is a good indicator of the distribution of power in society. In particular, E. E. Schattschneider, in his book *The Semi-Sovereign People*, has stressed the importance of defining alternatives in the political debate. Thus he argues:

> Political conflict is not like an intercollegiate debate in which opponents agree in advance on a definition of the issues. As a matter of fact, *the definition of the alternatives is the supreme instrument of power*, the antagonists can rarely agree on what the issues are because power is involved in the definition. He who determines what politics is about runs the country, because the definition of the alternatives is the choice of conflicts, and the choice of conflicts allocates power.[3]

Indeed, Schattschneider sees most political theories as being related to the question of 'who can get into the fight and who is excluded'.[4] He is deeply worried by the bias that he believes exists in terms of the class background of people who do actually manage to get into the fight.

This concern arises from the class bias of what American writers tend to call associational activity. Basically there is a tendency in virtually all political systems for the middle class to be more active in pressure groups – even those pressure groups whose objectives are entirely linked to increased benefits for the working class. To Schattschneider the pressure group system is not one that enables all sections of society to enter the political fight. It only makes sense '... as the political instrument of a segment of the community. It gets results by being selective and biased; *if everybody got into the act the unique advantages of this form of organization would be destroyed, for it is possible that if all interests could be mobilized the result would be stalemate*'.[5] The more groups there are, the more difficult it may be for any one group to gain a real advantage, although this takes no account of the sanctions that particular groups possess. For example, university lecturers might be as well *organised* as power station workers or motor manufacturers, but it is obvious to all (and especially to governments deciding the level of university pay) that lecturers possess few if any effective *sanctions*. Several thousand academics marching along Westminster Bridge may be an impressive organisational achievement, but it hardly brings society to its knees.

But we would certainly accept Schattschneider's central thesis that 'All forms of political organisation have a bias in favor of the exploitation of some kinds of conflict *bias*. Some issues are organized into politics while others are organized out of it.[6] All issues are therefore not equal. The fact that a pressure group makes a demand that the government should (or should not) do something does not constitute a political issue. Thousands of demands on government are made each year but only a small proportion of these demands are taken on board by the political system, debated and *possibly* acted upon. Most are stillborn or suffer a premature death. Moreover, as politics is centrally concerned with the management of conflict, then the displacement of conflicts is 'a prime instrument of political strategy'.[7] One conflict can be used to displace another, perhaps more important conflict.

Schattschneider cites such US examples as McCarthyism being used to destroy liberal causes, urban-rural conflict being used to check the political excesses of the labour movement, and the revival of sectional antagonism driving a wedge between the western and southern branches of the Populist movement.[8] A more spectacular and recent UK example is the way in which producer interests have utilised the issues of inflation and unemployment to drive environmental protection off the main political agenda.

The whole concept of agenda setting is well understood by groups. Thus Frank Field, director of the Child Poverty Action Group (CPAG) wrote in 1972 '... long before 1969 the Labour Government had, to put it mildly, run out of steam. As a result, poverty was just one of the many issues that were struck off the political agenda. The first task, therefore, seemed to be to get this back into the political debate'.[9] Recognising their relative weakness in terms of their power to force 'poverty' back into the political fight, the strategy adopted by CPAG was to formulate an alliance with the trade union movement, as that part of the Labour movement having a veto power over a Labour government.[10] It is interesting that in the UK we have had a great deal of discussion about the need for more 'open government' yet little or no discussion on the more crucial process of agenda setting.

There is some evidence that the process has become a little more open in recent years, although it would be too optimistic to accept the view that '... with ambitious sponsors and an active press hungry for news, it has become next to impossible to deny a hearing to "an idea whose time has come".[11] Even if it has become easier (at least in Western nations, but possibly in the Eastern bloc too) to get an issue a 'hearing', there is always the danger that as new issues get forced onto the agenda, they will damage or remove others in doing so.

But many writers would not concede that agenda setting has been significantly 'democratised'. Space does not permit a full discussion of the lively debate about the nature of political power, but in an important development of Schattschneider's notion of mobilisation of bias, Bachrach and Baratz have developed the concept of 'two faces of power'.[12] In criticising both the elitist and the pluralist characterisations of democracy, they too highlight the importance of issue emergence and non-emergence or *non-decision-making*, which constitutes the 'other' face of power. The pluralists, by concentrating on decisions, are ignoring a vital element in the power structure – the power not to make decisions in give policy areas. Thus, 'power is exercised when A participates in decisions that affect B' but it is 'also exercised when A devotes his energies to creating or reinforcing social and political values and institutional practices that limit the scope of the political process to public consideration of only those issues which are comparatively innocuous to A'.[13]

So researchers should be as interested in those areas where decisions are *not* made as where they *are* made. If he ignores non-decision-making he is neglecting one whole facet of power.[14] Thus, 'individuals and groups, both liberal and conservative, who are bent upon maintaining the correct allocation of values are likely to focus on preventing demands for reallocation of values from reaching the decision-making stage, rather than running the risk that hostile demands will not be voted down when they are ripe for decision'.[15]

Perhaps the most widely quoted study of an example of agenda control is Crenson's study of the un-politics of air pollution in two us cities.[16] The starting point for Crenson's study is the fact that two us cities faced with similar air pollution problems – Gary and East Chicago in Indiana – exhibited marked differences in the way they dealt with them. In particular, it was not until the mid-1950s that air pollution became a public issue in Gary, yet East Chicago passed an ordinance relating to air pollution in 1949.[17] The explanation, according to Crenson, is that industrial interests in Gary were more influential in preventing air pollution from becoming an issue than were industrialists in East Chicago.

It is, however, important to note that Crenson's analysis of this influence is rather subtle. It was not simply a case of the industrialists in Gary applying pressure on politicians, it was more a case of the mere *existence* of the industrialists influencing the actions of decision-makers.[18] A pressure group can thus exercise influence simply by being there – they do not necessarily have to take any action. Politicians are perfectly aware of groups and the attitudes they are likely to adopt in a given situation and will often avoid action that is likely to provoke the groups into greater activity. Thus, in Gary, 'Though US Steel never really threw its weight against anti-pollution forces, its weight was felt all the same.... In spite of its political passivity, US Steel seems to have had the ability to enforce inaction on the dirty air issue'.[19] It was helped in this influence by anticipated reactions to the fact that it was the dominant industry in the city. In contrast, East Chicago was not the creation of a single company and so 'The apparent fractionation [*sic*] of industrial power may have emboldened the partisans of pollution control.'[20]

Also industrialists in East Chicago took an active interest in the anti-pollution issue and indeed influenced the political outcome. But by doing so they were at least recognising the issue and were prepared to see attempts to resolve it. Their counterparts in Gary, in contrast, frustrated the anti-pollution activists by conceding that pollution was bad, but never actually doing anything. Crenson concludes from his study that 'Decision-making activity is channeled and restricted by the process of non-decision-making [and that] the power reputations of people within a community may deter action on certain sensitive or politically unprofitable issues'.[21]

In discussing the power of groups to prevent the emergence of issues onto the political agenda, it is important to recall our suggestion that it was desirable to use a fairly wide definition of the term 'group' on some occasions. We argued that it was often the case that government departments and agencies and individual companies were capable of exhibiting all the characteristics of what are normally recognised as pressure groups. This phenomenon can be particularly important in deciding the content of the political agenda. For example, departments may try to restrict consideration of issues, raised by outside groups, that are a potential threat to its own programmes and staffing. Thus, pressure groups opposed to road schemes in the UK argued for many years that at public inquiries they should be able to challenge whether a road or motor-way was actually needed. It was only in 1973 that this right was conceded by the Government.

This resistance is easily explicable in terms of departmental interest. Quite simply it did not suit organisations such as Road Construction Units (within the Department of the Environment) to permit a challenge to the basis of their own existence – the generation of new road schemes. Even where a department or official agency does not set out to prevent a specific issue emerging, it may have the same effect by restricting the range of groups who are consulted in a particular policy area. The 'process of consultation' is an integral part of the policy process. Indeed, the very fact of consultation is used to reduce the power of Parliament itself, as the government is able to use the argument that the 'affected interests have been consulted and have agreed to this measure'. But who gets consulted and who does not is then of central importance. If nothing else it puts a high premium on being organised. If an 'interest' is not organised it cannot be consulted, and if it is not consulted decisions will be made, policies crystallised, before the community at large is able to exert pressure.

An interesting UK example of new groups managing to 'enter' a specific policy area that had been dominated by well-established interests for many years is the case of 'construction and use' lorry regulations. New groups made sufficient noise, gained wide media coverage and as a result were included on the department's con-sultation list for the future. Thus, discussions of construction and use regulations now cover wider environmental implications than was the case in the past and this is because new groups bring with them new issues. Similarly, discussion of road schemes now takes into account the wider environmental implications as a result of new groups 'getting in on the act'. Yet another example is provided by Friends of the Earth and their campaign against non-returnable bottles and cans. They have been brought into departmental con-sultations and have gained representation on departmental working parties as a result of their well-publicised 'events'.

Indeed, it is important to remember what at first sight is an obvious point – namely that the political agenda *does* change. Whilst writers such as Bachrach and Baratz have highlighted a most important aspect of political power – that of the power to *prevent* decisions being made – there is evidence that it is increasingly difficult to exercise this power. Much of this, we would argue, is due to the ability of new pressure groups in modern democracies to *force* issues onto the agenda, whether or not governments or existing groups like it, or whether or not they are insider groups having insider status. It is to this more positive aspect of group behaviour that we now turn.

FORCING ISSUES ONTO THE AGENDA

A glance at any daily newspaper is enough to convince the reader of the key role played by groups in getting issues onto the political agenda. As Finer suggests when discussing the question of governmental 'interference' in the economy, it is not usually a case of foolish or misguided governments interfering with the market, it is the other way round: 'for firms and trade unions actively seek the intervention of the political power in one shape or form. It is not so much the politicians who interfere with the market as the market – firms and unions – that interferes with the government.'[22] A good example of a group actively seeking the 'interference' of the government is provided by the Institute of Plumbers in the UK. In early 1978 they pressed for legislative action requiring the registration of all plumbers in an attempt to control what they saw as 'cowboys' who were competing unfairly with Institute members. Similarly, British shipowners tried to persuade the government to set up a Norwegian-style state agency to guarantee the industry's large and increasing debts. In January 1978 the British cutlery industry produced a rescue plan that demanded the tightening of controls on low-cost Pacific imports, together with government aid for some companies. This provoked reaction from the British Importers Confederation who set up a committee to protect the interests of cutlery importers and sent a study to the Under-Secretary of State for Trade arguing *against* import controls.

In practice, Finer argues, sectional groups seek to manipulate the *entire* environment in their favour. As an example he cites the British trade unions who wanted prices frozen (by the government), low-income bracket taxes cut (by the government) and surtax and company taxes increased in order to pay greater welfare payments (by the government), yet still demanded free collective bargaining.[23]

It is important to note that promotional groups are just as active in pressing their own pet schemes before politicians in the hope that they may gain a place on the agenda for action. Voluntary agencies concerned with homelessness attempted to draw attention to the plight of the growing number of homeless girls in Britain and expressed concern that the government was not providing more money to the agencies in order to provide accommodation. The agencies had cooperated in a survey that had revealed that, in contrast to earlier surveys, a new 'problem' had emerged. Previously there had been a small population of older female 'dossers', whereas now 'there had been a dramatic change and now young girls had become homeless in numbers large enough to cause deep concern among social and voluntary agencies'.[24]

Pressure groups were performing an important role in the policy process – namely helping in the process of problem *identification*. The first stage in any national policy process must be effective problem identification, and groups may well be more efficient at this than official policy-making structures such as central government departments. Indeed, departments may well encourage them in these tasks, as 'new problems' provide new opportunities for the departments too.

A classic example of a pressure group plugging away year after year to convince government and Parliament that a serious problem existed, needing legislative action, is provided by the National Society for Clean Air. Formed in 1929 (as the Smoke Abatement Society), its policy was to convert 'informed opinion' before trying to gain popular support for its cause.[25] As Sanderson suggests, the Society had to avoid any accusations of crankiness as 'in its early days it was often dismissed an organisation of eccentrics'.[26] Over a period of years, using exhibitions, gaining press publicity, producing factual reports, the Society has helped 'air pollution' to get on the political agenda. More specifically, he suggests, 'the Society has been responsible for the propagation of the two ideas which have been the main vehicles of smoke abatement in recent years'.[27] These ideas were 'smokeless zones', now widely accepted, and the principle of 'prior approval' for the installation of fuel-burning appliances. Not that the Society can be accorded all the credit for the eventual legislation, the Clean Air Act 1956, which is now the foundation of UK air pollution policy. Events and personalities, as is often the case in the policy process, played an important part. In particular, the great London fog of 1952 and the activities of a backbench MP, Gerald (later Sir) Nabarro, helped to dramatise and politicise what was still a rather technical subject.

An important success for the Smoke Abatement Society was the setting up of an official committee of inquiry into the problem. This gave official recognition that the problem of air pollution had indeed arrived on the political agenda. As Sanderson argues, the setting up of a committee of inquiry of some kind is often an important goal for promotional groups. This, he suggests, is because they are otherwise consulted much less frequently by governments than are sectional groups. While this is true, we might also add that it also reflects their lack of what Finer calls 'socio-economic leverage'.[28] Though they may be consulted, promotional groups can hardly *demand* that the government take action on, or at least give very serious consideration to, a particular issue. (Indeed the adoption of such an attitude may be quite counter-productive. For example, the Standing Committee on National Parks was seen by the Secretary of State for the Environment as being too strident in its demands for reform of the National Parks administration during discussions of local government reform in October 1971. The result was that it did not even receive a copy of the subsequent consultation paper!)

On the other hand, if an official committee of inquiry (or royal commission) comes forward with proposals in line with those previously advocated by the group, then the issue is more likely to take root and bear fruit in terms of government and parliamentary action. Some groups, openly recognising this, have even resorted to setting up their *own* 'commissions' in the hope that this will raise the status of the issue they are trying to launch. For example, environmental groups involved in transport policy set up a 'commission' in the early 1970s. In contrast, seven large mining companies set up a Commission on Mining and the Environment, chaired by Lord Zuckerman, in an attempt to meet growing criticism from such groups as Friends of the Earth.

The importance of committee reports can be seen by the report of the Advisory Committee on Trunk Road Assessment, published in January 1978. This government-appointed committee proposed quite radical changes in road planning. Its report was seen by groups like Friends of the Earth as vindicating '... the protests of motorway objectors and exposes the heavy-handed methods of the

Department of Transport road planners'.[29] In essence, the Committee accepted many of the criticisms of road planning made by environmentalists for years without success and immediately gave their ideas greater status and importance. Thus the issue got firmly on the agenda, in a two-stage process. In stage one, the groups agitated for a change of policy without success, but made themselves such a nuisance that the government decided to appoint the Advisory Committee to look into the whole problem. This, temporarily, submerged the 'issue' again. In stage two, the Committee reported and the 'issue' had bounced back again with an 'official' label attached to it. Moreover, the groups were still around and active in pressing for its implementation.

The setting up of a committee or commission to look at a problem does not, of course, guarantee that the problem will in fact become an issue. All observers of politics are familiar with the use of committees to delay action on problems. The setting up of a committee can thus effectively *remove* an item from the political agenda for several years – by which time other, seemingly important issues will be under consideration, thus preventing the 'old' item from returning. Many a dusty committee report must be lying on the shelves in Whitehall departments labelled 'problem gone away' (or at least 'no one of political importance interested in problem'). However, the activity of groups at the time of publication of these reports can be crucial if the issue is to be revived.

The process that led to the Deposit of Poisonous Waste Act in 1972 shows the difficulty of getting a subject on the agenda.[30] The problem first 'surfaced' in 1963 when farm animals were killed by chemicals from a nearby factory. Partly as a result of this the Government set up the Key Committee in 1964. This recommended much stricter controls, but did not report until 1970. By that time the problem was 'off the agenda' and the Government merely published a circular (in August 1970). The matter was again raised by the Royal Commission on Environmental Pollution, and the Working Party on Refuse Disposal in 1971. Thus, no less than three official committees of inquiry had drawn attention to the problem, but progress to legislation was pedestrian. The Department of the Environment wanted to shelve the matter until local government reorganisation was finalised. In the meantime preliminary consultations with groups such as the CBI were initiated.

Although the problem was undoubtedly important, there was no effective *pressure* for change. No significant group, no powerful interest, was forcing the issue to the top of the pile of issues facing the Department at that time. However, in November 1971 a lorry driver employed by a national waste disposal contractor gave evidence to the Warwickshire branch of the Conservation Society concerning unauthorised tipping of poisonous wastes. (He had earlier been rebuffed by local government officials.) The Warwickshire Conservation Society sent his evidence to the relevant ministers and in a meeting with DOE officials it was promised stronger measures on 'dumping' at the end of the Parliament (i.e. 1975).

Regarding this offer as unsatisfactory, the group released the story to the media. The story was given dramatic coverage and this publicity generated more allegations of the dumping of toxic waste. The publicity turned a technical matter into a political issue. Nonetheless, by February 1972 the issue was beginning to 'fade'. It looked as if the Government had weathered the storm and would be able to revert to a more leisurely timetable. But the developing calm was upset by the discovery of thirty-six drums in a derelict brickyard used by children as a playground. The drums contained sufficient cyanide waste to poison half the Midlands, and a local MP soon questioned the Secretary of State for the Environment. He was told that the Government intended to introduce statutory control to put into effect a code of practice that was being agreed between the Department and the National Association of Waste Disposal Contractors. The Opposition offered their cooperation to the Government and an issue that had been around for years was dealt with under emergency legislation in eighteen days.

So here we have a case where group activity – the Conservation Society aided by the media – transformed what was a serious problem into a salient political issue. It is also significant that the terms of the solution had to be agreed with the relevant trade association. Undoubtedly chance events were also important, but these were exploited by the interested groups. Similarly, the role of MPs was also important as exploiters of issues. Backbenchers are 'scavengers' for potential issues, particularly if constituency interests are involved. While MPs rarely play a major role in the identification of a problem or the formulation and passage of solutions, they are effective in 'running with the ball' when groups have given them the chance. Given sufficient parliamentary activity, it is difficult for the government to refuse to 'accept the pass' eventually.

THE MEDIA AND THE AGENDA

In discussing the emergence of toxic waste as a political issue, we indicated that the role of the media can be a crucial one. Indeed, Sir Edward Boyle has commented, reflecting on his experience as a Cabinet minister, that 'The Cabinet increasingly, as the years go on, tends to be most concerned with the agenda that the press and media are setting out as the crucial issues before the nation at any one time'.[31] Pressure groups are as aware of this as are ex-Cabinet ministers and they act accordingly. Virtually *all* pressure groups seek media publicity for their cause or interest. They may not see media coverage as their prime target,[32] but groups that are so clearly 'insiders', such as the CBI and the TUC, are nevertheless keen to gain publicity for most of their objectives. For example, the TUC, as both an insider group and one possessing plenty of 'muscle' too, is nonetheless sufficiently concerned to have set up a committee to monitor media coverage of industrial affairs. Its aim is to seek what it considers as fairer and more balanced reporting of industrial matters (particularly industrial disputes). The danger of 'biased' reporting, from the point of view of the unions, it that it produces a climate of opinion generally hostile to some of their activities and this could, in turn, cause the re-emergence of trade union reform as a political issue.

But just as the TUC may be anxious to avoid 'bad publicity' (and likewise many immigrant organisations are disturbed by publicity surrounding immigration statistics, etc.) for fear that new 'hostile' issues will emerge, so other groups are most anxious to create a climate of opinion out of which legislation will emerge. The development of 'the environment' as a political issue is a case in point. Many observers have suggested that 'the environment' emerged suddenly as a political issue in the late 1960s and early 1970s. As Gregory (writing in 1972) has argued, the preoccupation of the communications media with 'the environment' transformed hitherto 'low visibility' decisions into 'highly conspicious and therefore palpable indicators of a Minister's personal scale of values'. Sounding a warning note to environmental pressure groups, he suggested that politicians, in granting greater weight to environmental factors in their decisions, were not reacting to mass opinion; '... rather it is the possibility of hostile criticisms from the mass media and a relatively small circle of supposed opinion-leaders that has influenced their thinking'.[33]

The dangers to environmental groups, he suggests, were obvious: 'The media thrive on fashion and do much to create it. Fashions are ephemeral; new ones regularly drive out the old... environmentalists must make rapid headway in the task of embedding what is still a somewhat limited and superficial concern for amenity far more deeply within the British political and social culture.'[34] Many would now (1978) believe that this warning has been proved by subsequent events to be well founded.

It could be argued that the media themselves are a pressure group. Indeed, in terms of 'the environment', a group of journalists did form a pressure group *within* the mass media, called Environmental Communicators Organisation, with the aim of securing more environmental coverage in the press, radio and television. They built up links between the media and environmental pressure groups by providing the latter with the names of sympathetic journalist to whom 'copy' could be sent. In a similar way the National Union of Journalists has attempted to influence the way in which race-relations news has been presented and indeed has produced a code of practice, designed to prevent what it sees as 'biased' race stories being published.

The difficulty for environmental groups today is that 'the environment' as an issue is probably in what Anthony Downs has called 'the postproblem' stage.[35] Downs has suggested a theory of issue emergence that sees issues as passing through five stages:

(1) *The pre-problem stage* in which the problem exists, is recognised by experts and groups in the field and is usually far worse than when it eventually gets recognised.

(2) *Alarmed discovery and euphoric enthusiasm.* This is often the result of some dramatic event, e.g. the Torrey Canyon oil tanker disaster in the UK in 1967, or the cyanide discovery in 1972. The general public are alerted to the issue and there is enthusiasm for 'dealing' with the problem.

(3) *Realising the cost of significant progress.* People realise the cost of actually solving the problem is likely to be very high.

(4) *Gradual decline of public interest.* Having realised the cost of solutions, people get discouraged, bored or refuse to contemplate the problem anymore. This process is helped by the emergence of new issues, driving out the old.

(5) *Post-problem stage.* The issue has lost its primary position on the

agenda and received only spasmodic attention, although is still in a slightly better position than stage (1).

One of the main tasks of pressure groups is, of course, to prevent their problem from entering phases (3), (4) and (5) – the last being a potential disaster for most groups. On the other hand, just as we suggested, following Bachrach and Baratz, that some groups try to prevent the emergence of issues, then so some groups try to hasten 'hostile' issues along the Downsian progression and into relative oblivion. For example, polluters have been active in stage (3) of 'the environment's' progression by emphasising the cost and employment consequences of dealing with pollution. In this case 'costs' is used in the financial sense, but groups may emphasise *political* costs as well. Thus, the trade unions in Britain have fairly successfully killed trade union reform as a political issue by demonstrating the political costs to any party that dares to raise it.

POLITICAL PARTIES AND ISSUE EMERGENCE

Many governmental policies originate when the governing party is in opposition. In so far as governments try to control events, rather than react to them, they do so by trying to decide in advance of becoming the government what they would do in particular policy areas. So the political parties are themselves important agents for the emergence of issues. As observers of British politics are aware, party ideology can be an important source of policy initiatives and can influence governmental response to events as they occur. Pressure groups readily recognise that contact with opposition parties can bear fruit at a later date. For example, the close links between the trade union movement and the British Labour party have been a vital mechanism for the unions to bring forward policies with a reasonable chance of them being implemented.

The Labour Government's 1945–50 programme of nationalisation can in part be traced back to trade union influence within the party over a long period. Similarly, the commitment to nationalise the shipbuilding industry in the 1960s owes a lot to pressure from the shipbuilding unions through the Labour party. The securing of a promise from the Labour party in opposition to repeal the Conservative's Industrial Relations Act was part of a bargain struck by the unions in agreeing to a 'social contract' with a future Labour government. This close liaison was maintained in 1978 as the election approached with meetings of the TUC–Labour Party Liaison Committee, in 'rehearsal of policies to put before the electorate'.[36] The TUC, to take one example, was able to press for a commitment on the part of the Labour party to introduce a Bill on industrial democracy if it was re-elected. Quite clearly the unions could secure a 'shopping list' of policies from the Labour party because the party's ability to 'get on with the unions' was seen by the party as an electoral asset. Ministers, as *The Times* argued, felt that '... regular policy talks with the unions must be maintained in a realistic way if the Chancellor is to have any chance of getting union support for any form of continuing wage restraint'.[37] A similar, though less institutionalised (and less publicised) strategy was being adopted by business groups towards the Conservative party.

Though, as suggested, party ideology may be a generalised source of issues and may act as a brake on group influence, this does not mean that groups cannot persuade governments to go against their ideology. For example, the Federation of British Industries (now CBI) played an important role in getting the then Conservative Government to introduce some form of national economic planning in the UK. The Chancellor, Selwyn Lloyd, was greatly influenced by a conference held by the FBI in Brighton in November 1960, under the title 'The Next Five Years'. The Brighton 'revolution', as Sam Brittan terms it, helped to convince the Conservative Government that some form of 'indicative planning' was necessary and eventually the National Economic Development Council was formed.

But of course, more usually, groups will not attempt to push a political party in a policy direction that is thought to be against the ideological grain. Normally groups will select the 'appropriate' party. For example, the road haulage industry worked very closely with the Conservative Opposition between 1947 and 1951 in formulating a policy for denationalising road haulage. In this case, the Conservatives' ideology and the interests of the Road Haulage Association (RHA) were rather close and as a result the RHA was able to play an important role in the formulation of Conservative policy, which the Conservatives tried to implement when elected. In fact, the advice that the RHA had given proved to be rather bad and the implementation of the policy was far from a success. Not surprisingly this resulted in a decrease in the influence of the RHA, and by 1956 the Conservatives had decided to end their attempt to denationalise the road haulage industry fully. This demonstrate, what Finer has termed the 'technical efficiency' of the lobby (or at least the lack of it) being an important factor in determining the influence of a particular group.

THE ROLE OF DEPARTMENTS

One major answer to the question of 'who decides that some problem or other is an issue requiring governmental action?' is that the initiative is taken within the administrative machine. In other words, 'within puts' are an important component of the British policy process and can be part of the game by which departments as interests jockey for policy space.[38] Occasionally in recent years individual civil servants have been singled out as being active in the creation of policy. For example, in July 1968 Crossman recorded in his Diary a Home Office proposal that the Cabinet's Social Services Committee should select twelve blackspots, each in a local authority area where social crises and tensions were at their highest. The Home Office paper argued that an inter-service team ›m the various component departments of the relevant local authorities should be given the task of assessing how the area might be improved – and of implementing the decisions. This proposal was recognisable as the start of the move leading to the creation of Community Development Projects. Crossman credited the idea to a civil servant, Derek Morrell, 'who had been an enormously important and dynamic factor at Education and who was now being transferred to the Home Office, where he is fighting the battle to make the Home Office the central pivotal office of social welfare'.[39] Morrell had been commonly credited as the driving force behind the Schools Council and the drafting of the Children and Young Persons Act.[40] He was obviously an extraordinary, untypical, civil servant. He was described by *New Society* as 'one of the great reformers in the government',[41] but consideration of his contribution does prove that on occasion the civil servant can 'set the ball rolling'. For the Community Development Programme it was the politicians such as Crossman and Callaghan who were putting forward the arguments of impracticability and unconstitutionality.

Another example of the breach of the convention of civil service anonymity was Edward Boyle's tribute to William Pile. He claimed that the decision to expand teacher training in the early part of 1963 could be attributed 'to the quality of Mr Pile's briefing... Without his briefing, I don't think it would have happened'.[42] Yet another example can be drawn from our own study of the Water Act, 1973, which we have discussed earlier. That Bill was referred to in the specialist press as the 'Beddoe Bill' after the under-secretary in charge of the measure. Immediately before Beddoe took over 'water' in the autumn of 1968, departmental policy was undecided, but within the course of a few months he had forged a clear policy in favour of multi-purpose regional water authorities.

However, these examples must be acknowledged as unusual; the real influence of the department is less dramatic, but probably more significant. This stems from the civil servant's role as gatekeeper of information, which is the main basis of the view of civil servants as policy influencers. The 1972 Report of the Tribunal into the collapse of the Vehicle and General Insurance Company claimed that 'well under 1%' of the work of the department was referred to ministers.' The Crossman *Diaries* contain many examples where Crossman frankly reveals his ignorance of what was going on in his own department.[43] Thus he was surprised when he discovered that his cousin was engaged in listing historic buildings for the Ministry of Housing and Local Government and it was a revelation to him that such a division of the Ministry existed.[44]

These twin facts that the departments, in the main, administer most policies and that they filter what goes to the minister, mean that it is within the ministry – probably about assistant or under-secretary level – that defects in existing policy often reveal themselves. It is at this level that proposals for change can often emerge, or at least the need for a major departmental policy reappraisal can be established.

The Civil Service would be open to criticism if they did not bring forward plans in response to difficulties with existing arrangements. It was one of Fulton's criticisms that too little attention was given to long-term policy thinking and planning. 'Planning units' were proposed to 'study the problems and the needs of the future and possible means to meet them'. A recent account of the development of criminal policy planning in the Home Office defines policy planning as the identification of issues, the definition of objectives and the analysis of ways of achieving them.[45] This definition makes clear how these developments are part of the managerial/rationalist phase described in chapter 2. In a sense such planning is necessary and commendable, but it does mean that suspicion of the Civil Service as a policy initiator will be exacerbated.

Crossman has pointed out how departments have their own preferences, which they attempt to 'sell' to ministers. He argued that the Civil Service take a long-term view and realise that politicians move on – governments are defeated and individual ministers move on even more quickly. Crossman claimed that the civil servants knew that any ideological crusade to carry out the mandate would be blunted by failure, electoral unpopularity and sheer exhaustion. Therefore, 'they are prepared to concede quite a lot under the impact of an election victory. But when it is over they resume quiet defence of entrenched departmental positions and policies against political change.'[46]

Earlier he had argued (in partial contradiction) that it was the time of change-over that provided the greatest opportunity for Civil Service power. At that time the minister was likely to be less experienced and he would face 'the well-organised ceaseless pressure of a disciplined body of intelligent dedicated men and women who know that, whereas they were there for keeps, he was unlikely to be with them for more than two or three years'.[47] Crossman said that, in observing the Tories enter office in 1970, he could see his successor being 'peddled' a number of departmental policies that he, himself, had refused to buy.

One senior civil servant has acknowledged and defended the fact that major departments have 'states of mind' that are absorbed and transmitted by successive generations of civil servants.[48] 'Not a bias, rather an ethos.' However, critics have seen departmental policies as more specific and more dangerous. One participant has claimed that since the early 1960s the Treasury has been infected by a desire for a compulsory incomes policy and that the run on sterling on 30 June 1975 was the result of a Treasury plot to ensure such a compulsory pay policy.[49] A less extraordinary claim is made in Bruce-Gardyne and Lawson's case study on the introduction of the Bill to abolish Retail Price Maintenance (RPM).[50] They explain that from the end of the war to its merger with the Ministry of Technology in 1970, the Board of Trade was possessed of a departmental philosophy of free trade and free competition. Accordingly, RPM was anathama with its essential aim of curbing price competition. Bruce-Gardyne and Lawson trace the eventual abolition under Edward Heath in 1964 back to the Labour White Paper of 1951. Although the Labour Government was defeated before a Bill was drafted, the Board of Trade still favoured the policy.

Bruce-Gardyne and Lawson show how RPM abolition was a constant part of the Board of Trade's portfolio of policies. Heath was appointed to the presidency of the Board in 1963 and, despite the fact that there was only a year to run before the next election, looked for some measure that would make his personal mark and take the initiative from the Opposition. He asked his departmental officials for a list of measures and the department, 'more or less as a matter of course, included the abolition of RPM, but they did not press it, assuming that so contentious a proposal was hardly suitable for the last few months before a General Election'. However, in November John Stonehouse, MP, drew first place in the ballot for Private Members' Bills. He decided to introduce a Bill to abolish RPM. As the abolition of RPM was now 'on the agenda' with the help of this piece of good fortune, the senior civil servants presented Heath with the submission that had been shown to his two immediate predecessors. Heath accepted the brief.

Undoubtedly the involvement of civil servants in policy-making has been underestimated in the past. It is difficult to know, not least because too few studies have been made, how significant is their involvement. Given the right set of circumstances, departments have a stockpile of policies from which they are only too willing to thrust items on to the agenda. We thus see departments playing a very similar role to outsider groups in agenda setting.

CHAPTER 5

The Processing of Issues

THE PRIVATE MANAGEMENT OF PUBLIC BUSINESS[1]

A superficial glance at the British policy process might suggest that characterisation of the process as 'private management of public business' is rather misleading. There are a number of examples where the government apparently behaves rather openly. For example, in April 1978 the Government announced that it was no longer certain that it had universal support for the introduction of metric units. The Minister of State for Prices and Consumer Protection wrote to more than 100 organisations representing the retail trade, wholesalers, industry and the consumer, asking if they supported the full introduction of metrication to an agreed timetable. One does not need to be a cynic to suspect that the purpose of this manoeuvre was to establish publicly that there was widespread group support for the Government's plans and to put into perspective the sniping ridicule that was aimed at the change-over. In a parliamentary answer in December 1977, the Under-Secretary of State for Trade stated that over 600 organisations were invited to comment on the consultation document *Airport Strategy for Great Britain*. The Departments of Energy and Education and Science were active in 1977 with 'great debates' on fuel and education policy. Conferences, ministerial tours, consultation papers were the apparent style of policy-making.

The 'participation' we discuss in this chapter differs from (and is probably more genuine than) the ritualistic consultation described above. Issues are handled in a multiplicity of fashions, but it is worth noting that there is a preferred relationship that Whitehall attempts to establish – and that generally very much suits the interests involved. Thus the decision on how much money is released each month by building societies to finance private building house purchases is made at the Joint Advisory Committee on Mortgage Finance where representatives of the government and the building societies reach 'understanding'. This is an example of a regularised, routinised relationship, which appears to be the normal response to problems that automatically reappear on the agenda. Our suggestion is that over time any governmental/interest group relationship on a matter of substance will evolve a special machinery – such as a standing committee, joint advisory committee, etc.

The reasons for the 'consultation' phenomenon in British government are various and include:

(a) a lack of confidence by civil servants in their own legitimacy to enforce decision;
(b) a realisation that implementation of policies is affected by a cooperation (or lack of it) by groups;
(c) a recognition that in other aspects of the subject or at other times the department will depend on the interests for political support, aid in policy implementation or the provision of detailed information;
(d) a desire to maintain professional relations with the officers of relevant groups.

For these and other reasons consultation takes place, and of course the development of committees is the extension of this consultative tide. By the use of committees with some continuity of existence there is administrative convenience – a process is established that obviates the need for decisions on procedure and protocol on each issue. But the formalisation of consultation has a greater importance. With a longer term perspective, the possibility of a gradualist solution becomes more likely.

One of the main points in the earlier chapters was that group competition is as prevalent within Whitehall as it is between Whitehall and outside bodies. But it is conflict constrained by an overall sense of community. This sense of community is illustrated by some of the chapter titles in Heclo and Wildavsky's study of the expenditure process – 'Kinship and Culture', 'The Treasury', 'Village Life in Civil Service Society: Department–Treasury Bargaining'.[2] The essence of this present chapter is to extend their insights concerning the importance of 'community' within Whitehall to relationships outside Whitehall. For example, in their discussion of how the Treasury operates, they dwell not on intellect or ideas, but on emotions. They claim that the Treasury's 'supreme skill lies in personal relations. When the Treasury succeeds where others fail, it is due to the recognition of the over-riding importance of getting a personal commitment. Bringing colleagues along with you makes sense . . .' This observation seems as important in understanding, say, DOE/local government relations as relations between the Treasury and DOE. Heclo and Wildavsky go on to say,

> 'Ultimately, British Treasury men know that their desires cannot prevail unless they maintain a community to support them . . . coercion has its uses and is not to be despised. Far better, however, to create a nexus of interests so that cooperation flows from a sense of mutual advantage ... You go along with the Treasury, then, because you must, because you expect to gain, and ultimately, because you are part of a civil service society that wants to do so.'

We subscribe to this view and add that the 'community' is far wider: many other groups are bound into the policy process by this sense of respectability and responsibility.

In fact, not all groups are considered part of the 'community'. The question of whether a group is 'accepted' or not has been used as a basis of classification of groups. For example, Kogan makes a distinction between legitimised and non-legitimised (non-accepted) groups.[3] Change in this status can be a primary group goal. In 1978 the National Farmers' Union of Wales (formed in 1955) was formally recognised by the Government as having a *right* to be consulted on matters such as the annual review. This was hailed by the group as their major achievement.

Dearlove, in analysing the role of pressure groups at the local level, classifies groups into helpful or unhelpful – according to the perceptions that councillors have of them.[4] However, as Grant has suggested, it may well be politically necessary for local councils, and indeed national governments, to consult, and bargain with, groups that are unhelpful or that, by challenging the government, cannot be considered legitimate. Indeed, this 'unhelpful' activity can be one means of gaining access.

Grant chooses to make the distinction on the choice of strategy of the group.[5] 'Insider' groups actively seek consultative status and rely on a close relationship with government. 'Outsider' groups either reject, or cannot obtain, a close or even symbiotic position. There is, then, an important distinction between groups that are invited by central government departments to submit their views on topics related to their concerns and those that are at best tolerated to the extent that they are allowed to send occasional deputations. In the main, of course, such distinctions tend to merge and the major groups we principally discuss in this account are 'legitimised', 'helpful' and 'insider'. It is these established (and establishment?) groups that form the substance of the system we are describing. Groups such as the Trades Union Congress, National Farmers' Union, Association of Metropolitan Authorities, etc., enjoy an automatic right to consultation in their fields of interest. Necessarily the relationship varies with the precise subject. The TUC was not interested in detailed consultations with the Heath Government on their industrial relations proposals, but this breakdown on this (albeit important) front did not inhibit the 'normal' relations on wider business.

While our main interest is in the clientele type relations at the centre of the British policy system, one must acknowledge that other styles exist. Some groups perforce have to adopt outsider strategies: few would voluntarily use that channel. There have been attempts to make some systematic connection between the kind of policy in question and the style of relationship that emerges. Theodore Lowi has claimed that distributive, regulatory or redistributive policies produce different processes.[6] The proposition has some validity, but in the British context it is difficult to see the pattern working out so neatly as the theory suggests. One reason might be the breadth of involvement of groups. After all if the TUC enjoys one style of relationship on the detail of safety at work, it is unlikely permanently to accept a very different connection on old age pensions, pay policy or the length of the working week.

This chapter is about the 'operating understandings' under which the major groups are granted participation; the process by which and the atmosphere within which most policy-making is resolved. Groups have traded off certain rights to frustrate the government by all possible means – in return for the predictability, the insurance of consultative status and the 'standing' in the policy-making community that insider status confers. Notwithstanding the publicity that group non-cooperation obtains, in the pressure group/government nexus, a stress on conflict avoidance has developed. There are relationships that must be maintained. The task of the civil servant and his counterpart on the pressure group side is to minimise conflict. The civil servant who cannot 'manage' his group is a liability to his minister. It seems useful to begin by looking at a few concepts borrowed from other fields, but that appear to provide useful insights into group/departmental relations.

NEGOTIATED ORDER AND NEGOTIATED ENVIRONMENT

This negotiated order model was first applied by Strauss and his colleagues to the study of psychiatric hospitals – but it was hoped that it would be applicable to other organisations.[7] The appropriateness of the model for our purposes can be seen by noting the similarity between their starting point and Heclo and Wildavsky's comment on the tension between policy change and the maintenance of community relationships. Strauss and his colleagues took their cue from Margaret Mead's comment in 1936:

'How can you bring . . . changes about in an orderly fashion and yet preserve order? To bring about change is seemingly to destroy the given order, and yet society does and must change. That is the problem, to incorporate the method of change into the order of society itself.[8]

Similarly, Heclo and Wildavsky argue that

There is no escaping the tension between policy and community, between adopting actions and maintaining relationships, between decision and cohesion, between governing now and preserving the possibility of governing later. To cope with the world without destroying the understandings their common life requires – this is the underlying dilemma facing the community of political administrators.[9]

'Negotiated order' is the concept that squares this circle. Strauss and his colleagues stress the importance of negotiation – the processes of give and take, of diplomacy, of bargaining, that characterise organisation life. They also suggest that social order must be continually 'worked at'. This is suggestive of the continuous reappraisal of problems implicit in 'incrementalism'. Parties to the dispute have to weigh up the risk of damaging long-term relationships if they adopt intransigent positions. Strauss sees the hospital as 'a professionalised locale'. Accordingly, the various actors involved draw on different backgrounds, values and specialities. But it is useful in extending the negotiated order idea to departmental/group relationships to observe the professionalisation of negotiations. Those involved tend to see their task as the efficient reconciliation of the dispute. If a committee has been created to deal with a matter, those operating the committee have some commitment to agreement. This is so when the negotiations are at a political level – (say) Minister of Agriculture and president of the NFU – but is reinforced when those involved are literally professional – civil servants and officers of groups. On both sides, then, it will be recognised that getting agreement is their prime role: the essence of their job. As we have seen above, not infrequently those negotiating have experience of the other side of the table, and because of their common situations vis-à-vis 'their politicians' they have an appreciation of each other's settings. A pattern of compromise is thus established. Neither side will push too far. Each will offer some kind of concession. To ignore these implicit rules is to infringe the professional ethic of negotiation.

A further dimension of negotiated order – at least as we extend its use – is a tendency to concentrate on small manageable problems. Part of the mode of negotiation is to translate large unbargainable conflicts into smaller negotiable items. Where there is unlikely to be agreement on the major aspects, specific points – perhaps details of implementation – can be put forward for discussion. This allows an impression of progress and permits concessions on detail that might undermine resistance to the overall concept. The negotiated order model suggests that the agreements reached in this complexity do not occur by chance: they are 'patterned'. The outcome becomes, to a certain extent, predictable. The re-constitution of this order can be conceived in terms of a complex relationship between the *daily negotiative process and a periodic appraisal process.* This seems a valuable insight into appreciating how groups and departments have constant contact over policy details, but this does not prevent, in the longer term, a change in the style of the relationship between groups and departments to emerge. The relationship between the Department of Transport (in its various manifestations) and, say, the motorway building lobby undoubtedly changed between approximately 1965 and 1978. The kind of understandings developed allowed business to be done but did not prevent other groups, other values, other priorities from gradually impinging so that ultimately the department/'motorway lobby' had a different relative position.

Johan P. Olsen has used a coincidentally similar label to 'negotiated order' in his explanation of why groups and departments become involved in these close encounters of a bureaucratic kind.[10] He deftly sums up March and Simon's *Organisations*[11] as being about organisations avoiding uncertainty by arranging *'negotiated environments'*. Uncertainty and risk, as well as conflict and competition, are avoided through the formation of stable relationships with environmental actors; standard answers to uncertainty include plans, contracts, laws, rules, norms, consultations, recruiting and cooperation, representation and joint ventures. This private world of decision evolves its own means of regulation.

ACCOMMODATION

A third concept that appears useful in understanding how policies are decided within the British policy system is Arend Lijphart's 'accommodation' – used to convey the process by which divisive issues and conflicts in the Netherlands are settled despite only a minimal consensus.[12] He claims that pragmatic solutions are forged for all problems. His explanation of the origins of accommodation in the period from 1878 to 1917 suggests that this spirit is a product of the singular circumstances of the Netherlands. But his seven 'rules of the game' surely have a wider validity:

Rule 1: 'The Business of Politics'. Lijphart quotes Alan D. Robinson's comment 'that doctrinal disputes should not stand in the way of getting the work done'.[13]

Rule 2: 'The Agreement to Disagree'. The determination to reach agreement leads on to the second rule – there is a pragmatic acceptance of the ideological differences. Lijphart says that 'the fundamental convictions of other blocs must be tolerated, if not respected'. He concedes that if this principle were always enforced paralysis in decision-making would follow. So on occasion it is infringed, but if a compromise cannot be reached, 'the other groups will go to great lengths in trying to avoid antagonising their opponents'. Winners should go out of their way to avoid antagonising the losers.

Rule 3: 'Summit Diplomacy'. Here Lijphart argues that the politics of accommodation entails government by elite. Matters of great importance tend to be dealt with by direct discussion among representative leaders of major religious–ideological blocs. This rule might be more particular to the Netherlands than the others he offers, but the British version of tripartism might approximate to the Dutch practice. In 1972 Sir Frank Figgures, director general of NEDO, Sir Douglas Allen, Permanent Secretary of the Treasury, Victor Feather of the TUC and Campbell Adamson of the CBI picked up the sobriquet 'the group of four'. When Sir William Armstrong, Head of the Home Civil Service, joined the talks as the Prime Minister's unofficial representative, the group became 'the five wise men'.[14]

Rule 4: 'Proportionality'. Lijphart offers the rule of proportionality as a procedural device capable of solving a host of troublesome problems. In three very important senses this extends to Britain. There is proportionality ('fair shares') in the allocation of financial resources. There is proportionality in the form of tripartite institutions such as the Manpower Services Commission and in the composition of various advisory committees. Various parts of the UK are also becoming very sensitive to their 'fair share' of regional aid, Civil Service jobs, miles of motorway, etc. Decisions are often justified (or attacked) on 'proportional' grounds.

Rule 5: 'Depoliticisation'. Perhaps we can interpret this rule in the British context as the attempt to solve matters by 'rationality' as outlined in chapter 2. There has been an attempt to make matters subject to technical criteria rather than value judgements – though with little success.

Rule 6: 'Secrecy'. This point is akin to rule 3 on 'summit diplomacy'. As successful accommodation requires flexibility, the negotiations are best kept secret. Members are apt to confuse bargaining positions and realistic demands and they are best kept out of the discussion.

Rule 7: 'The Government's Right to Govern'. This rule is a useful corrective to parts of this book where we would argue that the government is just another group. It is a player in the game but it has special status. At times its special status will be ignored – as in the late 60s and early 70s, or in special cases where the Urban District Councillors of Clay Cross failed to implement the 1972 Housing Finance Act. The government can indulge in coercion, in 'elective dictatorship', and it is often important to realise that there is this right in the background. For example, in case studies of water reorganisation, or the abolition of retail price maintenance, or the introduction of the 1957 Housing Act, or the negotiation of the annual arrangements for agriculture, etc., there is an appreciation that the government is 'in the driving seat'. But that said, it is equally important to remember Heclo and Wildavsky's maxim quoted at the start of this chapter: '... coercion has its uses and is not to be despised. Far better, however, to create a nexus of interests so that cooperation flows from a sense of mutual advantage'.

Each of these rules implies that the policy system has a strong tendency to 'accommodate' interests wherever possible.[15]

THE LOCAL GOVERNMENT COMMUNITY

Our claim that policy is made within these professional communities, and is determined by a wish in the community to avoid direct conflict, stems from our assumption that most decisions are made without involving party politicians. Most issues are not politicised in the party sense. In the rest of this chapter we look in more detail at the 'communities' of local government and agriculture, but we would argue that the kinds of relationship described here are by no means unique. What has emerged in the local government case is the (inevitable) compromise whereby central government attempts to influence a nominally independent local government. Central government itself does not have the capacity to monitor the impact of policies at the local level, but what it can do is respond when its attention is drawn to difficulties. This response can follow direct bilateral links between a departmental section and an individual local authority, but it is here that the local authority associations are a particularly useful channel.

So 'consultation' between central government and the main associations – Association of Metropolitan Authorities (AMA), Association of District Councils (ADC), Association of County Councils (ACC) – is not a generous concession but is the inevitable response in a situation where the centre lacks detailed control. The associations act as filters, ranking matters according to importance, aggregating individual cases so that wider implications can be recognised. The frequency of contact between the associations and central government is impressive. The office diary of the AMA shows officer/officer level meetings occur practically every day of the year outside August and Christmas. Member/minister meetings average two to three meetings a month – and are of increasing frequency. Exceptionally contact is made between ministers and whole AMA committees. Contacts are then more or less continuous – particularly at officer level. Indeed, so routinised are relations that it is difficult to convey the frequency, but any meeting of the AMA Policy Committee is likely to be in touch with government departments on subjects as varied as population projections (and the implication for planning in metropolitan areas), finance, pay policy, industrial democracy, public sector pensions, employment of children, arts subsidies, etc.

The competitive group basis of central government means that the relations between central government and local government are complex. While the DOE is the main point of contact for the local authority associations, local government has much wider interests, and contacts are needed with the DHSS, the Department of Industry, the Home Department, etc. The Central Policy Review Staff report on *Relations between Central Government and Local Authorities* argues:

> Central Government is, in fact, a federation of separate departments with their own Ministers and their own policies. The aims of the Treasury and of the DOE in its capacity as the 'Department of Local Government' often cut across those of the spending or service departments. They in turn compete with each other for scarce resources. The development of an inter-departmental view about a local authority service is a rare achievement.[16]

The CPRS report acknowledges some 'joint' working in central government vis-à-vis local government, but their main argument is that it inevitably follows from the 'plural nature of central government' that joint behaviour is the exception. Most circulars, for example, relate to a single service and are drafted and circulated by the single department responsible.

It follows from this that the contacts between central and local government are varied – with local government in contact with different departments and indeed different sections of departments.

A feature of the relationship is the multiplicity of committees and joint bodies between central and local government – the Housing Consultative Council, the National and Local Government Statistical Liaison Committee, Working Group on the Management of Higher Education, Joint Working Party on Local Authority Fees and Charges, Waste Management Advisory Council, etc. The relations between central and local government provide confirmation for the theme of earlier chapters with regard to central government's departmental pluralism. The prevalence of committees also confirms the importance we allotted to this device. But we also want to return to the earlier part of this chapter and the generalisation that cooperation is the main means of policy development. Much has been written about the centralising tendency that is said to be undermining local government.[17] Alternatively, it can be argued that the variety of service provision by individual local authorities is so great as to make untenable the image of a strong directing and determining central government.[18]

We would, however, stress a third dimension to the debate and that is the extent to which directions from the centre stem from discussions *between* central and local government. While policy requests/demands might appear to the individual local authority as sudden and arbitrary, it is often the case that the policy will have been discussed exhaustively in the labyrinth of central/local consultative machinery. Consultation between government and the various local government organisations is accepted as the regular convention, as can be seen by a deviant case where sufficient consultation did *not* take place. A circular in July 1970 was intended to give local councils greater freedom over their pattern of secondary education. Although the contents were broadly welcomed, complaints about the lack of prior consultation were still made.[19] It can, then, be misleading to view the stream of circulars from the centre as evidence of central government always attempting to regulate local authorities. It can be seen in part as self-regulation by local government. Various standards are agreed in the central organs of local government in discussion with central government and then promulgated by the departments.

The pattern of multiple contacts between specialist services of local government and their relevant sections in various departments in central government remains, but since 1975 a new instrument has been developed to provide a more ordered and convenient forum for the vital financial discussions. The Consultative Council on Local Government Finance (CCLGF) was set up in May 1975.[20] It has no formal terms of reference but its main work, as its name implies, concerns levels of expenditure and grants. But given this useful mechanism, central government has been unable to resist using it to discuss wider issues (such as the Health and Safety at Work Act).

The local government side of the Consultative Council broadly consists of the chairmen and some of the leading members of the local authority associations. Central government is represented by the Secretary of State for the Environment (who chairs the meetings). He is supported by the Chief Secretary to the Treasury and ministerial representatives from other interested departments – such as the Department of Education and Science and the Department of Transport. Much of the detailed work goes on in a parallel committee of officers and civil servants – the Official Steering Group (OSG). This is chaired by the DOE Deputy Secretary (Finance and Local Government) and is attended by officials of other departments and secretaries and advisors of the associations. Ostensibly the main purpose of the OSG is to filter out and deal with items of lesser importance and to clarify issues for the 'political' side. Of course, in practice, matters of substance can be dealt with in the technical setting. A second tier of officers' groups have specialised remits and report to the Consultative Council through the OSG.

Thus the relationship is developing along the lines suggested in the earlier part of this chapter – closer and more formal contacts, a predilection for policy to be passed to more technical levels for resolution, a reluctance to act without predigestion of the policy in the consultative machinery. This is not to say that the local authorities always welcome the results. The associations have differences between and within themselves. The DOE (or whatever department) sometimes fails to win a large enough budget to satisfy local authority demands. And plainly, on occasions, the DOE interest and attitude clashes with that of the associations. Even so, the type of arrangement that recurs frequently in association minutes is 'a small working group of officers from local authorities and the DOE have been working . . .', or 'the Secretaries of the three local authority Associations have been discussing with officials of the DOE', or 'an officer level working group has been set up with the DOE'.

This machinery has operational difficulties. One criticism has been that while ministers can speak on behalf of the government, the association's representatives cannot commit individual authorities. Some authorities view the technical discussions at CCLGF with some suspicion and some authorities inevitably do better than others. What is important for our argument is the manner in which the local authorities are involved in the discussions of the formula that will be applied. The norms of behaviour between the DOE and the local government lobby demand collaboration, even though conflict occasionally breaks out.

THE LOCAL GOVERNMENT 'STRIKE'

The idea of 'negotiated order' is useful in understanding the process that led to the Water Act in 1973. 'Negotiated order' helps explain why the Ministry of Housing and Local Government went to such trouble to consult the industry when it had its own clear policy preference with regard to water reorganisation in the period 1968–73. An internal Ministry working party in the summer of 1969 came out in favour of four to twelve regional, multipurpose water authorities. The extensive bargaining that nonetheless followed was a good example of negotiated order. The Ministry decided change was necessary, but attempted to avoid as much direct conflict with the groups as it could. Accordingly, it involved the interested parties in discussions, such as on the Central Advisory Water Committee, and in direct negotiations. These were intended to educate the groups as to the need for a change and most importantly to assuage resentment by those involved. 'Consultation' is one of the rules of the game and it would aggravate the matter if groups had not at least the courtesy of futile consultation. There is a French proverb to the effect that it is unnecessary to consult the frogs when draining the swamp: the reverse is true in Britain.

    The core of the new scheme – the replacement of a local government by a managerial system – could not be compromised (although the local authorities eventually claimed that they had gained nineteen specific concessions). The relatively unsuccessful challenge by the local government associations meant that they were faced with the decision – how far could their 'pressure' escalate? And how much could they afford to embarrass general relations with Whitehall for the sake of one particular topic? The following incident also demonstrates the cooperation between the associations in a 'common cause' campaign.

It has been suggested to us by one participant that the strength of feeling engendered in local government by the proposed water reorganisation stemmed from the fact that 'water' was the end of a long list of local government functions 'lost' since World War II. The secretary of the then County Councils Association (CCA) expressed something of this in a letter to the Government in December 1971: 'It has been our hope, and indeed the Government's stated intention to use a strengthened local government for the devolution of powers from Central Government. The taking away therefore of further functions ... at this time is bound to be a matter of grave concern to the Association.' More materially, there was also the argument that with the loss of water supply and sewerage disposal functions, the viability of the proposed (post 'Redcliffe-Maud') district councils, from a technical services point of view, was questioned: there was not the work to maintain such a team.

The initial reaction of the associations to the Government's proposals in December 1971 was produced by the secretaries of the four associations involved. No formal coordination machinery was set up; informal collaboration – at secretary level – was sufficient. A joint memorandum was prepared in May 1972 that suggested a more 'evolutionary' transformation of the water industry. On 9 June the DOE asked the local authorities to participate in local working parties and steering committees to prepare the way for the setting up of the proposed Regional Water Authorities (RWA). The groups were to produce a report for the new RWAS with proposals for action. These innocuous sounding means and ends were not uncontroversial.

On 7 March 1973 a letter appeared in *The Times* from the vice-chairman of one of the RWA steering committees. Members of the standing committee considering the Bill in Parliament raised this anticipation of legislation in moving towards reorganisation before the Bill was through. Graham Page (Minister for Local Government and Development) explained that 'those so-called steering committees were set up, at the invitation of the Department, by the British Waterworks Association (BWA). *Whilst this action is in no way official* [our emphasis], we were glad that those interested in such questions are getting together to consider the future . . .

The Committees have been set up merely at the Department's invitation, and are in no way departmental committees.'

In fact, when we queried this account with BWA they suggested to us that the Department played a somewhat larger part in the creation of the committees:

> The water supply steering committees and working parties . . .
> *have been set up by the Department of the Environment* [our emphasis] to consider certain aspects of the reorganisation proposals. The Associations' part in this exercise was limited to providing facilities for water undertakings to meet together to determine whether or not they should co-operate with the Department of the Environment in setting up of water supply steering committees and working parties, in advance of the publication of the Water Bill.

The formula of a departmental invitation to BWA to arrange the initial meetings appears to have been an administrative improvisation by the Department to circumvent the restraint's of the parliamentary timetable – a neat example of our earlier comments on the pragmatic style. It also, however, demonstrates how useful good relations with a group, such as BWA, can be for a department.

That episode provoked a minor crisis of constitutionality in the standing committee, but the local authority response proved another difficulty. Initially, the associations recommended cooperation, but subsequently their line changed. On 23 June the CCA wrote to the DOE that 'It would be inappropriate for the local authorities to undertake detailed work on the basis of the Department's present proposals until the general method of reorganisation has been settled in the light of the ultimative proposals of the four associations'. On 20 July the Association of Municipal Corporations (AMC) General Purpose Committee carried a motion that the setting up of committees and working parties was premature, 'in view of the fact that the Department's proposals are contrary to the advice of the local authority Associations and that the Department's action in requiring the setting up of the steering committees and working parties appears to have been designed to pre-empt legislation on the subject'. By 28 July the official policy of the associations had crystallised and a joint letter was sent out advising constituent members to 'boycott work on the transfer of water and sewage services out of local government'. This boycott was confirmed at the end of August when concessions by the Department were judged insufficient. A letter from the associations read; 'We think that we should tell you that the preliminary response to our consultations indicates that concessions which you are offering fall far short of meeting the associations' case.'

The Permanent Secretary of the Department wrote to the AMC on 27 October in an attempt to obtain progress at the working party level:

> He [the Secretary of State] is also anxious that the difficulties of the transitional period are minimised. It is for this reason that he has proposed the establishment of Steering Committees of members of local authorities and of Working Parties of officers to prepare for the change. The British Waterworks Association and the Association of Joint Sewerage Boards have co-operated in these arrangements. The Secretary of State regrets that your Association together with other associations of local authorities have not felt able to do the same.

He argued that the work would be essentially similar whatever form of reorganisation was adopted and that delay could lead to a risk to public health. After this moral carrot, the Permanent Secretary ended with a thinly veiled stick: '... [Co-operation] is desirable if the discussions between the Department and the Associations on the substantive proposals to be enacted in legislation are to be helpful and fruitful.' This threat that concession would be withheld if cooperation was not forthcoming had no effect and the policy (described by the AMC as 'reluctant hesitation') continued.

The policy of non-cooperation was eventually rescinded on 9 March 1973. By that time the concession allowing district councils to undertake certain sewerage functions for the RWAS on a 'controlled agency' basis had been developed by the officers and civil servants. This followed a meeting of the officers with the DOE in September 1972 when it had been agreed that the Department would draft a compromise proposal. This was discussed at further officer/civil servant meetings. Another draft was (confidentially) sent by the Department to the association in December and further meetings were held in January and February. As described on p. 129, the 'heads of agreement' were completed on a confidential basis while the parliamentary spokesmen for the associations were left pursuing a more radical tack.

At first sight this breakdown of normal relations between the Department and the associations might appear to be an unlikely example of our argument that a 'local government community' exists. But, of course, the existence of community does not preclude conflict, and in following the dispute one was struck by the reluctance with which the associations pursued their tactics. It appeared to be recognised that such action was outside the 'rules'. The associations could have maintained their boycott to secure bigger concessions, but before that could happen the associations felt obliged to accept the Government's view – to accept the government's right to govern. The Department has claimed to us that the 'strike' had little effect, but there must at least have been some nuisance value as the period between the Royal Assent to the Act in July 1973 and the vesting of the new authorities in April 1974 was already very short. Our assessment is that non-cooperation was withdrawn, not because it was ineffective or because the authorities were satisfied with the concession, but because it was thought that it was an inappropriate form of behaviour in view of the normal central/local relationship.

THE AGRICULTURAL PARTNERSHIP

The relationship between local government and central government is not, we think, untypically close. Indeed, the view has been expressed that the relationship with the central authorities is insufficiently close. From the government side the suggestion was made in the November 1977 Green Paper on Local Government Finance that better consultation was yet possible. In turning to the relationship between the agriculture lobby and the Ministry of Agriculture, Fisheries and Food (MAFF), we are turning to what is often thought to be one of the closest departmental/pressure group partnerships. It is certainly one of the best-documented cases.[21]

There are approximately 188,000 full-time farm businesses in England and Wales. The National Farmers' Union of England and Wales claims a membership of approximately 85 per cent of full-time farmers. The most important link between the MAFF and the NFU follows from the nature of the annual review that takes place in February between the government and the union. This determines the anticipated level of profitability of farming in the next year. The Agriculture Act of 1947 obliges the government to consult 'such

bodies of persons who appear to them to represent the interests
of producers in the agricultural industry'. Until 1978 this meant
the NFU, but from 1978 onwards the newly recognised Farmers'
Union of Wales has also been consulted. Self and Storing describe the
reviews as having 'been shaped by a series of understandings
(written or unwritten) arrived at by the two participants. The most
significant, if least admitted of these, is that the final settlement
(which, constitutionally is of course the Government's sole responsibility) shall be broadly acceptable to both parties.'[22] By 1958 the
union had disassociated itself from only one review, but since then
it has disassociated itself from about half. Of course, the tendency
to fail to agree to the price review does not necessarily imply that
the NFU is unhappy at MAFF's attitude – but it means that the union
is unhappy at the deal that MAFF has been allowed to give by the
Treasury and other forces in Whitehall.

The price review as it developed in the 1960s had a PESC-like
style. It begins with a technical evaluation of the state of the
industry, with economists from the NFU and MAFF meeting to establish the existing situation. In February each year the discussion
moves to bargaining at a more senior level.[23] One prerequisite is
that the NFU should produce authoritative spokesmen.[24] This can
lead to a kind of 'summit diplomacy' because the Ministry will not
allow the NFU to take Ministry proposals to a vote, or even debate,
in the union's council. The union's position must therefore be stated
and formed by its full-time representatives. The NFU cannot mandate
its representatives and nor can the representatives properly report
back for guidance without breaking confidence. When the NFU first
became closely involved in setting agricultural subsidies in the
1940s, the chairmen of its council's specialist committees were
involved in decisions with the government. This led to differences
in priority between exponents of the NFU case, which antagonised
the Ministry and weakened the authority of the union. Accordingly,
chairmen were soon banished from major discussions and the NFU
case was left to the president and the senior officers.[25]

Throughout the year the NFU is in constant touch with MAFF –
'almost hourly contact' as Graham Wilson describes it.[26] 'Thus it
is only natural that a community of shared beliefs and attitudes
should develop between the officials of the two organisations in
such close contact.' He reports an acceptance of a form of neo-
pluralism by civil servants within the Ministry (akin to the picture

we suggested in chapter 2). He was told, 'We cannot worry about everything, so we leave some factors to other Ministries to worry about'. Another said, 'The duty of the MAFF is to present the arguments for help for farming. Other Ministries will soon bring forth criticism based on trade policy implications for public expenditure'.[27] Self and Storing significantly dedicate their book on agricultural politics 'to Partnership, properly understood'. The partnership they describe so fully seems consistent with the broad generalisations made at the start of this chapter – though they themselves might have been reluctant to put their case in such terms. Their chapter describing the historical basis of the relationship is entitled 'The Quest for Stability'. This fits in well with the negotiated environment idea, where both sides benefit from an ordered and predictable situation.

The closeness of the Ministry/NFU embrace has been tightened by the British entry into Europe.[28] One Minister has told us that the union knows 99 per cent of the British information and arguments. The union can further these arguments in the COPA (Comité des Organisations Professionnelles Agricoles – the 'umbrella' organisation for the various national agricultural lobbies) or by its direct lobbying in Brussels. This means that when an agreement is reached not only does the Minister have to get it accepted in Cabinet, but the interest group leadership has to 'sell' it to its own membership. There is consequently a dilemma for the leadership – either it attacks a deal to which it was, in practice, a party or it is seen by the membership to be acquiescing to whatever the Ministry delivers. Domestically the lobby is very often 'making the bullets for MAFF to fire', and the European dimension has certainly reinforced this tendency.

IMPLICATIONS

These examples cannot prove the argument that policy-making is carried out in governmental sub-systems in an essentially co-operative and consensual atmosphere, but they may have illustrated the kind of practices that prompt the generalisation. The overwhelming proliferation of committees and regular meetings means that one cannot fully catalogue and describe what goes on. In local government there are so many bodies in specific areas – such as the Housing Consultative Council (HCC), which was set up as 'a forum for discussions between central and local government' and was intended 'to foster the concept of partnership between the two' – that listing is tedious. The HCC consists only of representatives of the department and the associations, and in turn relates to other machinery for consultation with the construction industry, the building societies and the housing association movement. The (relative) absence of such a number of committees on the agriculture side is because the relations are so close as to make such formalisation less necessary.

The Whitehall preference in the processing of policies is to internalise the required debate within some structure or institutions. Our general proposition is that the atmosphere in a standing body is likely to be more fruitful than in an ad hoc body. In a standing body, the norms of behaviour – with the longer term perspective – will be more conducive to settlement, the possibilities for trade-offs on timing more obvious. The possible combinations of the nature of the problem and the type of forum are presented in Table 5.1.

TABLE 5.1   *Internalised processing of problems*

| Type of forum | Nature of problem | |
	'One-off'	Recurring
Regularised	(1) e.g. Central Advisory Water Committee	(2) e.g. Joint Advisory Committee on Mortgage Finance
Ad hoc	(3) e.g. Fulton Committee on the Civil Service	(4) e.g. pay conflict

The regularised arrangements represent the more likely options. One can see a drift to the establishment of more and more of these instruments over a wider and wider range of policies. They can be used for recurring problems, but they can also be used to 'process' 'one-off' issues such as water reorganisation in the Central Advisory Water Committee or the Layfield Report in the Consultative Council on Local Government Finance. They are convenient for dealing with 'one-off' issues and they are also (ideally) imbued with the correct, cooperative atmosphere. Developments of the Fulton type are also part of the 'bureaucratisation' of problems that we have identified, but since there was no convenient forum that would be politically credible an 'ad hoc' body was created. We see discussions of pay conflict in the late 1970s as being fully compatible with this simple scheme. The common arguments for systematic bargaining, for kitty bargaining, for negotiation rather than strikes, etc., can be seen as an implicit attempt to accommodate the pay issue in machinery similar to that existing in other policy areas – subject to the same consensual values. The ambition appears to move pay from cell (4) to cell (2). Perhaps, in a discreet fashion, that has been achieved in some phases of pay policy. Agreements have been reached between the union leadership and the government, but the arrangement had not by 1978 achieved the predictability and permanence that existed in other policy areas.

Of course, processing of problems in such a fashion does not mean the resolution of all issues. Some obviously spill over into the party/parliamentary/political area. But just as writers in the 1950s saw public campaigns by pressure groups as a sign of the breakdown – the failure – of group strategies, so we would argue that the need to bring in parties and Parliament to resolve an issue is a failure of both department and outside group strategies. Both 'sides' try to reach agreement *before* issues go to Parliament for formal ratification. So the cases where Parliament is called in to resolve a conflict are comparatively rare. These are instances when the normal processing system has 'blown a fuse'.

CHAPTER 6

Legislation, Decisions and the Role of Groups

POLICY OUTPUTS

There tends to be a concentration on the *legislative* process in textbooks on political systems. The passage of Bills is often seen as the central function of the political system – for legislation is seen as the tangible *output* of the system. Whilst we do not dispute that a great deal of energy and effort is used in passing legislation and that legislation once passed does have an important impact on daily life, we wish to stress the extent to which many of the outputs of the political system do not take the form of formal legislation. Increasingly, modern governments make decisions that do not go through the normal legislative process and are not subject to effective legislative scrutiny or control.

One aspect of the problem has been the debate (and growing concern) about 'delegated legislation'. For example, in February 1978 the Joint Committee on Statutory Instruments condemned the recurring tendency of ministers and departments to by-pass Parliament through the use of statutory instruments that left out details and left the way open for ministerial discretion. The issue has been further complicated by Britain's membership of the EEC where 'decisions' from the Commission in Brussels may have more impact than some of the legislation passed by the House of Commons.

Of perhaps even greater significance are decisions such as those flowing from the influence of the International Monetary Fund (IMF) in reviewing the British economy. Both left and right in British politics see UK economic policy (say in terms of monetary targets, etc.) as being largely determined by the team of economists from the IMF. It has become doubtful as to what role the UK Cabinet, let alone the House of Commons, plays in the formulation of the package of policies. Even when we look at decisions that are clearly taken inside the UK political system, we can see the extent to which the actual process of legislation is rather irrelevant. For example, the Labour Government's decision in 1977 to build the Drax 'B' coal-fired power station was taken as a result of a process of bargaining between Department of Energy and various outside interests. The protagonists were the Central Electricity Generating Board (CEGB) and the two main turbo-generator manufacturers in the UK (C. A. Parsons and GEC) together with various trade unions, the National Coal Board and the National Union of Mineworkers, the Central Policy Review Staff and Mr Wedgwood Benn and the Department of Energy. The issue at stake was whether to build a new coal-fired power station at Drax 'B', in Yorkshire, even though the CEGB considered that it did not need the new station in order to meet anticipated demand. However, in the event the Government decided to go ahead with the station in order to save jobs in the equipment manufacturing industry. The actual *decision* to go ahead, the selection of the policy, was taken quite outside the normal parliamentary legislative process. Only several months later was minor legislation required to compensate the CEGB for the extra costs involved in agreeing to build the power station.

In fact, pressure group activity can be directed at the avoidance of legislation – a classic example in the UK being the battle over the Labour Government's proposal to introduce industrial relations legislation in 1969, contained in its White Paper *In Place of Strife*. Having started out with the clear intention of *legislating* in order to achieve better industrial relations, the Government ended up accepting what it had earlier refused to accept – an *undertaking* from the TUC to achieve similar results by action *within* the trade union movement. Thus in June 1969, after a long battle between the Prime Minister and Mrs Castle (Secretary of State for Employment and Productivity) and the TUC, the latter agreed to a 'solemn and binding' undertaking to change its roles in order to deal with unofficial strikes.[1] As a quid pro quo the Prime Minister had to agree to drop his plans for legislation. Subsequent events have, of course, led journalists to ridicule the value of this agreement to such a degree that 'Mr Solomon Binding' has now achieved a special place in British pressure group history. Quite simply, the Government was unable to legislate because of the resistance of a powerful pressure group and its parliamentary supporters.

Similarly, the process by which incomes policy has been formulated and applied in the UK during the period 1974–78 has been characterised by a marked lack of legislation as such. In 1977/78 the Government chose to use existing statutory powers, which had nothing to do with pay or prices policy, in order to enforce a policy decision that lacked legislative backing. Thus the 'black list' of companies who had breached the 'guidelines' and who as a result were not given public contracts highlighted an important constitutional issue – namely the power of governments to take decisions without recourse to the legislative process. Many observors saw the pay policy, as it was being operated, as an alarming example of a developing trend in which governments sought to 'manage' society without parliamentary approval. A further aspect of the pay policy, in early 1978, was the Government's attempt to get firms tendering for government contracts to sign a pledge to abide by all *future* pay policies. These policies had not even been formulated by the Government at that time, let alone approved by the House of Commons.

There are, of course, quite formalised processes by which decisions are reached between groups and the government and in which the legislature plays only the most minor of roles. The UK annual agricultural review is an excellent example of this phenomenon. The House of Commons merely comments upon the arrangement once it has been agreed between the government and the National Farmers' Union. The influence of the Commons is 'indirect as either a forum where rival MPs can back up the pressure from the NFU or the forum for party competition for the farm vote'.[2]

As the relationship between groups and government gets closer (more symbiotic), then it becomes easier for either side to 'lean on' the other in order to achieve a particular result. Decisions or policy outputs 'emerge' from the rather grey area that may or may not require formal legislative action. An apt example of this 'government by influence' occurred in March 1978 when the Government persuaded the Building Societies Association to reduce the amount of funds available for house mortgages. The Government's policy objective was to prevent a sudden and large increase in house prices, and it considered that one way of achieving this was to reduce the flow of money to potential borrowers. The most interesting aspect of the case was that the Building Societies Association agreed to the proposal, without any legislative backing behind it and *against their own better judgement*. Thus it was reported that 'angry as building society leaders are at the corner they find themselves in, there is little likelihood that they will rebel against the Government *instructions*. The more moderate among the council argue that *the Government has the right to govern*, no matter how misguided the societies may feel its conclusions to be.'[3] Here was an important policy decision that had been reached by a process of consultation between the government and an organised group, yet no *law* was needed to put it into effect. An excellent example in fact of what has been described as 'ear stroking' by governments. Thus governments achieve their objectives in handling groups, as with handling donkeys, by the use of the stick, the carrot and by stroking ears. Conversely, groups get governmental action by the same process. Sometimes they threaten, sometimes they offer cooperation as a quid pro quo and on other occasions they too resort to car stroking in the cosy confines of Whitehall.

But as groups and government get more adept at manipulating each other in terms of achieving desired policy outputs, what does this mean for the role of Parliament, the traditional processor of policy outputs?

THE DECLINE OF PARLIAMENT

Peter Self, in an article attempting to answer the question 'are we worse governed?', ends with what at first seems a curious postscript – 'This article hardly mentions parliament. I suggest the reader asks himself why'.[4] In identifying a number of trends, he points to modification of majority rule by pluralism and the 'spawning of public boards onto which representatives of interests are co-opted'.[5] Thus the Manpower Services Commission's members are appointed after consultation with the TUC, CBI, local authority associations and professional interests. Moreover, he argues, 'the inequality of pressure groups has meant that it is the big economic and professional interests (including those of the Civil Service itself, as a vast and largely self-regulating body of workers) who dominate the scene'.[6] The significance of Parliament in this struggle is its very insignificance. By and large the big decisions in society are not made in Parliament at all. Pessimism runs deep. Thus S. A. Walkland, writing in 1977, observes that '. . . its ineffectuality in ordering or

influencing the course of events, even in real crisis, is discerned as
never having been lower'.[7] This, of course, is despite a decade of
parliamentary reforms that Walkland concedes as puny '. . . in the
extent to which they have failed to grip the essential problem'.[8]
The essential problem, as he correctly observes, is political. The
issue is 'whether the Commons has the political power to make
its views heeded in the decisions of government, or whether government can at all essential times control the decisions of Parliament'.[9]
As we saw over such issues as devolution and even the levels of
taxation during the period 1976–78, the House of Commons did
occasionally impinge upon the policies proposed by the Government, but the surprising thing about the operation of a minority
government in Britain is the extent to which the vast bulk of
policy-making was carried on in exactly the same way as before –
namely through the process of consultation (increasingly drifting
into a process of bargaining) between the Government and the
affected interests. It was only on a limited range of issues, where
the minor parties had a particularly strong policy commitment or
where they saw the potential of electoral advantage, that the House
of Commons, as a legislature, began to play a significant role in
the policy process.

It is not surprising therefore that most writers on pressure group
tactics see attempts to influence Parliament as relatively low in
terms of the priorities adopted by groups. The 'pecking order' of
targets emerges as (1) Whitehall, (2) Parliament, (3) the public.
Good contacts with the executive/bureaucracy come first, followed
by good legislative contacts, followed by ability to mobilise mass
opinion. This reflects the gradual decline of legislatures and the
aggrandisement of power in centralised executives – a trend that
has been fairly consistent with only relatively minor setbacks, such
as the post-Watergate situation in the USA and the 'untidy' election
results in the UK in 1974.

Nevertheless, despite this decline in legislative authority, are we
correct, in terms of the activity of pressure groups, to relegate the
role of, say, the House of Commons to a postscript?

GROUPS AND THE LEGISLATURE

In attempting to assess the impact of the House of Commons on
governmental legislation, J. A. G. Griffith has calculated that over

93.7 per cent of the amendments to government Bills that were agreed to in committee, were in fact, ministerial amendments. During the period under investigation (1967–71), only one ministerial amendment failed and only just over 4 per cent of the opposition's amendments were accepted (and even this is an 'inflated' figure – in reality Griffith considers it is nearer 2 per cent.)[10] Usually, government amendments do not in fact reflect pressure from the standing committee, '. . . they reflect later developments in the thinking of civil servants in the department, often reflecting pressures from interest groups'.[11] He concludes that the committee stage of Bills has very little impact indeed as during the three sessions under investigation the government was forced on only sixteen occasions to modify a part of a principle.[12]

On the other hand, the government did appear to be more responsive in report stage, and over the same period approximately 125 amendments of some importance were moved by the government as a result of points raised at committee stage. In more general terms, eleven Bills of importance were 'markedly affected' by their passage through the Commons during the three sessions, but, as Griffith points out, 'against these achievements must be set the long debates, the hundreds of aborted attempts at amendment, the scores of bills, including some of the greatest importance, which remained effectively unchanged despite the efforts of Opposition Members and, to a lesser extent, of Government backbenchers'.[13] We shall come on to discuss whether this type of analysis may in fact *undervalue* the influence of the House of Commons in the policy process (as Griffith himself suggests, debates perform functions other than amending bills), but we do believe that the nature of empirical studies of pressure group activity has an inbuilt tendency to *overestimate* the importance of legislatures. This is because pressure on the legislature (or indeed attempts to influence public opinion) is more easily researched. It is more visible and less confidential than other forms of influence. Thus to concentrate on pressure group *campaigns* (as many writers do) is in a real sense to misunderstand the nature of the bulk of group influence. Pressure groups are about relationships. Campaigns are the currency of unsuccessful groups; permanent relationships are the mode of the successful. The difficulty for the researcher is that this very relationship is the most difficult to research because its very basis is one of confidentiality and mutual trust between group and, say, government department. The result is that, not surprisingly, the tip of the pressure group iceberg receives the most attention from researchers. We thus need to set against the fairly large amount of literature on pressure group 'campaigning' the evidence supplied by researchers such as Griffith that suggests the House of Commons is relatively unimportant in the legislative process.

Even in systems where the legislature is thought to be relatively powerful in comparative terms, groups will 'cultivate' the administration because that is where the initiative for policy change often originates. The legislature may be useful as a means of deflecting or amending the initiative that has been taken elsewhere, but it is an unwise group that waits for the policy proposal to arrive on the legislative timetable before taking defensive action.

None of this is to suggest that legislatures, even notably weak ones such as in the UK and France, have no significance for groups or indeed to policy-making as a whole. Whilst in chapter 5 we discussed the intimate relationships that groups develop with government departments, there is of course a parliamentary dimension to group activity. The case of industrial relations reform in the UK, discussed earlier, though illustrating the importance and effectiveness of group sanctions, also illustrates the importance of the legislature too. An important element in the Government's decision not to go ahead with legislation was the Chief Whip's intervention to the effect that he could not guarantee a majority for the Government.[14] Ultimately the Government had to back down because it could not get the legislation through. And this, of course, is not the only example of such an occurrence.

An equally significant case concerns the proposal to build a third London airport and the fight by the Wing Airport Resistance Association (WARA) to prevent the siting of the airport at Wing/ Cublington in Buckinghamshire.[15] Having presented a well-researched and well-argued case throughout the Roskill Commission (the Commission set up by the Government in 1968 to recommend the most suitable site for the airport) nonetheless, WARA realised, by June 1970, that the technical case had been lost. The selection of Wing/Cublington had emerged as the recommendation most likely to be made by the Roskill Commission. WARA had discovered that the Government was likely to allow a fairly lengthy period for discussion between the publication of the Roskill Report and the announcement of the Government's own decision.

This gave the Association an opportunity to use its political contacts at the parliamentary level. Having consulted local MPs, a press statement was issued announcing the formation of an All-Party Committee of Backbenchers[16] with the object of coordinating opposition to the selection of *any* inland site for the third London airport. The All-Party Committee adopted three main tactics in developing its parliamentary campaign.

(1) It organised a series of visits and meetings designed to inform and persuade MPs. For example, the chairman of WARA addressed a meeting of the All-Party Committee at which he outlined WARA's case against the airport.

(2) The Committee set about organising widespread backbench opposition to an inland site. This opposition took the form of an Early-Day Motion (EDM) that opposed an inland site and advocated a coastal site (Foulness). The EDM was carefully drafted so that parliamentary supporters of all the anti-island site groups (there were several possible inland sites besides Wing/Cublington) could support it. The backbench MPs were in fact 'lined up' in advance of the publication of the Roskill Report so that an impressive and 'immediate' response could be demonstrated. Thus within a few hours of the publication of the Roskill Report the EDM had been put down and had attracted over 160 signatures – the eventual total being 219 backbenchers. This was a very impressive demonstration of parliamentary opposition, all the more so because it was drawn from all parties in the House.

(3) The All-Party Committee went on to 'stage-manage' the ensuing debates in both houses of Parliament. When the House debated the Roskill Report, in March 1971, half of the forty-two speakers had earlier signed the EDM. It was against this background of fierce parliamentary hostility that the Government had to formulate its airports policy.

With a divided Cabinet, the Government eventually took the line of least resistance and selected a coastal site, contrary to Roskill's choice of Wing/Cublington. There is little doubt that WARA's parliamentary efforts had played a crucial role in the final policy outcome and that the Government had made an important tactical error in allowing sufficient time for WARA to mount its parliamentary campaign. But the campaign was in the nature of what Finer has aptly termed a 'fire brigade campaign'.[17] WARA was faced with a clear possibility of a hostile decision and it had to act to 'put the fire out'. As with Labour's industrial relations reform, Parliament could ultimately pull the mat from under the Government's policy. However docile Parliament might be generally, it still has to deliver the vote to the government if governmental policies are to survive.

On other occasions, of course, parliamentary pressure might be used, not to put out the fire, but to start one! This is particularly true of Private Members' legislation where the parliamentary side of group activity becomes quite crucial. For example, the Abortion Act of 1967 was the eighth 'abortion bill' to be introduced into the House of Commons. The 1964 election brought into the House a group of young Members who were more sympathetic to the Abortion Law Reform Association's (ALRA) aims, thus encouraging ALRA to put a lot of effort into locating and developing parliamentary support for its cause.[18] By 1965 it had located approximately 150 MPs who were prepared to give some support and by 1966 had found 340 MPs who were prepared to see some measure of parliamentary reform. By the time David Steel's (eventually successful) Bill had reached its second reading in 1967 the number of MPs giving some measure of support had grown to nearly 400. Not that parliamentary support was the only factor in ALRA's success. As Hindell and Simms argue, it was important for ALRA to demonstrate to MPs that 'public opinion had finally caught up with the views it [ALRA] had been expressing for thirty years'.[19] By demonstrating this (by the use of public opinion polls, etc.), ALRA convinced most MPs that there were few risks in supporting such an emotive cause as abortion reform.

Does the ALRA case perhaps illustrate a more general conclusion about the role of the House of Commons? Is the function of the House to define what has reached the political agenda, in the sense that once an issue has achieved sufficient parliamentary support, then that issue is reasonably certain to be 'processed' into a policy output? This is not to suggest that problems do not generate policy outputs *until* Parliament has accepted the problem as an issue. Indeed, the main argument in this chapter has been that the House of Commons, in common with most legislatures, is presented with a flow of legislation/decisions that originates elsewhere out of the amalgam of government and pressure groups, and that the House is faced with a choice of either accepting the legislation or rejecting it. The evidence suggests that rejection is rare.

However, not all problems 'emerge' from the government/group relationship, if only because some groups find it nearly impossible to force their way into the 'consultative system'. In such cases Parliament can be used to force both politicians and administrators to 'accept' problems for processing that they have hitherto ignored or rejected. The case of the deposit of poisonous waste in the UK, cited in chapter 4, is a good example of this phenomenon. Here was a 'problem' of which the government (particularly the administrative side of government) had been aware for some time, yet it had chosen not to act. No policy proposal had emerged from the existing bureaucratic/established group relationship. It took two factors to force policy action from the Government: (1) the activity of a new pressure group – the Conservation Society; (2) parliamentary interest, stimulated by mass media coverage of the problem, which helped to embarrass government ministers into taking emergency action.

An interesting variation in the use of parliamentary pressure to influence policies is the case of the controversy over heavy lorries in the late 1960s. The consultations between government and 'affected interests' regarding the size and weight of lorries running on Britain's roads had hitherto excluded groups whose interests can be broadly defined as 'environmental'. It was as a result of pressure on the Minister of Transport from a backbench MP who represented a constituency badly affected by heavy lorry traffic that groups such as the Civic Trust and the Council for the Protection of Rural England were included on the 'consultation list' for future policy changes.[20] The significant aspect of this example is, of course, that the backbencher was instrumental as an agent securing the opening of what had been a closed door rather than in increasing parliamentary influence as such.

However, the heavy lorries issue does again illustrate the role of backbenchers as '*scavengers*' for policy issues. The whole heavy lorries controversy had not started in Parliament. It had arisen with the *Sunday Times* and with outside groups such as the Civic Trust. As with poisonous waste, it was a case of backbenchers deciding to run with a ball that someone else had already fielded. Even the most cursory glance at *Hansard* will quickly reveal the extent to which legislators are 'feeding' upon problems reported in the media or that have been thrust upon them by constituents and pressure groups. If the ball lands in the parliamentary area, and if sufficient parliamentarians decide to run with the ball, then government often feels obliged to respond.

So what do we conclude about the relationships between groups and Parliament? A number of generalisations can be made. By and large policies are not initiated in Parliament. Neither are policies that are initiated elsewhere subject to much effective parliamentary amendment. The main effect of this 'weak legislature' situation is that group activity tends to be at its most effective where initiative lies – with the executive branch of government.

This does not mean that groups ignore the legislature. As we have seen, even the House of Commons can on occasions be important as a veto power on legislation and can play an important role in getting a problem recognised as needing political action. Even where policies are initiated by the government and are not being vetoed by the House of Commons, groups can and do use the amending process. Few groups will fail to 'brief' friendly MPs or fail to propose amendments. Indeed, the briefing of MPs and the proposing of amendments through them is by no means incompatible with a very close relationship between a group and the government. It is not uncommon for amendments that have been agreed informally between the groups and the department to be 'parcelled out' – the government agreeing to put some down in its name and asking the group to get 'its people' (i.e. its sympathetic MPs) to put down others. Because of this close and usually amicable relationship it is difficult to discover the true origin of amendments to legislation. In such a situation, backbenchers begin to look more like postmen than legislators – effectively being 'used' by both group and government.

Indeed, Parliament as a legislature can be devalued by the process of consultation between the government and groups. The Water Bill struck deeply at powers exercised by local authorities in the water supply and sewage disposal field. It was not surprising, therefore, that there should be detailed consultations, indeed negotiations, between the government and the local authority associations. As it happens, the *constitutional basis* of these negotiations became an issue in the standing committee considering the Water Bill. The constitutional issue was sparked off by the most esoteric of policy areas – sewerage and sewage disposal. During discussions of clause 14 (sewerage and sewage disposal) the Minister (Graham Page) sought to indicate where the line between local authority and

Regional Water Authority responsibility for sewerage and sewage disposal was to be drawn. His reference in the course of his explanation to 'heads of agreement' almost monopolised the committee for the next three and a half hours.[21]

Mr Page explained that district councils could retain control of sewerage, but not of sewage disposal.

> In pursuance of what I have called a controlled function [sewerage] we have been in close consultation with the local authority associations and *model heads of agreement have been drawn up between my Department and the associations.* I believe that this will prove a good partnership and that under the model agreement now agreed, it will work effectively and far better than it is working under the existing fragmented sewerage functions.

In his reply, Denis Howell (Labour) concentrated on the practical point that any future conflict over this function could not be resolved by examination of the Bill: 'When the public want to know in future what is to be done should a conflict arise, they must look not only at Clause 14 but *at some heads of agreement which in the privacy of his Ministry, the Minister is drawing up.*' Unfortunately for the Government, Arthur Jones (Conservative) referred to 'the form of contract – I have not yet seen a copy, but there is one being passed around – that heads of agreement between regional water authorities and district councils –'. The Opposition quickly seized on the point that the Government benches were favoured with a document not available to their side of the table. Eldon Griffiths (another Government minister) did not succeed in calming the storm by claiming that because the Regional Water Authorities had not yet been set up there could not be formal agreements; 'as yet there are no such documents as heads of agreement'. The Opposition nevertheless insisted that the document referred to by Page as containing 'heads of agreement' be circulated. The chairman of the standing committee emphasised that, unless the document had been directly quoted, there was no technical obligation to have it tabled, but added that in fairness to the committee it should be produced. George Thomas (Labour) added that in his twenty-eight years in the House, he had never known a government of any political colour distribute papers concerning a debate only in confidence to some of its own members and not to the whole committee.

Mr Page, for the Government, explained that he was anxious that the committee should see the heads of agreement – but claimed that the local authorities had not actually agreed to it but reserved their position: 'Therefore I believe that without the permission of local authority associations I am not at liberty even to place before the committee whatever there may be in writing on heads of agreement – I felt that I might quote two or three, because they were firm enough.' Thus, after Mr Griffiths had carefully explained that the document could not exist, Mr Page explained it could not be produced *unless the associations agreed*!

However, within five minutes Mr Page had obtained the permission of the associations to distribute the document, and the apparent conclusion to this episode was a complaint by the Chair on the unseemly nature of the previous sixty-five minutes:

> . . . It is hard lines on the Chair that during the course of a discussion, and an important point of principle relating to the dissemination of documents, negotiations can take place between certain individuals in the committee, or at their behest, and that an agreement reached after the row has taken place, and the committee told that it can have the document. It is not fair to the Chair and I resent being treated in this way by anybody in the committee.

But this was far from the end of the controversy. The indignation at not seeing the document seemed mild compared with the Opposition reaction once they had an opportunity to read the speedily produced copies. Denis Howell resumed after the adjournment:

> I shall try to measure my words, because having read this document, the committee is now placed in a situation which to my knowledge is unprecedented in our parliamentary procedure.
> This document fills us with the greatest despair over local government. I am sorry to have to tell the Minister that it is an attempt by the Government to reach an agreement with local authorities on matters of legal responsibility of sewerage and sewage disposal and the expenditure of local authority services and to do it outside the scope of the Bill. The document is usurping the powers of Parliament . . .
> . . . If there is to be any method of distributing responsibility as the document does, if there is to be an attempt to divide up responsibility between regional water authorities on one hand and local authorities on the other, it is not a matter to

be dealt with in a hole in the corner of a Ministry. It is a matter for a Bill. Its proper place is in a proposed Act of Parliament, where it can be discussed by Members of Parliament. Our functions and purpose have been totally usurped by the document . . .

Mr Howell noted that the heads of agreement 'required' certain responses of the district councils. He attacked both the fact that such agreements anticipated parliamentary discussion of clause 14, and the fact that such agreements were too many and important to be dealt with outside the Bill and outside the normal scrutiny. Mr Rowlands (Labour) picked up and extended the attack. He described the Bill as no more than an enabling Bill '. . . to allow an enormous amount of detailed arrangement and delegation of financial and administrative responsibility to be dealt with behind the scenes or *by agreement between pressure groups and representative bodies and the Government outside the Commons and its Committees'*. Mr Rowlands saw this as a developing process:

> At one point it was at least controlled because under statutory instruments, legislative proposals, schedules of Bills and the Bill itself we had procedures for dealing with it. Under statutory instruments, Orders in Council, and so on, there are procedures – we have a Prayer procedure – where at least things can be debated, if nothing else. But this document is a further development in the process.
> Then we had this curious thing called codes of conduct which was the next stage. It came under the Industrial Relations Act and it has come again under the Price and Pay Code. Codes of conduct were developed and we had to find parliamentary ways of scrutinising this type of delegation away from the legislative procedures of the House. We can now add something else to our list – heads of agreement – which is a new form of abrogating and avoiding the responsibilities of Government and undermining the responsibilities of the House and Committees such as this.
> When one looks at the nature of this document, putting aside the actual content of the issue, I cannot help reinforcing the point made by my Honourable Friend. Look at the terms used – requiring, enabling, empowering –

Mr Howell (intervening): 'Directing'.
Mr Rowlands:

> Directing. These are legislative terms which should be found in clauses: that the regional water authority 'should require'

councils to do this; all district councils 'should be empowered' to do that. These are terms which are part and parcel of our legislative language. Yet they have been included and wrapped up in documents which have been the basis for discussion outside this Committee.

I am a student of the legislative process and I should perhaps say that I conduct a seminar on legislative processes at the Law Department, London School of Economics. This document, and what is going on in this Committee, will keep the seminar going for a couple of weeks with some practical case work on the way in which the processes have altered and amended – not by coming to the House and changing Standing Orders or through Select Committees on procedures, but insidiously, almost without our knowing, by these informal arrangements which are developing to avoid and bypass the legislative process.

George Thomas (Labour) again pursued the original constitutional issue of access to documents:

. . . It is clear as a pikestaff what happened this morning: some people went out of the room, and in a moment the Minister could say that he had the permission of the local authorities and could say what was in the document.

No Committee in the House has been put into the position, in the middle of deliberations, of having to hold up its proceedings in order that permission should be obtained from some official outside the House, as to whether it should see the documents . . .

In reply Graham Page presented what might be termed the pragmatic basis for what had been termed a 'constitutional shambles'.

It is not unusual that a Government should hope that a Bill may become law as they originally presented it; I do not think it is arrogant to say that, because I believe it right for a Government to prepare for what they hope Parliament will accept, therefore, in anticipation, I and my Department, particularly my Under Secretary, have been anxious to give assistance both to water authorities and to local authorities to prepare for when the Bill is enacted.

He then described the talks as reasonable and prudent steps to examine the position with the local authority associations to see what they are prepared to accept. The Minister went on to turn the initial controversy of access to the 'heads of agreement' into farce, for he informed the committee that *The Surveyor* had published in full the heads of agreement. Thus both the Opposition's zeal to see the document and the Minister's concern at receiving the permission of the associations seemed somewhat misguided!

Eventually the committee divided on the original amendment after Mr Page had undertaken to reconsider the fundamental point that was left after considerable energy was expended. Mr Page agreed at least to consider setting out a schedule to the Bill or, in some other way, the procedure by which local authorities and regional water authorities would be encouraged to reach the necessary agreements.

Although the initial constitutional issue of circulation of the heads of agreement turned out to be an unnecessary diversion, the question as to whether such agreements could usurp such areas of policy outside the Bill is still valid. There obviously remains the question whether or not such agreements between the department and interested groups can remain outside Bills; but whether or not they do, they clearly can be of more importance than the parliamentary stages.

And as Mr Rowlands mentioned during the course of the Water Bill discussion, the trend of 'consultation paper' and response directly by the interested parties probably furthers these practices. 'The draft circulars are sent out, and all sorts of bodies discuss them and they are consulted about them – all except the Parliamentary Committee which has spent hour after hour trying to scrutinise the Bill, to check that it is a good Bill.'

As a final point, which underlines the devalued status of Parliament, it is worth noting that standing committee members sponsoring amendments to the Water Bill on behalf of the associations were *themselves in ignorance of what was going on*. As Arthur Jones explained,

We have all had representations from various interests affected by the Bill, and we are asked to put down amendments. A number of us are closely associated with local authority associations and we accept in good faith amendments and supporting memoranda from them. We then find that on matters in which we are acting as advocates for local authorities, the Government are in negotiation which completely undermines the whole purpose of amendments which the local authority associations have asked us to put down.

Essentially, the backbenchers had been left stranded by the private negotiations between the Government and the groups. The 'water' case illustrates, albeit as farce, the way in which backbenchers, *even when acting as group spokesmen*, can be squeezed between the groups and the government, even though the parliamentary 'show' goes on.

On occasions it is publicly admitted that the involvement of the legislature would be positively harmful to the delicate relationship between the 'interested parties'. For example, during the 1978 investigation of the British Steel Corporation (BSC) by the Select Committee on Nationalised Industries, Sir Charles Villiers, Chairman of BSC, claimed that while in principle he was keen to answer questions put to him by the Committee, to do so might upset delicate negotiations between the BSC and the unions.

However, on occasions, the reverse can be the case – namely that the backbenchers develop such a close relationship with the minister that *they* can veto attempts by a group to get its amendments proposed in the Commons. For example, during the passage of the 1953 Transport Act members of the Conservative backbench transport committee refused to propose 'group' amendments that the Minister of Transport was unlikely to accept. Having developed a good working relationship with him, they did not want to be involved with any 'hostile' amendments. So, as groups proposed amendments to the committee, these would be taken to the Minister for informal 'clearance' before being put down on the Order Paper. In this rather unusual case the backbenchers were also involved with the civil servants in 'agreeing' amendments. The process in fact became rather complex with the Minister and his civil servants sitting round the table with the Conservative backbench committee to discuss amendments, some of which had been proposed direct to the Ministry by the groups and others that had been proposed by the group via the backbench committee. In a very real sense the legislative process, such as it was, has shifted from the official House of Commons committee towards the *party* committee.

The House of Commons can be used as part of an attempt by groups to create a 'climate of opinion' out of which favourable (to them) policy proposals may emerge. Ministers feel obliged to respond to the 'sense of the House' and a concentrated parliamentary campaign (as the Wing Airport Resistance Association recognised) can help transform a problem into a political issue. As a corollary to this, most groups recognise that it is important to ensure that their case is put in the legislature, even if the legislature is normally weak. This is because opposing groups may succeed in creating a 'hostile' climate of opinion if the 'defence' case is not put. Thus the anti-abortion forces made a tactical error in allowing the Abortion Law Reform Association to build up a climate of opinion in the House favourable to abortion reform.

We thus begin to see legislatures like the House of Commons as a sort of insurance policy for groups. This 'insurance' operates in two senses: (1) the importance of climates of opinion – either creating or preventing them; (2) occasionally legislatures such as the Commons can actively influence legislation that has been proposed by the government. This is most likely to be the case, as Finer suggests,[22] when a pressure group can squeeze the minister between the official opposition and his own backbenchers.

In the case of the Water Bill, the backbenchers were used as a long-stop in the battle between the groups and the Government. The bulk of the concessions were agreed in private bargaining between groups and Whitehall, but the backbenchers were useful as a possible threat to the Minister as the groups were always capable of organising sufficient backbench opposition for the Water Bill to be considerably delayed. So we need to remember that legislatures may *appear* weaker than they really are, because (a) just as groups exercise influence 'behind the scenes', so too do legislators; (b) the *threat* of trouble in the legislature may lead the government *not* to introduce legislation or to modify its contents in advance of introduction. Thus, the case of industrial relations reform in 1969 must be a deviant case in that normally governments are much too sensitive to introduce legislation that will run into resistance in the House of Commons. While we would not wish to stress this argument too strongly, anticipated reactions can act in a legislature's favour even though it leads us to underestimate the power of that legislature.

Finally it should be noted that if groups see the legislature as a relatively unimportant channel of influence (and again we should stress that the US Congress appears as a deviant case), this is sometimes due to the fact that legislation that has been introduced has often *originated* with the groups themselves. The Labour party's nationalisation of the shipbuilding industry in the UK is a perfect example of the involvement of groups in the actual formulation of the legislation. The proposals to nationalise the shipbuilding industry were developed in opposition between 1970 and 1974 in conjunction with the TUC and the Confederation of Shipbuilding and Engineering Unions.[23] Much of the nationalisation and employment protection legislation in the UK has originated with the trade unions and it is therefore not surprising that they see little need to mobilise support in the House of Commons when the legislation is being processed. Similarly, Shelter (the organisation representing the homeless) had a good deal of influence over the content of the 1978 Green Paper on Housing. A close examination of Shelter's pre-1974 'manifesto' and the Labour Government's Green Paper reveals a more than coincidental likeness. The Consumers' Association can also take a lot of credit for the detailed content of recent consumer legislation. When groups become embedded in the policy *formulation* process, it is little wonder that they see MPS as the last resort. They also, of course, recognise Parliament as what B. Smith has described as 'a constitutional procedural device for legitimising decisions'.[24]

CHAPTER 7

Groups and the Implementation Process

Modern governments are becoming increasingly aware of the fact that the real test of power is whether or not they can get their policies *implemented*. Getting a policy approved by the legislative may be difficult, especially under a minority government, but Acts are not worth the paper they are printed on if the policies break down at the implementation stage – hence the great emphasis on consultation. We have come to realise that in fact rather a high proportion of policies do fail to achieve their objectives. There is often a huge gap between the intentions as framed in the legislation and the actual policy that gets delivered. Why is this? Why do policies fail?

THE IMPLEMENTATION PROCESS: THEORY

Political scientists have tended to neglect the study of policy implementation and policy delivery for the same reason that they have neglected the processes by which issues arrive on the political agenda – because they have been almost totally absorbed in the legislative process. How did this law come to be passed? How was that decision reached? Just as we argued in chapter 4 that it is of equal importance to know why governments are addressing themselves to this or that problem at all, then we would also argue that it is of equal importance to study the circumstances under which policies are likely to be successful and those under which they are likely to fail. Christopher Hood, in his book *The Limits of Administration*, outlines a model of 'perfect administration' that would produce perfect policy implementation.[1] It is, of course, a theoretical model the function of which is to help us to understand why perfect policy implementation is hardly ever achieved. The rest of his book is a detailed explanation, including case studies, of the limits that exist in the real world and that prevent the achievement of the ideal administration outlined in his theoretical model. Here we do not give a full discussion of Hood's theory, but one particular category of 'limits' is of special interest to anyone concerned with pressure groups and the policy process. He identifies 'political limits' as 'those cases where policy implementation fails as a result of the application of political power...'. Using the example of taxation, he cites the case of the French *bouilleurs de cru* (local distillers who were exempt from the alcohol tax), 'whose influence was sufficient to defeat attempts to include them in the alcohol tax for over 100 years, beginning in the 1830's'. Thus, Hood argues, the 'limits of what is politically acceptable to dominant groups typically 'distort' policy programmes in a number of familiar ways'.[2]

An example of the 'distortion' is the fact that governments tend to favour schemes that benefit several areas of the country rather than concentrating resources in one particular territorial area. The political benefits are greater to the government if it spreads aid around, even though this might undermine the particular pro- gramme objectives. If aid is concentrated in one area the government will be subject to great pressure from the areas not favoured. Inter- estingly, in terms of our inclusion of 'the bureaucracy' in our definition of 'pressure group', Hood sees the 'influence of high officials in political decisions' as part of his category of political limits on administration. He quotes such examples as Lloyd George's People's Budget of 1909, 'which was held up for months because the Parliamentary draftsmen asserted that the policies in- volved were impossible to write into law'.[3] A more recent example of bureaucratic pressure affecting implementation is the case of Mr Leslie Chapman, formerly director of the Southern Region of the Property Services Agency (PSA), who has produced evidence to show that civil servants deliberately disregarded instructions from ministers to implement in other regions the type of economies that he had achieved. This outright obstruction of the implementation process even went so far as the Property Services Agency supplying inaccurate information to the Public Accounts Committee in 1975 in order to justify the non-implementation.[4] This is a good example of Tullock's claim that bureaucrats try to resist cuts by the use of superior knowledge.[5] In this case the PSA claimed that there were special circumstances in Mr Chapman's region that enabled him to make spectacular costs savings (the special circumstances were said to be that there had been a movement of troops *out* of his region, thus enabling him to effect savings) and that these circumstances did not apply in other regions. This explanation was accepted by the Public Accounts Committee. After all who should know better than the Agency itself? In fact, the 'superior knowledge' claimed by the Agency was quite false as, if anything, there had been troop movements *into* Chapman's region, as a result of the British withdrawal from Aden!

Pressman and Wildavsky have also attempted to produce a theory of implementation, though it pre-dates and is less refined than Hood's approach. However, their theory is of perhaps greater relevance to our primary interest. In particular, Pressman and Wildavsky introduce the notion of 'decision-points' and 'clearances'. A decision-point is reached when 'an act of agreement has to be registered for the program to continue...'.[6] Each instance in which a participant is required to give his consent is termed a 'clearance' point. In their case study of an employment creation programme in Oakland, California, the authors list the number of clearances involved in the various decision-points they identified. Put simply, their theory suggests that the greater the number of decision-points and clearances involved in a policy programme, the greater the likelihood that the programme will fail to achieve its objectives. Indeed, they are extremely pessimistic about the chances of any programme succeeding. Thus they argue that 'Our normal expectation should be that new programs will fail to get off the ground and that, at best, they will take considerable time to get started. The cards in this world are stacked against things happening, as so much effort is required to make them move. The remarkable thing is that new programs work at all.'[7] The reason is that, for programmes to succeed, agreement is needed at so many decision-points. In the real world the chances of agreement being reached all along the line are rather small, yet if the programme is to succeed, they argue, the probability of such agreement must be high. So policies need to be relatively simple, designed with problems of implementation in mind and involving relatively few clearances and decision-points. In all probability of course, this ideal situation is unlikely to arise. The evidence suggests that policies are increasingly complex, are often formulated without much reference to implementation needs and certainly involve increased numbers of participants. In particular, the growth and proliferation of agencies for delivering policies increases the number of decision-points and clearances quite significantly.

We have, as Anthony King has argued, arrived at a situation where 'the number of dependency relationships in which government is involved has increased substantially'. This, together with the fact that 'the incidence of acts of non-compliance by the other participants in these relationships has also increased substantially', is at the heart of the increasing difficulty that governments are experiencing in the UK.[8] Because of the increasing interdependence in modern advanced economies, governments have become more vulnerable to acts of non-compliance by sections of the community. He contrasts the effect of the 1974 miners' strike with their strike in 1926. In 1926 we could manage for a long period without the miners. In 1974 the country was soon reduced to a three-day week. But it is, of course, not just that we have become more interdependent; it is also that, as King suggests, groups are more willing to use the power that interdependence gives them. The miners in 1974 were not behaving significantly differently from 1926 (though we had become dependent upon them). But increasingly *other* groups, such as doctors and nurses, firemen and schoolteachers, have begun to behave in the same way. They have begun to realise that they too can cause quite considerable inconvenience and disruption to the rest of the community. For example, teachers who refused to supervise children at lunchtime caused quite severe difficulties in 1978 for those families with working mothers.

Much of policy implementation depends upon the good-will and cooperation of participating groups for its success. Because of this, and because more groups have come to realise it, we need to shift our focus, as political scientists, to 'what Gross terms "the nastier problems" which have to do with persuading, manipulating or coercing people to act in accordance with decisions that are (somehow or other) made'.[9]

THE BEST LAID SCHEMES...

We do not need to look very hard in order to find examples of groups who either sabotage public policies or have a considerable effect on their implementation. For example, the Ministry of Defence (MOD) was subject to 'blacking' when the West Midlands Haulage Association refused to move a dozen Scorpion tanks from a Coventry test track. The boycott was decided after the MOD withdrew a contract from a Coventry firm that had breached phase III of the pay policy. One immediate union response to a Post Office plan to introduce a special cheap 5p Christmas post rate was that the Union of Post Office Workers let it be known that it would refuse to handle the extra work.

Increasingly, the task for the decision-maker is to discover the limits set by those who will implement the decision. In November 1977 the National Union of Teachers asked its members not to cooperate with the Government's questionnaire on the curriculum that had been sent out to all local education authorities. The questionnaire contained over fifty detailed questions on curriculum contents, policy and control. The idea behind the questionnaire was that the Government would ultimately give guidance on how the practice of local authorities could best fit national needs. The teachers' union decided on non-cooperation because they feared that the questionnaire could lead to 'interference' from the central government in the curriculum in schools, i.e. the exercise could eventually threaten the monopoly that the teachers have exercised over the curriculum in our schools.

In the same year the Prime Minister was warned that the Government's much publicised £80 million grant aid scheme to the iron foundry industry in the UK was being undermined by shop floor opposition to new methods of working in the re-equipped foundries. The chairman of the Ferrous Foundries National Economic Development Committee was reported as saying that he had personally told the Prime Minister that there was an urgent need for closer cooperation between union leaders serving on the 'little Neddy' and their members on the shop floor. The whole process of attempting to modernise and restructure the British steel industry has been delayed by the powerful resistance of both the national unions and more particularly effectively organised local resistance groups opposed to steel plant closures.

Similarly, the failure of the Fulton reforms of the Civil Service can in part be attributed to the effective resistance of the civil servants themselves to any radical changes in the way the service operates. In each case, of course, the groups concerned were playing a perfectly legitimate role. It is the function of the steel union, for example, to defend the jobs of its members and the internal politics of the union would demand that union leaders should oppose plant closures. On the other hand, such activity does have profound effects on the success of public policies, and in the study of issues we must be aware of these effects. We may have every sympathy with groups who oppose plant closures, motorways or expenditure cuts in the Health Service, but this does not negate the fact that such groups make governing more difficult. Sometimes, of course, group activity can be so effective that a policy simply cannot be implemented. The Industrial Relations Act, passed by Parliament with a comfortable majority, was an almost complete failure in terms of it's primary objectives because the Government did not have sufficient power to implement it against the resistance of the trade unions. Again, the reader might have every sympathy with the opposition to that legislation, but it does raise the rather important question of the position of an elected government and legislature when faced with well-organised opposition to its policies.

Opposition to the implementation of policies that have been formulated can take a number of forms. It may be perfectly 'constitutional': for example, the use of the courts by anti-nuclear protesters in the USA has been rather effective as a means of slowing down the US nuclear energy programme. In contrast, the 'Carlos Committee' in France organised a series of bomb, fire and machine gun attacks in France in November 1977 as part of its campaign against the development of nuclear energy in France. A letter signed by the Committee attempted to justify the attacks with the argument that 'the fight against nuclear energy cannot be confined to the legalistic opposition of the parties and unions. It is essential to intensify the acts of sabotage which directly affect the authority's economic interests and *delay or halt the construction of* generators, mines and factories linked to nuclear power.'[10]

Similarly, anti-nuclear groups in West Germany have clashed with police at building sites for nuclear power stations in Brokdorf and Grohnde. These citizen action groups (or *Bürgerinitiativen*) have proliferated in recent years and some 850 of them have formed the Federal Association of Citizens Action Groups. The chairman of the Association is on record, in 1977, as claiming that the Federal Government's nuclear policy could lead to a threat to liberty and the rule of law. The Association has published a manual that lists sixty examples of civil disobedience – including delaying tactics over paying taxes and boycotting the products of firms involved in the atomic business. Perhaps the most spectacular example of pressure group activity preventing the implementation of a policy is the case of the new Tokyo airport, the opening of which was delayed several years by protesters.

But it is a truism in pressure group studies that the public aspect of pressure group activity is merely the tip of the iceberg. The bulk of the activity lies below the 'water line' and this is particularly true of pressure group influence on the implementation process. Once a decision is reached, once a policy is announced, once an Act is passed, there is a tendency for the issue concerned to leave the political agenda. In the eye of the public, 'informed' by the media, 'the problem' has been 'dealt with'. There is little concern about what actually *happens* after that point. So groups are able to work quite effectively at the *erosion* of public policies away from the glare of publicity. The groups are rather like the waves of the sea continually eroding the base of the cliff until the cliff face gradually falls into the sea over the years. The set battles, like the TUC's victory over the Conservative Industrial Relations Act, are not typical. Much more typical is the case of the local authority associations, whose pressure on the Government in 1977 led to a weakening of the code of guidance under the Housing (Homeless Persons) Act. Originally, the Government had hoped to get local authorities to change their policies towards the homeless, and an earlier draft of the code had suggested that the use of bed and breakfast accommodation for the homeless should only be a last resort and that homeless families must be given permanent accommodation as soon as possible. These views were toned down as a result of local authority pressure and indeed certain statements of principle, originally included, were removed altogether as a result of their pressure. Moreover, the manner in which the Act has been implemented by the local authorities again shows the importance of local authority attitudes.

The concept of policy erosion is, of course, well understood by groups themselves and can play an important part in the type and nature of amendments that they propose during the passage of legislation. It has generally been argued that groups rarely try to change the *principle* of a Bill that has been proposed by the government. They recognise, so the argument runs, that once the government has made a policy commitment in public, then it cannot be seen to 'back down' in response to sectional pressures. Whilst not denying this as a general principle, we would argue (a) that, as indicated in chapter 4, groups can be quite effective at preventing issues emerging in the first place, and (b) that they recognise that it is quite often unnecessary to attack .the principle of a Bill when they can so affect its implementation as to achieve the same result. For example, the British Civil Service was not so unwise as to attack the Fulton Committee proposals head-on. They appeared to be responding to the climate of opinion that prevailed at the time. The reality, critics argue, is that 'appearances and titles may have changed, but little of significance has altered'.[11] In fact, groups may well seek to amend legislation as it passes through the legislature in such a way as to allow the maximum possible scope for erosion of the principles involved when the legislation comes to be implemented. Thus, detailed procedures to be followed, the structures and institutions to be employed to deliver a particular policy, the type of personnel to be involved in the policy programme are all extremely relevant so-called 'technical matters' that concern groups during the passage of legislation. Such matters are of increasing importance as the amount of delegated legislation increases. The more scope given by Parliament to ministers to decide the details of policies, the more scope for groups to influence what actually happens at the point of policy delivery.

A good example of group activity designed to influence the procedures and structures used to implement a broad policy decision is provided by the Restrictive Trade Practices Act 1956. The Conservative Government had decided to legislate against restrictive trade practices as operated by industrial trade associations. The industrial interests recognised that legislation was inevitable (indeed some of them thought it desirable) and so made no attempt to oppose the principle of controlling such activity. But they showed very great concern about the kind of institution that should be set up to implement the proposed legislation. They were particularly concerned that the enforcement of the Act should be carried out through a court or court-like institution. Thus the Federation of British Industry argued that cases of restrictive trade practices should be investigated by an independent tribunal.[12] Similarly, the National Union of Manufacturers (later to merge with the FBI to form the CBI) argued that a judicial rather than an administrative tribunal should be set up. Furthermore, all industrial interests were concerned not only that a court should be set up, but that a case by case approach should be used. They were most anxious that particular categories of restrictive practice should be outlawed in principle. Each case should be judged on its merits. No definition of the public interest should be attempted, the tribunal should be left to hear all the evidence and should be left to decide on balance which way the evidence lay. Also, it should make its judgements in the light of judicial precedent.

All of this pressure is easy to explain. Experience had shown over the years that the courts were not particularly effective instruments for controlling monopolies and restrictive practices. Put simply, the industrial interests knew full well that they would have a much greater chance of being able to continue with their trade practices if the implementation machinery was judicial in nature and adopted a case by case approach. Their pressure was, in the event, almost entirely successful as the government department then responsible, the Board of Trade, was only too willing to hand over the rather unpleasant task to what became the Restrictive Practices Court The Board was, in this case, an example of a general ideology in the British Civil Service that, as Shonfield argued, meant that civil servants 'were anxious above all to ensure that the exercise of new powers of government did not saddle them with the responsibility of making choices, for which later they might be accountable'.[13] In the restrictive practices case the self-interest of the bureacracy (the Board of Trade) coincided with the self-interest of the outside pressure groups.

Another example of the crucial importance of the locus of responsibility for implementation, in terms of pressure group interests, is provided by the 1973 Water Act in England and Wales. During discussion of the proposed reforms, the question of who should retain responsibility for land drainage became an important issue. One of the main objectives of the various outside interests concerned with land drainage (e.g. the National Farmers' Union, NFU, the Country Landowners' Association, CLA) was that central administrative responsibility for land drainage should remain with the Ministry of Agriculture, Fisheries and Food (MAFF). For example, the CLA's position was that land drainage should be administered by authorities covering areas no larger than the existing river authorities, that these authorities should have their own sources of finance and that they should be under the control of MAFF.[14] As it happens, like the case of restrictive trade practices, the interests of the outside groups coincided with the interests of a government department. MAFF was just as keen to defend its administrative territory as were the agricultural interests. Consequently, MAFF and the agricultural interests acted as a joint pressure group (they were known as the MAFFia by their opponents) against the Department of the Environment which wanted to remove land drainage from MAFF control and place it with the proposed Regional Water Authorities. In the event the MAFFia won the battle. MAFF retained control over land drainage and, although at regional level land drainage is included in the function of the Regional Water Authorities, there are separate land drainage committees within each RWA as requested by the agricultural lobby. In essence, the administrative system for land drainage is the one most favourable to the organised groups and their allies in the Ministry of Agriculture, Fisheries and Food. Yet again, the question of who administers the policy and through what processes was seen by the groups as an issue of crucial importance to them.

Even where groups have not made great issue of procedures and processes at the time legislation was passed, they may subsequently see opportunities in the implementation process radically to affect the way policies operate. For example, development authorities like the Central Electricity Generating Board have found that environmental groups are increasingly inclined to use existing planning procedures with the result that the planning and building of even conventional power stations has become more difficult. As a consequence of this increased utilisation of long-established procedures, the time taken for the planning and completion of such developments has been lengthened considerably – so much so that the Generating Board considered the contruction of much larger power stations (five times the size of existing generating stations) as a solution to the growing public resistance to an expanding network of smaller power stations.

Moreover, the actual threat, by a group, of the use of existing machinery can cause changes in the way in which a policy is implemented. Developers, both private and public, are willing to modify their proposals rather than face considerable delays caused by opposing groups who use the opportunities offered by planning procedures. Equally, as we suggested earlier, the question of the degree of cooperation that groups will give in the administration of a proposed policy is of vital concern to the government. As Finer argued, 'our whole framework of public administration presumes that private associations will give freely of their advice and assistance. It would be seriously dislocated if they were withheld'.[15] Thus both sides realise the importance of the implementation process – after the set legislative battles, which change little, the real business of implementing, interpreting and modifying policy begins.

So far we have tended to stress the negative or disruptive impact that groups may have on the implementation of public polcies. But there are numerous examples of cases where groups have played a positive and constructive role in the implementation of public policies. Indeed, the quotation above from Finer suggests that most of the time groups do cooperate with and assist the government in the formulation and implementation of public policies and that our system of public administration assumes that they will do so.

One important aspect of their role in the implementation process is as part of the *monitoring* function of existing policies. A small example drawn from local government illustrates the point. Groups like the Council for the Protection of Rural England have a system of local branches and much of the work of these local branches is to act as monitors of existing policies. The Sheffield and Peak District Branch of the CPRE is one such local society, which is rather well organised and capable of alerting the local authorities in its area to possible 'erosion' of policies. For example, in 1977, they noticed a case of unauthorised tipping in the area and notified the North East Derbyshire District Council of the situation. The Council took prompt action on receipt of the information from the Society and the tip was graded and covered with soil as a result. A small case, but it does illustrate the role of groups as early warning systems to policy-makers when existing policies are not working.

The case of the dumping of poisonous waste, discussed in chapter 4, is a more important example of the same phenomenon. In that case the action of the Warwickshire Conservation Society was important in publicly demonstrating that the existing policy setting was quite inadequate as a system of control. So groups can play a positive role in the monitoring of existing policies. Unless the government has an army of bureaucrats whose task is to monitor the implementation of policies, then we must rely on interested groups to do the job for us. Even in key policy areas – such as incomes policies – groups can play a central role in the monitoring process. For example, during the 1977/78 wages policy the Government appeared to have no effective mechanism for monitoring the actual level of pay settlements. They relied on the CBI's data bank for information on whether or not the policy, which was central to the Government's economic strategy, was successful or not. Similarly, the CBI's Industrial Trends Survey is the most reliable guide on business confidence, new orders and level of output.

But pressure groups can and do play a role in the actual *administration* of policies as opposed to just the *monitoring* of the administration. The best-documented examples of groups becoming part of the machinery of government occurred during the two world wars when trade associations were directly responsible for the administration of war-time controls. In World War II '... trade associations were authorized, as government agents, to allocate markets, fix output and prices and ration materials...'.[16] Indeed, the close relationship that developed between the government and trade associations (and trade unions) during World War II is seen by some observers as the foundation of the corporatism with which we are so familiar today.[17]

Although the war saw the closest involvement of groups in the machinery of government, the process is perfectly well known in more recent times. Thus, the Royal Automobile Club and the Auto-mobile Association have been directly involved in the administration of petrol rationing in the UK at various times since the war. The numerous voluntary associations in the field of social welfare have been involved on a much more regular basis in the 'delivery' of policies. Even in a welfare state it appears that the voluntary movement plays an important role in our social and environmental services. The contribution that these societies make in such areas as help to ex-offenders was recognised in 1977 by an official committee chaired by Lord Wolfendon.[18] There is no doubt that governments see advantages in using outside groups in the implementation of public policies, particularly in policy areas that are not thought to be politically sensitive. For example, in 1977 the Government promised to give all possible backing to the Save a Baby campaign organised by the Spastics Society. The objective of the campaign was to prevent thousands of babies from being born with needless handicaps. The minister responsible promised talks between his department and the society to see how the government might help – suggesting priority for deprived areas of the inner cities. In the same year the Manpower Services Commission went out of its way to reassure local authorities and youth organisations that they would be involved in the Government's new opportunities programme for the young unemployed. The programme 'would require participation of a wide range of institutions, groups and interests at community, local authority, regional and central government levels'.[19]

Occasionally, however, the close relationship proves to be uneasy. At the end of 1977 the Government also announced that it was to cease funding a group called Fair Play for Children. The group was in receipt of some £27,000 a year and acted as coordinator of groups concerned with children's play needs. In fact, the question of public funding of voluntary organisations has proved to be a rather thorny one, both from the government's viewpoint and from that of the groups themselves.

However, it is by no means uncommon for voluntary organisations, which in part are acting as pressure groups on the government, to be in receipt of public funds. For example, the Keep Britain Tidy group receives an annual grant from the Department of the Environment, as does the Development Commission towards the expenses of rural community councils. Similarly, the National Council of Social Service receives grants from government departments. An official report, in 1972, on the role of voluntary organisations and youth in the environment, estimated that at the national level the Departments of Environment, Education and Science, and Health and Social Security, spent approximately £1.5 million per year in grants to voluntary organisations of various kinds.[20] The report argued that the government should substantially increase its financial support for voluntary movements 'especially in areas (e.g. community development) where voluntary movements can provide a non-statutory service of a higher quality than any which the government can provide'.[21]

The implication of this statement is, of course, that under certain conditions outside groups are *more able than the government to deliver policies effectively*. There may be a number of reasons for this. The group may, for example, be regarded as more legitimate – more acceptable – by the potential recipients of the policy in question. They may have more local knowledge than the official bureaucracy and they may have more manpower. They may also develop a degree of technical expertise in a particular policy area that the public authorities do not possess. In such cases the group may play a more important role in the policy process than the public authorities themselves. After the blizzards of January 1978 had caused livestock losses in Scotland, a National Farmers' Union–UK Agricultural Departments' compensation fund was created. The NFU (Scotland) was seen as the most suitable body to deal with compensation to Scottish farmers who lost livestock in the 1978 blizzard. They established a fund to which the Government and the EEC contributed. Criteria for eligibility for compensation were negotiated between the NFU (Scotland) and the Government. This was an example of a scheme where it was held to be administratively easier for the union to manage the operation – and the Government was freed of some of the risk of criticisms of arbitrariness and lack of generosity.

Another excellent example of this is provided by the Civic Trust for the North-West (CTNW).[22] The Trust was formed in 1961 by a group of environmentally conscious businessmen in the North-West. Local industry and local authorities in the area subscribe to the Trust, enabling it to employ full-time staff. The Trust has three main functions: (1) it plays an educational role in the region by stimulating an awareness of local problems through lectures, exhibitions, publications, etc.; (2) it plays an advisory role in showing companies, local authorities and individuals how environmental problems can be tackled; (3) it carries out technical studies that result in fairly detailed environmental schemes.

One such scheme in which the Trust became very closely involved was an improvement scheme for the Tame Valley. In 1965 a number of local authorities bordering the River Tame decided in principle that joint action was needed to improve the valley. It was soon realised, however, that because so many public authorities were involved (at least ten local authorities plus other public bodies such as the British Waterways Board and the River Board), action to improve the valley was unlikely unless some coordinating mechanism was created. Fortunately, a local businessman who was a trustee of CTNW intervened with a grant of £1000 to CTNW to help promote the improvement of the valley. CTNW decided to use this gift to formulate a detailed strategy for the valley. CTNW was thus in a position to provide both the necessary coordination and the detailed planning for a scheme to move forward.

The Tame Valley Advisory Committee was set up in 1969 in order to provide a link between CTNW and the various local councils involved. Though formally the policy-making body for the Tame Valley scheme, the Committee delegated planning and design work to a project team within CTNW. The CTNW team originally comprised two full-time staff but eventually was expanded to a total of seven. This was made possible because the central government introduced a national Special Environmental Assistance Scheme in 1972 and hence extra finance became available. As the improvement scheme was developed by the CTNW team, the role of CTNW increased in importance. Effectively, the local authorities delegated their responsibility for the actual site work to CTNW, with each local authority merely countersigning papers submitted to them by CTNW. Similarly, the Department of the Environment, as the department responsible for granting funds under the Special Environmental Assistance Scheme, agreed to deal direct with CTNW as effective coordinator/ planner of the Tame Valley scheme, rather than with each statutory local authority. CTNW thus played a crucial role in both the formulation and actual implementation of the improvement scheme, having considerable delegated authority and supplying both technical expertise and administrative coordination. In effect, CTNW acquired the status and respectability of a statutory body, even though it was a pressure group.

Issues like the improvement of a valley are, of course, relatively uncontroversial in political terms (although CTNW did exhibit very considerable political skills in managing to coordinate so many different public authorities). However, groups are often involved, in a constructive way, in the implementation of policies of much greater political significance. Thus in 1971/72 the CBI originated a voluntary prices initiative and 'for a time it seemed as if the initiative in the management of the economy had passed to the CBI and that the organization might emerge as the body which had set the economy on a new road'.[23] The new Conservative Government in 1970 was keen to reduce the level of wage increases and, 'eager to play its part, the CBI attempted to foster employer solidarity by facilitating discussions among negotiators from those large firms which were seen as "wage leaders"'.[24] Despite this, the rate of inflation increased, and fearing the introduction of a *statutory* prices and income policy (which it had always opposed) the CBI decided to initiate a *voluntary* prices policy. It consulted its leading members, plus other interests, about the possibility of undertaking a voluntary limit on price increases for twelve months. It was hoped that as a quid pro quo the Government would reflate the economy.[25] The Confederation's hope was soon realised as the Chancellor announced cuts in purchase tax, the abolition of hire purchase restrictions and better capital allowances.

Grant and Marsh argue that, 'in the short run, the initiative had been a great success ... in the long run the prices initiative left a nasty taste in many industralists' mouths'.[26] No doubt the same comment could be applied to the role of the TUC in wages policy during the period 1974–78 and referred to in Section I. But even though the CBI and TUC have incurred costs (particularly in terms of organisational stress) in participating in the implementation of these politically controversial policies, there is little doubt that they *have* played a quite crucial role in whatever success these policies have achieved. For example, during the 1977/78 period the success of the TUC in implementing the Government's pay policy was a key factor in determining the shape of the Chancellor's budget in Spring 1978 and in the fixing of the Government's monetary targets. If it is accepted that wages play a key role in determining the rate of inflation (and it should be noted that there is considerable disagreement amongst economists on this), then ultimately the rate of inflation rests upon the ability of pressure groups like the TUC to deliver a policy of wage restraint.

Another key policy area in which groups in the UK have come to play a key role is the formulation and implementation of industrial policies. In November 1975 the Government launched its industrial strategy, which was claimed to be a common approach agreed between government, management and unions. As a result of this agreement some thirty-seven Sector Working Parties (SWPs) were set up within the National Economic Development Council structure. Within each SWP, management, unions and the Civil Service have been engaged in 'searching for practical solutions to practical problems'.[27] The Treasury itself, in discussing the progress of the SWPs, has stressed that whether or not the strategy (basically designed to increase productivity and win back markets) succeeds '... depends very much on managers and workpeople becoming fully involved...'.[28] In a memorandum on the industrial strategy, the Government stressed that 'even after identifying what needs to be done ... SWPs will have to persuade individual companies within their sectors to adopt these strategies in pursuit of sectoral improvement...'.[29] Many would argue that it is at this very point – when the strategies need to be implemented – that the power of groups will be most felt, because the strategies will call for sacrifices and changes in behaviour of well-organised and powerful sectoral interests. If the cooperation of these groups is withheld, there is little doubt that policies like the 'industrial strategy' will be almost completely eroded.

IMPLEMENTATION AND POLICY FORMULATION

Throughout the book we have examined the policy process as not *one* process but a series of sub-processes. All of these are closely linked. If the implementation theorists are correct, the link between policy implementation, or policy delivery and policy formulation ought to be particularly close if policies are to 'succeed'. To quote Pressman and Wildavsky,

> The great problem, as we understand it, is to make the difficulties of implementation a part of the initial formulation of policy. Implementation must not be conceived of as a process that takes place after and independent of, the design of policy. Means and ends can be brought into somewhat closer correspondence only by making each partially dependent on the other'.[30]

In other words, policies are more likely to succeed if at the policy design/formulation stage the problems likely to be encountered at the implementation stage are recognised and taken account of. As we have argued, one of the main problems at the implementation stage is likely to be resistance from affected interests, be they bureaucratic organisations or 'outside' pressure groups, and this is one very good reason why policy-makers are so anxious to integrate the groups in the policy process. Put simply, a policy that can be eroded or sabotaged by a powerful group or agency is not worth the paper it is written on.

SECTION III:

Assessment

CHAPTER 8

Pressure Groups and the Political System—Broader Comparative Perspectives

The trends described in previous chapters are based on evidence mostly drawn from the UK, but they are in fact not uniquely British. There is considerable evidence to suggest that there are broad transnational political forces at work. In most European countries, discussion of the policy-making system has moved from a parliamentary, elective perspective to the functional representation area. A large number of labels have accumulated – e.g. corporatist, neo-corporatist, corporativist, neo-corporativist, liberal corporatist, quasi-corporatist, estatist corporatist, societal corpo. st, pluralist, segmented pluralist, limited pluralist, institutionalised pluralist, pluralist corporatist, corporate pluralist, new corporatist, statist pluralist, etc. One aim in this chapter is to draw attention to the resemblances between our description and the equivalent processes in other states that have generated this plethora of labels.

The chapter attempts to link our own description to four strands of post-war literature,[1] which can be broadly grouped as follows:
  (a) British pluralists
  (b) American post-pluralists
  (c) British corporate state debate
  (d) New comparative government?
These strands in many ways are self-consciously incompatible, and in discussing them together we are not implying that they represent a homogeneous whole. But we are claiming that their vocabulary is part of the same language and that they are attempting to explain the same phenomena. The terms they introduce seem as necessary as the more conventional vocabulary, such as executive, legislature and judiciary, checks and balances, etc.

THE BRITISH PLURALISTS

The detailed study of pressure groups in Britain only dates from the 1950s. There had been earlier and acute observations. Sir Ivor Jennings for one, in his study *Parliament* in 1939, wrote that 'much legislation is derived from organized interests ... most of it is amended on the representation of such interests, and ... often parliamentary opposition is in truth the opposition of interests'.[2] It was between 1954 and 1963, however, that major studies opened up the subject and these British studies have presaged much of what we have had to say in earlier chapters. For example, McKenzie argued that the electoral anomaly by which the Conservative Government took office in 1951, having obtained fewer votes than Labour, was offset by the fact that they could not administer the economic affairs of the country unless they paid very close attention to the demands and the opinions of the trade unions. Eckstein concluded his study on the British Medical Association by observing: 'that decisions relating to medical policy are made in Britain by the interaction of "authorized groups" is undeniable. In negotiations about such policy the general public plays no role, except only when its views are represented by the Treasury.'[3] Samuel Beer, writing in 1956, argued that 'the main substance of this [British] system is continual, day-to-day contacts between public bureaucrats in the government departments and private bureaucrats in the offices of the great pressure groups'.[4] Beer stressed the 'cultural context' that favoured pressure groups and indeed referred to the 'rules of the game'. In using the ideas of 'negotiated order', 'negotiated environments' and 'accommodation', we were ourselves making a similar point. By 1957, the role of the pressure groups was sufficiently well known for Paul Johnson to be able to sum up (perhaps too strongly) that 'acts of policy are now decided by the interplay of thousands of conflicting interest groups and cabinet ministers are little more than the chairmen of arbitration committees. . .'[5]

The trends that were observed in the 1950s have, we argue, intensified. If some of the claims then were contentious, they are now confirmed by subsequent developments and might even be regarded as routine, so established has the system become. In functional terms, groups are not only involved in 'articulating demands', they are also participating in the 'politics of conversion' and implementation. There was an awareness of this in the early studies, but

writers got absorbed in a classificatory debate and still retained
a parliamentary focus. Pressure groups were down-graded into 'just
another facet' of the political process. Even as late as 1968 one could
find a standard textbook on British politics relegating pressure
groups to a short twenty-page chapter, compared with over 160
pages on Parliament![6]

Samuel Beer's work was least easily incorporated into conventional political interpretation. He was clearly discussing an *alternative* system rather than an accretion to earlier concepts. He took
his cue from Herring's argument that the more the government
becomes involved in controlling industrial and commercial interests,
the more those interests must be allowed to participate in and indeed
to consent to policy changes.[7] Beer saw this develop particularly
in World War II and claimed that despite the relaxation of controls
after the war a system of quasi-corporatism remained.[8] He later
developed his ideas and coined the term 'new group politics'.[9] This
meant that the ideological gap between the parties had narrowed
and public policy emerged from an intricate system of bidding and
bargaining involving the government and consumer and producer
groups. New group politics can be seen as a specific example of the
pluralist interpretation that coloured British and American political
science in the post-war era. Accommodation, the pluralist mode of
adjusting conflicts, rests on multiple centres of power. The image of
a pluralist society as depicted by American pluralists such as Dahl
sounds very similar to our own description of British politics. He
suggests that in almost any year in American history, 'Important
government policies would be arrived at through negotiation, bargaining, persuasion and pressure at a considerable number of different sites in the political system...'[10] To the American pluralists the
accommodation of interests was the way to contain conflict – their
version in fact of the 'negotiated order'.

In Britain there is relatively little discussion of pluralism – even
though it can be read into many case studies. The editorial in the
Political Quarterly special issue on pressure groups in 1958 was
unusually explicit in the British context when it argued that 'pressure
groups give us today a genuinely pluralist society... And without
pluralism we should indeed be helpless before the great Leviathan'.
But while that is a rare explicit mention of British pluralism, the
various early studies fitted that framework of analysis rather than
any other.

THE AMERICAN POST-PLURALISTS

The early British material still offers a rich supply of detail of practices and relationships, but in the United States the pluralist interpretation has been challenged. This alternative literature pays far less attention to the parties and Congress. The pluralists seemed intent on reconciling groups and the elective political machinery, whereas the post-pluralists tend to present them as alternatives. Thus, in the polemical *The End of Liberalism*, Lowi describes how the US-notion of a government limited to a specific set of activities was discarded when it became too confining. Lowi claims that 'the result – which only at first exposure appears paradoxical – was not the strong, positive government of which the pluralists spoke but impotent government, no less impotent because it was getting bigger'. Lowi discusses the American 'interest-group liberalism philosophy'. He sees it as a vulgarised version of pluralism:

(1) Organized interests are homogeneous and easy to define, sometimes monolithic. Any 'duly elected' spokesman for any interest is taken as speaking in close approximation for each and every member.
(2) Organized interests pretty much fill up and adequately represent most of the sectors of our lives, so that one organized group can be found effectively answering and checking some other organized group as it seeks to prosecute its claims against society.
(3) And the role of government is one of ensuring access particularly to the most effectively organized, and of ratifying the agreements and adjustments worked out among the competing leaders and their claims.[11]

Lowi claims that from the single policy area of agriculture 'manifestations of the corporate state' appeared more widely. For example, in discussing the War on Poverty, he notes how Sargent Shriver insisted on group involvement – 'governmental groups, philanthropic, religious, business and labor groups and the poor'. Lowi notes how 'governmental groups' were simply one more type of participant.[12]

What effects do these opportunities for group access have on policy-making? Some observers see a process of the colonisation of government by groups and the exploitation of public policy in the groups' own interests. In such a situation the distinction between public and private becomes rather blurred and the function of public policy-making may be delegated to particular groups. Government itself gets fragmented and the fragments in turn are beholden to the associated interests. The agency system in the USA does nothing to prevent this colonisation. For example, Selznick and Bernstein argue that agencies also get captured by their clients. Far from 'crusading', they end up protecting the interests of the people they are supposed to be regulating.[13]

THE BRITISH CORPORATE STATE DEBATE

The third set of material that we think usefully extends our own account is the 'corporatist' discussion that emerged in Britain in the 1970s. Just as the post-war pluralists' interpretation of British politics had seen an earlier manifestation in the guild socialist writings of G. D. H. Cole and the Webbs, the corporatist style is an idea that had been discussed by an earlier generation of commentators. However, by the early 1970s the term 'the corporate state' was beginning to connote the 'corporation state' – implying that the government was dominated by giant business corporations. A more traditional concept of the corporate state, as a system where government 'organises' cooperation rather than leaving it to pluralistic bargaining and compromise, re-emerged in the early 1970s in Britain. This had precursors such as Andrew Shonfield's *Modern Capitalism* (1965),[14] which viewed the 'corporatist formula for managing the [British] economy as one in which the major interest groups are brought together and encouraged to conclude a series of bargains about their future behaviour which will have the effect of moving economic events along the desired path'. In 1972 Nigel Harris examined the post-war Conservative party in the context of two versions of corporatism. He contrasted '*estatiste* corporation', which rested on state direction and planning, with a 'pluralist corporation', which was more conservative, more inclined to recognise the autonomy of groups.[15] Despite such works, the 'corporate state' debate in Britain failed to arouse much critical attention at that time.

In 1974, however, Pahl and Winkler largely revived the corporatist discussion in Britain.[16] The essence of their evidence for the 'coming corporatism' was drawn from economic management and research into the behaviour of firms. They seem to have found little enthusiasm there for competition. Instead, what was wanted was stability and predictability. Indeed it was the (then) Federation of British Industry that helped to persuade the Conservatives, in the early 1960s, to adopt some form of economic planning in order to make business life rather more predictable. Winkler defined 'corporatism' as 'an economic system in which the state directs and controls predominantly privately-owned business according to four principles: unity, order, nationalism, and success'. The kernel of the Pahl and Winkler contribution is that Britain is moving towards a new economic system. With the state moving from a supportive to a directive role for industry, a new phase – neither socialist, nor capitalist – has been created. The Industry Act 1975, which sought to initiate a system of planning agreements by which the major companies would inform the government of intentions in the area of prices, investment, productivity, exports, import saving, etc., is clearly a development that neatly fits this model. Winkler has argued that the impulse to this corporatism has been pragmatic, not ideological, adaptive problem-solving, not the intentional imposition of a coherent economic strategy.[17] It was the pragmatic *regularisation* of long-established relationships in the 1960s that prompted observers to view Britain as a corporatist rather than a pluralist system. Much of this and subsequent corporatist writing looks at the economy and industrial relations. For example, the emergence of incomes policies is a good example of the use of existing voluntary associations as agents of social control. But the economy is an area where evidence for symbiosis is possibly less strong than elsewhere. The economy is perhaps the most intractable area in the corporatist advance. We have tried to indicate a range of policy areas where it has been more easily established.

The 'corporate state', or 'corporatism' in its many formulations, is an unresolved item on the agenda. We have no authoritative verdicts to hand out. For our purposes the interest in the topic is more significant than any particular version of it. Pluralism has been particularly identified with American society, corporatism with fascist regimes. Accordingly, at first sight there appears a great discontinuity between the two, but in practice the gap is not too wide: both treatments are reactions to the same trends in society.

It seems unlikely that any rigorous definition of corporatism will be applicable to Britain. And this is itself significant. Whereas rigorous criteria might demand formal agreements between the state and trade unions or industry, in Britain informal agreements are the norm.

Philippe Schmitter has attempted the difficult task of distinguishing between corporatism and pluralism as follows:

Corporatism
Corporatism can be defined as a system of interest representation in which the constituent units are organized into a limited number of singular, compulsory, non-competitive, hierarchically ordered and functionally differentiated categories, recognized or licensed (if not created) by the state and granted a deliberate representational monopoly within their respective categories in exchange for observing certain controls on their selection of leaders and articulation of demands and supports.

Pluralism
Pluralism is a system of interest representation in which the constituent units are organized into an unspecified number of multiple, voluntary, competitive, non-hierarchically ordered and self-determined (as to type or scope of interest) categories not specially licensed, subsidized, created or otherwise controlled by the State and not exercising a monopoly of representational activity within their respective categories.[18]

Schmitter sees pluralism and corporatism as sharing a group-centred view of the political process. In Britain one can identify developments in legislation dealing with trade union recognition that seem to represent moves to a 'limited number of singular, compulsory, non-competitive, hierarchically ordered and functionally differentiated categories, etc.'. The granting of consultative status to a group often, in effect, means concession of representational monopoly. But all these matters are contentious, and Britain's pragmatic evolution of arrangements means that it is impossible to be sure of the extent to which Britain has moved from pluralism to corporatism.

THE NEW COMPARATIVE GOVERNMENT?

The British corporate state debate mulls over many examples, practices and phenomena that we would readily absorb into our own description of how policy is made in Britain, but analytically our own description of the British policy process is closer to the literature (mainly about Europe) that at its most ambitious represents an alternative approach to comparative government. The earliest of what we see as a genre were probably the Norwegian studies by Eckstein and Rokkan.[19] Rokkan's seminal article was entitled 'Numerical Democracy and Corporate Pluralism'. The bulk of the article considers conventional 'numerical democracy' – electoral influences, results, etc. – but towards the end of his piece he moves on to consider how the vitality of the political system had been maintained despite the fact that Labour had been in office (almost continuously) for thirty years. He concludes that the opposition might lose the fight for votes but the interests it represented could still be defended through other channels: 'Votes count in the choice of governing personnel but other resources decide the actual policies pursued by the authorities.'[20] Rokkan thus presents a two-tier image of decision-making. There is certainly an electoral system, but a growth of a vast network of interest organisations and other corporate bodies means that 'ruling' is not a matter of obtaining '50 per cent plus' votes, but has also to do with a bargaining process between giant alliances of associations and corporations. In a key passage he argues,

> the crucial decisions on economic policy are rarely taken in the parties or in Parliament: the central area is the bargaining table where the government authorities meet directly with the trade union leaders, the representatives of the farmers, the smallholders and the fishermen, and the delegates of the Employers' Association. These yearly rounds of negotiations have in fact come to mean more in the lives of rank-and-file citizens than formal elections.[21]

Rokkan observes that although there was talk of creating NEDC-like structures, the protagonists in the conflict over incomes wanted to avoid too binding a system: 'the corporatism of the 'two-tier' system of decision-making is implicit and latent, not formal and institutionalized.' Similarly, Olsen has suggested that groups wish to avoid highly formalised relationships of the NEDC type.[22] This, of course, is precisely the same phenomenon of avoidance of publicly institutionalised machinery that makes much of the discussion of British 'corporatism' so vague.

This 'corporate pluralism' system is described in considerably fuller detail by Robert Kvavik in his 1976 study, *Interest Groups in Norwegian Politics*. He finds that groups have only a limited interest in contacts with parties, legislators and the courts, and instead finds them directly co-opted into decision-making, 'into the administration's advisory, managemental or policy-making commissions'.[23] His description of interest group involvement is strikingly similar to our description of Britain. He also notes that interest group bureaucrats can have worked in several organisations. Well over half of those interviewed had worked in the national administration or private corporations. Given the nature of their work in the administration and the uniform structures and procedures in the Norwegian system, shifting sides is relatively simple to do.

Kvavik acknowledges that Norwegian groups do have contacts in the public opinion–party–Parliament–Cabinet 'chain', but he concludes that groups focus more on the administration. When action is required in Parliament, interest groups do have channels to utilise, but parties are not the central target of group attempts to gain access to the political system. He establishes, however, that while the order varies by the interest of the groups, they tend to value informal contacts with the Cabinet and ministers and (especially) formal contact in committees more highly. He describes a system of

> ... the secularization of the administration through the inclusion of interest group representatives and outside experts and the expansion of neocorporate structures and behaviour patterns. Today one finds a large network of administrative committees constituting the central arena for neocorporate politics. Within this system, one finds extensive participation by interest group representatives in accordance with a distinct role system and recognizable norms and values governing group behaviour.[24]

He appears able to quantify with more confidence than we can in Britain. We cannot really produce material equivalent to his claims that interest group representatives fill 42 per cent of committee places, but Kvavik's emphases are similar to our own. He views Norway's political system as a mixture of competitive pluralism (a laissez-faire model of group behaviour) and 'corporate pluralism', which is distinguished by the interdependence and interpenetration of the private and public sectors in policy formulation. 'Corporate pluralism' appears to be the developing mode.

This claim is reinforced by the empirical work of Christensen and Rønning.[25] They produce highly relevant empirical work demonstrating the predilection of organisations to link through ministries/ directors rather than parties or Parliament. Moreover they provide useful data (which could be replicated in Britain) on how different types of organisation, with different sizes of secretariat and different subject matters, relate in different ways to government. Overall, their data confirm that the corporate channel of influence is over-shadowing the channel of numerical democracy.

In Sweden the recent literature has sketched a similar pattern. Nils Elvander argued in 1974 that the influence of Swedish interest groups is developed through informal contacts with decision-makers, through representation on investigative commissions and through the 'remiss' system asking for comments on commission reports and at the executive stage in the agencies.[26] As in Britain, the least significant target for pressure is Parliament (*Riksdag*), although contacts are maintained with the parliamentary groups. Between 1955 and 1963 the so-called 'Harpsund democracy' was developed. This entailed the Prime Minister inviting representatives from trade and industry and other associations to his residence at Harpsund for informal talks on topical questions. They were dis-continued under sharp attacks from the non-socialist parties who argued that the Parliament was being presented with *faits accomplis* of covert agreements. This Harpsund system *appears* to have been a dramatic example of group access to government, yet Elvander argues that the Harpsund conferences had no great importance as a channel for group influence on government. This seems to be similar to our reservations about NEDC and tripartism in Britain. Such high-level contacts might appear impressive, but they rarely lead to action. The informal contacts were of far more importance than the more visible conferences and planning councils.

The essence of the Swedish system is accommodation of group interests. Policy-making in Sweden is characterised by a search for agreement with the extremely powerful corporate interest groups. Again, this phenomenon will be very familiar to the British reader. The institutions of compromise may be different in Sweden in that the famous study commissions, which usually precede any policy change, are important as instruments of bargaining, but the *process* is very similar. However, Sweden may find corporatism easier to operate than the UK, as there is possibly less ideological dis-agreement between the political parties.

In the Scandinavian countries, the corporate pluralism approach (or its variants) constitutes the orthodoxy in political interpretation. Traditional corporatist thought has similarly been central in work such as that by Schmitter on Portugal before 1974. In other countries, however, one can find interpretations of policy-making along 'neo-corporate' lines – even though such interpretations might not be so extended or widely accepted by political scientists as in Scandinavia.[27] In France, for example, the question has not been posed in the same terms. There are several explanations for this. First, political scientists have had the new phenomena of the presidency and the changing electoral coalitions to follow. Second, and it seems by an accident of intellectual history, the commentators on France have tended to examine the 'administrative state' or 'technocracy'. The evidence gleaned for these discussions often seems similar to that concerning observers in Britain and elsewhere, but they discuss it in different terms. Third, it has been claimed that most students of French politics have stressed the French philosophical attitude to the role of pressure groups – and this attitude has been at odds with empirical practice. Suleiman has pointed out how the available studies of groups attempting to wield influence in France have centred on rather sensational cases – the alcohol lobby, the aid to parochial schools issue, etc.[28] Accordingly, he observes that such studies – on explosive issues and when normal relationships have broken down – do not provide an understanding of the complex continuing process whereby groups attempt to influence decisions. For example, it is estimated that there are 4,700 consultative councils, committees or commissions in France.[29]

In Suleiman's study of administrators' dispositions toward groups, his questionnaire results show that 70 per cent of directors met with groups 'almost every day' or 'very often'. There is evidence that the directors interviewed were suspicious of the power of groups: Suleiman's respondents make comments such as, 'It is only the politicians – the ministers, the cabinet – that are susceptible to pressures. The Directors do not let themselves be impressed by pressure from groups.'[30]

The directors apparently did not consider contact with interest groups as being indispensable, or even important, in aiding them to fulfil their tasks. But other remarks made by respondents seem to indicate that they were in practice in a closer relationship with groups than they suggested. For example, one director in the Ministry of Agriculture noted: 'If it were just a question of consulting, asking for opinions, that would be fine. But it has gotten to the point where it has become a permanent dialogue. And this starts from the formulation of a law and goes all the way after the law has been passed. They [the interest groups] make it extremely hard for us to work. As for me, I'm now trying to cut contact with groups to a minimum.'[31]

Respondents tended to stress how they were prepared to 'consult' groups merely as a means of communicating their own case, possibly supporting the view that groups in France can sometimes be more pressured than pressuring. It is one of the 'rules of the game' to be seen to be consulting – even if one ignores the response. While the norm within the French bureaucracy is less sympathetic to group access than is the case in Britain, it seems that notwithstanding the views of civil servants (coloured by their values of what *should* happen) and the organisational weaknesses of French pressure groups, extensive contact does take place. The administration appears to be particularly open to 'legitimate' groups: these are seen as being professional associations, rather than a 'lobby' of small shopkeepers (e.g. the *Petites et moyennes entreprises*). Despite the prevalent normative idea that groups distort the general public interest and are therefore undesirable, in the case of the so-called professional organisations there develops a close relationship of the clientelist type. It is important to remember that the anti-group rhetoric of de Gaulle does not necessarily describe the reality, especially after his departure. Since then, the tendency has been to resolve conflict by consultation with both party and pressure group representatives. Indeed, Suleiman notes that, with the close relationship between the administration and certain interest groups, there is a blurring of the distinction between the public and private.[32] This is, of course, very similar to the conclusions drawn by many observers of the American policy process.

In earlier chapters we borrowed extensively from Arend Lijphart's 1968 study of Dutch politics and the 'accommodation' styles. Other European studies have discussed similar patterns of 'pillared pluralism' in which ethnic/religious differences are reconciled. Lijphart has himself developed the concept of consociational democracy, in which stable government is attained in a plural society by cooperative, elite-level behaviour.[33] Discussions of 'segmented pluralism' in other European polities (e.g. Belgium, Austria, Switzerland) are strongly related to this cultural pluralism.[34]

The policy process in Holland is in fact very familiar – a high level of interest group activity, the blurring of border-lines between state and society, government intervention stimulating private interest organisation, a myriad of social organisations with increasingly complex relations to one another and to sections of the government bureaucracy. The pattern of interest group access exhibits all the 'usual' features – a formal system of advisory bodies, strong informal links among specialised groups and sub-sections of the bureaucracy. There does, however, appear to be a reaction against this rationalised pattern of interest group institutionalisation. The prevailing accommodationist style has provoked direct pressure methods of more loosely structured groups – 'new plebicitory style in politics poses a challenge to the habitual politics of accommodation'.[35] One might argue that the British interest in public participation is a similar reaction, but it is difficult to see much chance of fundamentally amending the co-optive closed style of decision-making.

A European Model?

There seems ample evidence for our general claim at the start of this chapter that in recent European studies a central feature has been the attempt to probe the growing influence of the corporate policy-making channel. The several claims for uniqueness in fact add up to a general interest. Kvavik thought 'few political systems are distinguished by as elaborate and active a network of interest groups as one finds in Norway'.[36] Takeshi Ishida, writing on Japan, found there 'was a particularly close triangular relationship ... among party, bureaucracy and interest groups'.[37] Elvander considers that 'Sweden has perhaps the strongest system of interest groups in the world'.[38] In the Netherlands, interest groups are seen to constitute a 'very dense and highly institutionalized network'.[39] Beer has argued that if it were possible to measure political power then pressure groups are probably more powerful in Britain than in the United States.[40] Miller reports that in Denmark the interest organisations play an important role: 'The groups are quasi-public bodies responsible for various administrative tasks and rule-making functions. They constitute, therefore, a branch of the state administration.'[41] Even the Soviet Union has been described in terms such as 'incipient pluralism', 'co-optation', 'competition' and 'polyarchism'.

Thus, each observer of a given political system tends to see group involvement as in some way unique, yet all are in fact describing the same phenomenon. The institutions of group involvement may be different from one system to another; the degree of influence of groups may vary through time. The very nature of the group system itself can vary, as in the Dutch case with the more recent phenomenon of de-pillarisation. There is, therefore, a strong argument for considering the description of Britain we have supplied as just one variant of a European model of policy-making in which interest groups play a central role.[42]

CHAPTER 9

Costs, Benefits and Development of the Group System

THE BASIS OF THE RELATIONSHIP

The contemporary style of policy-making stems from the increased scope of governmental objectives. Once intervention starts, for whatever reason, the interdependence of problems makes it difficult for the government to avoid further intervention. For example once it is thought necessary to restrict pay rises, the government then finds it politically necessary to control prices and dividends. Thus it gets involved in the examination of productivity schemes, hours worked, costs of raw materials, different formulae for measuring costs, etc. Intervention itself leads to further intervention.

The implication of this for pressure groups is that the interventionist style of government demands a particular kind of relationship between groups and government. Much of what the government aspires to 'control' is outside its direct influence and can be secured only, if at all, by groups. The government can manage its complex environment only through the cooperation of mediating institutions – the groups. Thus, the secretary of one local government association has claimed:

> it is no good if the individual local authority goes to government about some general issues because they will put it in the waste paper basket. They may not take much notice about what the associations say but at least they do hear the voice. *There-fore, central government will want to build up the corporate body because then they have somebody with whom it can do business.*[1]

Another ex-civil servant, currently directing a pressure group, argued to us, 'We do of course have excellent relations with both Ministers and with Government departments. We are indeed in daily touch with the latter. The business of government – and certainly the affairs of this Association – would be impossible to conduct on any other basis. The "lobby" ... has become an indispensable part of public affairs.'

We have been arguing that public policies are the outcome of a process of adjustment between organisations. No longer do the assets of government markedly outweigh the assets of any given group or set of groups in a particular bargaining situation. Increasingly, pressure groups and governments have come to recognise that they need each other in order to achieve their respective objectives. This has meant that the relationship has generally become closer and closer, bringing with it a proliferation of institutions and processes to enable the necessary accommodation, adjustment of respective interests. But is this accommodation desirable, necessary or indeed inevitable? What does a balance sheet of costs and benefits of the present system of close cooperation look like?

THE PUBLIC INTEREST

We all have some idea that there is the notion of 'public interest' and the belief that in a representative democracy it is the job of the government and the legislature to see to it that the public interest is protected. But in practice what *is* the public interest in any given situation and how do policy-makers identify it? One senior civil servant, when asked the question 'how do you decide what is in the public interest?', told us that there was no such thing as *the* public interest. From his viewpoint in Whitehall there were a number of 'special publics' on any given issue (what are normally described as the 'affected interests' in Britain) and his job was to attempt to strike a 'fair' balance between those various special publics. Pressed to explain just what these 'special publics' were, he confirmed that in reality this meant the sum total of pressure group active on any given issue. In practice, the public was equal to the organised groups pressing the government on that issue. No doubt we would all be inclined to use the operational definition of the public interest if we were sitting behind a Whitehall desk.

After all, given the difficulty of defining or discovering what is in the more general public interest, what else should we do other than try to respond to the actual, real, pressures being placed upon us? If the CBI or TUC are demanding this, that or the other, reference to such concepts as the 'general will' are of little help. One obvious consequence of this practical approach is that a very high premium is placed on being *organised*. The politics of influence has increasingly become the politics of organisation. If you want your voice to be heard (let alone taken account of), then by and large you must be organised. In other words, the business of influencing governments has become professionalised. The most influential groups are those who are expertly organised in terms of (a) their contacts with government (thus organisations such as the National Farmers' Union are extremely professional in the way they argue their case to government, in the way they gather what Finer calls 'advance intelligence'[2] on what the government's thinking is, and in the way they supply information that the government considers useful); (b) the way they organise their own membership to apply sanctions to which the government must respond. The great success of the National Union of Mineworkers in the 1970s was not so much in its professionalised contacts with the government but in the way in which it could organise its own membership to disrupt not only coal production but the supply of other materials to power stations. Those interests in society that do not possess effective organisation, on either or both of these fronts, are likely to remain relatively uninfluential.

Thus one direct 'cost' of the 'system of consultation', as we call it in the UK, is that the *unorganised* are usually undervalued in the policy process. Whereas Robert McKenzie saw (admittedly with important qualifications) the pressure group system as providing an 'invaluable set of multiple channels through which the mass of the citizenry can influence the decision-making process at the highest levels',[3] it can equally be seen as a rather effective device for *excluding* the mass of the citizenry from the policy process. The very nature of the process by which those interests are directly affected and brought into close consultation (and we have argued earlier that consultation often means negotiation) excludes those interests that are not organised, *even though those interests may be quite important numerically*. Numbers are far less important than group organisations. As we saw in chapter 3, Sir Edward Boyle, formerly Minister of Education, suggested that the starting point for educational questions was in the educational world itself.[4] The process by which education policy is formed in Britain is relatively closed, dominated by the professional interests. In a very real sense, UK education policy has been determined by the interplay of various groups, including the Department of Education and Science, which has its own interests to pursue, *within the education industry.* There is little or no evidence to suggest that parents, who clearly have a very direct interest in education policy, have had much influence on it since World War II. There is, of course, a very simple explanation for this total lack of influence – parents have never been effectively *organised* on a national basis. (Significantly, there are examples of parental influence at the local level when parents have become organised.) The same is true, until recently, of consumers. The introduction of consumer protection legislation in the USA and the UK has generally been a reaction to a new phenomenon – the growing consumer movement.

Policy-making in most Western democracies has, as we argued in chapter 3, become compartmentalised. The policy-making map is in reality a series of vertical compartments or segments – each segment inhabited by a different set of organised groups and generally impenetrable by 'unrecognised groups' or by the general public. In such a system, the key to unlocking the door of influence is to get on the ministry's 'consultation list'. Who do the civil servants count as the affected interests – who are 'the public' in the case in question? One cost involved in the increasingly close relationship between groups and governments is that the policy process has if anything excluded the general public from any effective influence. As a result of this, policy-makers have retreated into a definition of 'public interest' that may be rather narrow in that it tends towards assuming that public interest equals the balance of organised pressure in a given policy area. An irony of this situation is that the reality of influence has become more widely recognised in Western democracies, with the result that more interests have decided to organise themselves, which in turn means that policy-makers have a much wider range of *organised* groups to deal with in any given policy area.

This raises the difficult question of whether the process of consultation, because it has been rather closed and secret, has within itself the seeds of its own destruction. If organisation is influence, then eventually all interests will become organised. If the game brings rewards to those who are organised, then we will all join the game and the ball park will be so crowded as to ruin the game itself.

IN THE GOVERNMENT'S INTEREST?

In referring to a senior civil servant who defined the public interest as the balance of organised pressure at any given time, we saw some indication of the advantage, from the point of view of government, of the increasingly symbiotic government/group relationship. It is at least a practical way of proceeding in the absence of a wider concept of the public interest. It is simple to understand and indeed can even be used as a defence against pressures for a yet wider definition. The British government often meets parliamentary criticism with the answer that 'this has been agreed with the affected interest and so Parliament has no grounds for complaint'. As we saw in the 'water' example in chapter 6, this can lead to bizarre situations. It is difficult enough for modern governments to resolve the interests of competing organised groups without also allowing Parliament (which in some sense may be said to be the institutional expression of the public interest) or some theoretical notion of the public interest to have some impact on policy outcomes.

But the primary advantage, to governments, is that the close embrace between government and groups is a means of *conflict avoidance* and a means of hiding conflict when it cannot be avoided. As Hayward demonstrates, the British attempt at economic planning is a classic example of conflict avoidance through attempts to reach agreement with organised groups.[5] Characterising British economic planning in the 1960s as a 'toothless tripartism' or 'pluralistic paralysis',[6] he sees the British (in contrast to the French) as deluding themselves into a belief that, by getting the organised groups round a table, agreement could be reached thus avoiding the need for the government to make painful choices. Hayward would argue that this attempt to humour all factions means that the interests of all, in the long term, suffer. Whereas French planners saw their interests as being served by the imposition of their ideas on other competing groups, British planners saw their interests as being served by the avoidance of conflict – they were temperamentally unsuited to a policy style that resulted in winners and losers.[7] The test of a good policy, Hayward argues, became whether it was *agreed*, not whether it was likely to succeed by some objectively defined criterion. This strategy of seeking agreement was, of course, only possible if the groups were brought into the plan-making process to the extent of being partners, with an effective veto. The principle behind the strategy was that public conflict is somehow damaging to the government's electoral fortunes and that an agreed policy is likely to enhance the government's electoral standing. The disadvantage is that, though this may be true (and we know all too little about the impact of policies in general elections), it does little in terms of solving actual *problems*. Thus, some problems with which the government is faced may not be capable of being solved without disturbing at least one established group in society.

However, defenders of the system would argue that there is a more important and tangible benefit to governments: by bringing groups into the process of policy formulation, and even allowing them to veto certain policy options, there is an increased likelihood of the policies that finally emerge being implemented. What use is it, say the supporters of the system, passing legislation totally opposed by very powerful interests in society? The legislation is doomed to failure. This, of course, is the logic of the consultation process. If one wants to reform an industry, who better to consult than the people who actually operate the industry in question? They know better than civil servants and politicians what actually goes on inside the industry, so why should they not exercise a veto? The difficult question is where the balance should be struck. Has the balance tipped too far in favour of the groups when consultation becomes negotiation? Is that when the costs to the government begin to outweigh the benefits of group participation in policy-making? If, as Hayward believes in the case of economic planning, the close relationship produces policies that are likely to fail, then governments are paying a rather too high price for group cooperation.[8] The result might well be more policy failure than would result from a system in which the government distanced itself from groups and drew the line at consultation rather than entering into negotiations. Such policy failures may be to the long-term detriment of society and also of the government's own electoral fortunes. Thus, if a government draws too close to a particular set of groups it may find itself adopting policies that can prove unpopular with the electorate at large. Thus, it might be argued that the Social Democrats in Sweden were too influenced by the trade union organisation, LO, and adopted policy stances that were not entirely in tune with the Swedish electorate and this contributed to their defeat in 1976, after forty-four years in office.

IN THE GROUPS' INTERESTS?

All of what has been said so far suggests that it is to the advantage of groups to participate in the policy process. But are there not disadvantages for the groups, just as there are for governments? We would argue that it is extremely difficult to find examples of groups who refuse to participate *at all* in the policy process – groups who in fact will have no dealings with the government – but we would concede that this does not mean that there are not costs to the groups in participating. One difficulty in discussing the costs and benefits of participating in the policy process is that 'participation' can take a number of different forms, even within the same political system. Different forms of participation have different combinations of costs and benefits in different policy situations. In a valuable attempt to explore the costs/benefits balance for groups participating in the policy process, J. P. Olsen has concentrated upon the costs/ benefits of what he terms *formal* participation in government, by which he means situations where groups 'are given a formal right to participate routinely in public policy-making, through direct representation in policy-making bodies'.[9] He cites as examples of formal participation 'the network of government committees, commissions, councils and boards that initiate, design and advise and decide upon, implement and administer public policies'.[10] A good British example is the participation by the CBI in some governmental advisory committees of various kinds mentioned in chapter 2.

Olsen lists eight main benefits and costs (though he points out that the list could be indefinitely long) associated with formal participation by groups (or what he terms *organisations*).[11]

(1) *The benefits of influence on policy.* One of the opportunities that participation provides is the opportunity to be influential in the substance of public policy.
(2) *The benefits of cartelisation.* The government institutions bring together a group of organisations and public agencies that can benefit by coordinating their private and public activities. Their participation together affords an opportunity for the exchange of information and coordination that such cooperation requires.
(3) *The benefits of efficiency and divisions of labour.* By creating a representative and specialised role within the organisation for one person, participation increases the technical competence and specialised knowledge of the representative.

(4) *The benefits of legitimacy.* Participation confers public recognition and confirmation of the status of the organisation. Participation also makes the organisation share the credit and praise of public policy successes.

(5) *The costs of loss of freedom.* Participation incurs some costs due to implicit understandings that agreements will be observed and behaviours within the organisation controlled.

(6) *The costs of loss of purity.* Entering into a compromising system results in a loss of the pure ideological position that might be enjoyed by an organisation not participating.

(7) *The costs of responsibility.* By accepting a position within the system, the organisation and its leadership is associated with the actions of the system. It has to share the blame for public policy failures.

(8) *The costs of loss of control.* Specialised representatives with technical competence undermine the control of members and elected leadership over an organisation. It is difficult to delegate responsibility without giving up some options for control over the actions of the delegate and the institutions to which he is a delegate.

We would want to stress that it is necessary to introduce a system of weighting into this list. For example, benefit (1) – the influence over policy – is of far greater importance for most groups compared with, say, (6) – lost of purity. In other words, in normal circumstances the benefits that accrue to a group in terms of policy outcomes are usually so attractive as to lead the group to particiate formally, despite being aware of the costs that this will entail for the group. Olsen suggests that there are groups for whom purity is of paramount importance – particularly revolutionary and reform organisations.[12] Similarly, Gundelach argues, 'To the socialist grass roots organization the corporatistic development is bad because the involvement is likely to result in goal displacement'.[13] But even very radical groups may resort to some informal means of participation. In a study of black groups in Wolverhampton, Jacobs found that many groups professing a desire to have nothing to do with 'white authority', in fact were prepared to be involved with informal consultations with the council.[14] Thus, as Olsen notes, less formal, ad hoc participation may be more attractive.[15] But it is important to note that few if any groups shun *all* forms of participation. Even if they refuse to participate at all in one policy area, they continue to participate in others, often at quite a formal level.

There are some cases where groups withdraw because costs are too high. Olsen cites Norway where the major economic organisations have 'several times resisted governmental attempts to institutionalize participation in general economic planning and policy-making'.[16] For example, in 1975 the Federation of Trade Unions refused to participate in a new attempt to institutionalise a system of pressure group representation – though they did agree to a bargaining arrangement (in an attempt to reduce inflation) between the groups and the Government for one year to set wages and salaries for all groups. This reluctance to agree to a permanent formal arrangement was in contrast to their willingness to participate in committees dealing with more limited subjects.[17]

As Olsen argues, it may well be the case that the bigger the issue the more likely it is that groups will select an informal, confidential system of participation in the policy process.[18] Certainly, the more central the issue is to the very rationale of the pressure group, the more cautious it will become in terms of accepting modes of participation that reduce its scope for manoeuverability. So if the issue is wage and salary levels we might well expect caution on the part of trade unions, for there the potential costs are rather high. The British TUC certainly found this to be the case in 1977/78 during phase III of the 'social contract'. Though the 'contract' produced undoubted policy gains for the TUC (for example, the Government implemented a wide-ranging job subsidy scheme and the Spring 1978 budget was greatly influenced by the need to maintain TUC cooperation in any future wages policy), the costs became evident during the firemen's strike. During that dispute much of the wrath of the firemen was eventually directed at the TUC, which refused to lend its support to the firemen as this would have resulted in a breach of the 'agreed' wages policy. Similarly, many university lecturers who voted for TUC membership became disillusioned by lack of TUC support in their battle with the Government over pay anomalies. Thus the internal strains for the TUC became quite considerable as a result of its agreement with the Government. However, such strains did not result in non-participation – merely a shift in the form of participation. To refuse to participate altogether would be organisationally harmful as this would force the Government to 'go it alone' and would release the Government from its part of the contract, thus losing the very policy benefits that the TUC had cherished. But clearly any bargain involves restraints upon both partners – each sacrifices some sovereignty in return for calculated benefits. The main difficulty for the groups is the internal strains that this sacrifice entails, as they have the sometimes difficult task of explaining to their more militant members why they should refrain from 'rocking the boat'.

One rather specific, though important, cost that groups have to bear as a result of their increasingly close relationship with governments is that governments sometimes try to influence the very nature of the group itself. For example, the Government was instrumental in bringing about the merger of the Federation of British Industry, the National Union of Manufacturers and the British Employers' Confederation to form the Confederation of British Industry in 1965. The Government was keen on the merger because it simplified the process of consultation, it was easier to consult one organisation than three in order to get the 'views of British industry'. The difficulty from the CBI's viewpoint is that the larger it gets the more complex its internal politics become. In an attempt to increase its own status and influence by becoming the voice of British business, the CBI may in fact undermine its influence because of greater policy conflicts within its own organisation. Can one organisation adequately represent both multinational corporations and small companies at the same time? Do the interests of the two sections coincide? Similarly, the TUC has been anxious to increase its scope of representation, and indeed the 'social contract' with the Labour Government may well have encouraged unions to join the TUC, but this very process may help to undermine the TUC's influence in the long run. The wider the range of workers the TUC represents, the more difficult it will become for the Congress to formulate its own policies.

DEVELOPMENTS

Grouping the groups

A continuing trend is the development of umbrella or coalition groups. For example, in 1974 fifteen organisations concerned with mental health formed a joint group called the Mental Health Crisis Group in response to Health Service expenditure cuts. The new 'coalition' was able to adopt a more open campaigning style than certain groups would normally adopt. This type of umbrella organisation is a fairly typical example of the increasing number of permanent or semi-permanent institutional arrangements that groups adopt in order to give greater weight to their views. Transport policy has seen a particularly marked growth in these new structures. One group, Transport 2000, is a coalition of amenity and environmental groups together with representatives of sectors of the railway industry and the railway unions. It is particularly interesting as an example of promotional groups (i.e. the environmentalists) joining forces with sectional groups (the unions) in an attempt to use some of the leverage that sectional groups have but that promotional groups usually lack. In 1974 thirty groups opposed to motorway schemes came together to form the National Motorways Action Committee. Perhaps the best-known environmental coalition is the Committee for Environmental Conservation (COENCO), which brings together representatives of the main environmental organisations in order to present a common front on key issues.

The existence of these – and many other – coalition groups does not necessarily *guarantee* that they do have access to the governmental machine. For example, the Scottish Homeless Group – representing a range of pressure groups – which has been critical of Scottish local authorities, is still essentially an outside group. But obviously government is more willing to listen to an organisation that represents a large number of individuals than a very small group. More importantly, the quality of their argument can be raised by the formation of these coalitions. For example, a number of small localised anti-motorway groups have benefited greatly from membership of the Midlands Motorways Action Committee. Acting alone they have lacked the technical expertise to campaign effectively against road schemes. On joining the coalition they have received expert advice regarding traffic flows, etc., based on the wider experience of the Action Committee. A group like COENCO is also able to coordinate lobbying by using the particular strengths (e.g. special contacts) of its member groups in a more 'orchestrated' manner. The government too benefits from these umbrella organisations. Quite simply the process of consultation, seen from the government side, is much easier with one organisation representing a particular interest than several. There is also greater chance of using the group to 'police' a particular policy area or even to implement a policy.

The European dimension

The impact of EEC entry on group behaviour varies according to the influence of Brussels on each policy area. For example, agricultural policy is very directly affected by the EEC and hence the NFU has become very active at the European level. Other groups, such as local authority associations, are less affected by EEC membership, but even they are active in Europe. So too are environmental groups, who recognise the political importance of, say, the administration of pollution control policies and are therefore developing a system of coordination with their European counterparts.

The growth of European groupings is in part due to the formal EEC Commission rule that it will only deal with Community-wide groups, rather than purely national organisations.[19] This policy has necessitated the creation of 'Eurogroups'. Estimates suggest that there are some 350 groupings at the European level. Three major categories exist: employers, agriculture and the unions. The most notable grouping is that of the agricultural interests – reflecting the fact that agriculture consumes around 95 per cent of the Community budget. The national agricultural groups have joined forces in COPA (Comité des Organisations Professionelles Agricoles). Between 1972 and 1975 COPA's budget grew from $154,000 to over $600,000. It has been suggested that the main force behind the growth in the organisation is the British groups who want to see COPA work much more closely with the Community institutions – similar to the NFU's style in Britain.[20] The Commission has itself been keen to see this development both to improve communication and to establish the Commission's own popularity and legitimacy – being seen to consult the affected interests. Not all policy issues can be processed using 'Eurogroups' because national interests may be too diverse (e.g. fishing), so one should not place too much emphasis on the development of these European coalitions. On the other hand, lobbying in Brussels will increase in importance for national groups, as the harmonisation programme develops.

WHAT ALTERNATIVES?

New institutions: a House of Industry?

An increasingly popular school of thought, in Britain at least, is that some means should be found to legitimise and publicise the reality of the relationship between groups and government. In other words, many commentators and, equally important, many practitioners share the view of reality that we have tried to convey and seek to bring it more into the open. Somehow institutions and processes have to be devised for 'managing' the group system as it has developed. As one British civil servant is reported as saying, when discussing incomes policy, 'You have got to deal with these institutions that do have the power to distort the market. The alternative is very costly and possibly confrontational. You have got to seek to constrain people from using economic power.'[21]

One practical step is for governments to use the power of the group system itself to 'police' demands by any one group. As J. P. Mackintosh has argued, 'perhaps some institutional changes are needed to strengthen governments, to be sure that they have a larger measure of support and that *if one pressure group holds out, the support of others can be mobilized*'.[22] Effectively, this is what the 1977/78 'social contract' in the UK achieved. The Government used the TUC's power to 'police' the power of any one group that tried to hold out against the Government's incomes policy. Thus the fire-men's strike was beaten because the TUC (a) refused to back the fire-men's claim to any significant degree and (b) did not object to the use of troops by the Labour Government to break a strike. Similarly, the TUC offered to 'police' the rest of the trade union movement if Mr Heath would agree to make the miners a 'special case' in January 1974. Though the offer was rejected by Mr Heath, Mrs Thatcher (the subsequent leader of the party) is on record as saying that she believes that it was a mistake to reject that offer and she would be prepared to use the power of the TUC to control the rest of the union movement when the government itself was not in a position to exercise such control.

Though there is considerable disagreement over whether such institutions as the National Economic Development Council are really tripartist/corporatist-type structures, the debate over 'Neddy' illustrates the more general feeling, referred to above, that such attempts to formulate policy outside the traditional parliamentary representative institutions should be legitimised. For example, Peter Parker, chairman of British Rail, referring to Neddy, has argued that

... what you need is regularity and a constitutional position for the consultation of government with industry, which is corporate power.

The way to handle the threat of corporatism is to get the corporate bodies, which are both unions and industry, into one chamber, with an independent president and a constitutional position to invite down your Prime Minister and your Chancellor perhaps twice a year. Give it prior rights in looking at legislation in the fields of social and industrial policy and they would then have public debates which would be covered, a la Hansard. Politicians who had stumbled about in this morass of industrial relations would have had the advantage of a thorough debate in this chamber.

It would be a consultative chamber, exposing corporate power, incidentally forcing it to establish its legitimacy ...[23]

The director general of the National Economic Development Office was himself aware of this problem when, in 1977, he suggested that 'It is immensely important to find a way of linking the work of NEDO quite formally with Parliament. We ought to have a select committee dealing with it. That would avoid the charges of corporatism – of the "carve-up" behind closed doors – and it would help to achieve a bipartisanship in the approach to industry.'[24] Similarly, the CBI has argued that a parliamentary select committee should be set up to assess the economic climate and suggest what the nation can afford itself, so that Parliament can get involved in the determination of incomes policies.[25] Proposing a much broader institution, Nicholas Scott (Conservative) has argued that Britain needs an industrial forum of the type operated by many western European countries. The forum would include the leaders of major economic pressure groups who would have the opportunity 'to argue, debate, and perhaps reach a consensus on important matters of the day. It would also enable the various arguments and agreements to be reported to the public'.[26] The forum would be advisory and might be asked for its view on proposed legislation, with Parliament retaining its sovereignty.

A related proposal, with a rather long pedigree, is for some form of functional representation, in addition to the territorial representation through constituencies that we have at present.[27] There is, of course, considerable room for disagreement on the exact composition and powers of a 'House of Industry' or 'industrial forum' or 'economic and social council' although, as Bogdanor argues, to give it actual *legislative* powers would cause a clash with the House of Commons. The purpose of the House of Industry, he argues, 'should not be to interfere with the process of working out and implementing a political programme, but rather to mobilise a consensus on technical, economic and industrial issues so as to assist in the implementation of policy'. However, he rightly recognises that the referral of all legislation on economic and industrial subjects to the House of Industry would mean in practice that it had some legislative power, '... since the House of Commons would be unlikely to ignore either unanimous recommendations from the House of Industry, or even recommendations backed up by the preponderant feeling of that house'.[28] The wider the representation in such a house (e.g. consumers, MPs, etc.), the greater would be its legitimacy. Ionescu has also argued along similar lines, suggesting that multicameralism may well become a feature of national parliaments and that the European Parliament should take the lead. Such a step at the European level would give the corporate forces '... a forum for homogeneous and expert participation in policy-making'.[29] Ionescu is arguing for what he terms centripetal politics being '... the arduous and relatively humble task of seeing that power is shared by, and circulates freely among the multiple centres of real decision-making'.[30] However, as Finer suggests, there is relatively little evidence that such institutions are all that effective, and so we should be rather more cautious in our assessment of their potential. This view is echoed by J. P. Olsen, who points out that 'reservations, withdrawals and flights, from such councils into more informal and confidential forms of interaction, have been frequent'.[31] Holland is perhaps one of the more successful examples with its Economic and Social Council,[32] but even there, more recently, 'Relations between the social partners and between them and the government have become more formal and are even strained sometimes. All these seem to be less tied by the strong ties of corporatism.'[33]

Real democracy after all?

In discussing the role of groups in policy-making and its relationship to notions of democracy and representation, it is perhaps important to note that expressions of concern relate to one's definition of democracy. In particular, those who see the exercise of a veto by pressure groups as being anti-democratic reflect a particular notion of democracy. It is quite possible to view democracy in other different terms.

Writing in the first half of the last century, John C. Calhoun made an important distinction between a numerical majority and a concurrent majority. To Calhoun, government by a numerical majority alone is to 'confuse a part of the people with the whole people, and is in fact no more than the rule of the smaller by the larger part'.[34] On the other hand, in a concurrent majority the community is regarded as being made up of different and conflicting interests with these interests having an effective veto over the majority. Thus Calhoun argued

> It is the negative power – the power of preventing or arresting the action of government – be it called by what term it may – veto, interposition, nullification, checks or balance of power – which in fact forms the constitution. They are all but different names for the negative power. In all its forms, and under all the names, it results from the concurrent majority. Without this there can be no negative, and without a negative, no constitution.[35]

Calhoun's concern was in fact with the preservation of states' rights in the USA, though, interestingly, he drew upon the separate representations of the patricians and plebeians in ancient Rome (each having a veto) and on the British parliamentary practice for support for his theory of concurrent majority.[36] The concurrent majority is necessary, according to Calhoun, because under a system of numerical majority government could degenerate into absolutism.[37] From Calhoun's perspective, the developments traced in this book are desirable and progressive. For much of our argument has been that, as Stein Rokkan argues when discussing modern Norwegian politics, we have moved a very long way from systems of government that can accurately be described as by numerical majority. Increasingly, sectional interests are seen by observers as having attained the very powers of veto over the majority that Calhoun sought for the southern states in America.

As Finer has recently suggested, Calhoun's theory of 'concurrent majority' is probably a much more accurate description of the form of pluralism that we have developed than is the term 'corporatism'.[38] And, of course, many writers see the process of 'accommodating' groups in society as one of the key elements in a stable democracy. For example, Eckstein sees pluralism in society as one of the requirements for a stable democracy: 'a large number of "secondary groups", particularly organized associations, in which many members of society participate and which intervene between national authority on one hand and individuals and their primary groups on the other'.[39] The difficulty is that pressure groups are likely to represent minority interests in society. Sometimes those minority interests coincide with the views of the majority (or even the 'national interest'), but there is no *guarantee* of this. Any coincidence is fortuitous, even though all groups claim to be operating in the national interest. Moreover, group influence rests on *power*. Those groups who have the most power (or are thought, by decision-makers, to have the most power) have the most influence over the policy process. Power, like beauty or money, is not evenly distributed.

Wider participation?

Britain, like most Western democracies, has seen a challenge to existing policy processes from the 'participation movement'. Since the mid-1960s governments have had to try and accommodate demands for wider public participation in policy-making. Olaf Ruin has noted the same reaction in Sweden. He describes how in the 1960s Sweden presented a picture of nation-wide groups and close relations between these groups and the government. However, this pattern of group-orientated participation was challenged in the late 60s by a demand for individual-orientated participation. One example Ruin gives is of a wildcat strike in northern Sweden in 1969. In the view of many striking miners, the trade union leadership, the management and the government tended to coalesce into a remote, closely knitted elite.[40] Although the intention was to permit single individuals to participate in the decision-making, this access was facilitated through groups – a new wave of corporativism. Ruin thus notes a rhythm of a rather paradoxical nature. The demands for more individual-orientated participation meant the further integration of groups into the governmental process. 'Traits of corporativism evoke dissatisfaction that evokes more corporativism, and so forth'.[41]

One can certainly detect this kind of reaction within Britain to 'the new establishment' of insider groups. But that is not to suggest that change in the system will necessarily result. Ruin reports that the Swedish reponse to the demands for more individual participation was in fact again group-orientated.

GOVERNANCE OF MODERN SOCIETIES

In chapter 1 we began by outlining the elements of group theory. We feel we have sufficiently documented the case that, in understanding how policies are made, such considerations are central. We do not deny the possibility that ideology or 'rationality' or a concept of the public interest or electoral pressure can be important, but in looking at a wide range of policies we see little evidence that they better explain outcomes – or little evidence to justify the attention that such aspects of policy-making have been allotted in the past.

The policy implications of group theory are not static. Group theory was probably an accurate description of the political process when developed in the early part of the century. Since then the *character* of government has changed. The growth of interventionist government has meant that there are more forces to be taken into account. More latent groups have been mobilised. The intervention has given groups more 'clout' in that their cooperation is needed in implementation. Moreover, as we have argued, there has been a vast increase in the *number* of groups to be bargained with. Policy areas have become overcrowded not just because governments have become more active but because groups have become organised in order to make government more active. The irony is that the overcrowding itself helps to produce policy stalemates. Our argument is that a fundamental change in the political system is inevitable as a result of the kind of economic and social system that has been devised. Committees and consultation are a manifestation of a Keynesian 'fine tuning' democracy. A government could certainly do less, and this would reduce the need for the close interrelationships that characterise the current style. But is it likely that the state would so diminish its concept of itself to allow a change in style? Further, to do so would be to ignore the clamour for regulation, for assistance, for innovation from the groups. The alternative to 'accommodation' is risk. Much of the search for accommodation is to increase the element of certainty for the participants. Governments do not want to take the electoral risks of standing back from society, as things might go wrong. Industrialists do not necessarily want the risks of competition and the market. The 1970–74 Conservative government's change in style from non-intervention to intervention was not done for trivial reasons, but because of real political costs.

If this argument is credible, then we have experienced a more fundamental change in the political system than is often conceded. It is easy to list certain superficial ways in which the political system has changed in the past twenty years – the increase in the number of parties represented in Parliament, the reduced share of the vote obtained by the two major parties, the Liberal/Labour 'pact' and the prospect of coalition government, etc. These are the areas in which commentators tend to look for change in the political system. What we have been describing is a kind of change that would have happened (and would have been equally important) even if the electoral situation had been more stable and governments were regularly returned with solid working majorities. In drawing attention to this kind of fundamental change, we are implying that certain remedies for our political condition are misdirected – or at least not directed at the more important target. For example, how much impact would 'proportional representation' or a 'Bill of Rights' have in the areas of policy-making we have highlighted?

We have argued a degree of inevitability for the Bentleyan incrementalist system that we identify, but we are not so deterministic in outlook as to consider the system immutable in degree. However, in looking at possible changes, we must note that different kinds of concern have been expressed about the defects of group involvement in policy-making.

THE PROBLEM: CONFLICT OR CONSENSUS?

The more obvious complaint is that groups achieve their own ends by force. The miners' strike of 1974 is the most dramatic example, but the threat of action by the police in 1977 over pay can also be produced as an example of the threat of force, as can the actions of hospital consultants on occasions. Groups have such power that the UK government failed to implement an EEC directive on 'tachographs' in lorries for fear of union response. And the CBI too can use its muscle to bring about important changes in proposals for worker participation.

A more interesting line of criticism is, however, that conflict avoidance (and not conflict) is the main concern. J. E. S. Hayward has argued that the danger comes from over-institutionalisation.[42] He sees political inertia as stemming from the British culturally determined addiction to conflict avoidance. Essentially, he sees the danger to societal stability in *the practice of cultivating it to excess.* This criticism seems more convincing than the too-much-conflict school of thought. Although crises where groups refuse cooperation are newsworthy, the dominant characteristic of British society is surely that crises are 'managed' short of social conflict. If Hayward is correct, then the misidentification of the problem as conflict could be critical, as that interpretation suggests the kind of response that we have been considering in this book – incorporatism, cooperation, accommodation.

In a sense it might be argued that societies face a choice of policy style and that the selection of the style determines the nature of the relationship between government and groups. This choice is related to one's value judgement regarding the primary functions of the policy process. Those who see the primary function of the policy process as solving problems in some objective sense may tend towards a rationalist or heroic policy style. The attitude of the Ministry of Housing and Local Government in 1968 is a rather good example of this 'value' at work. It chose to force through a reform of the water industry in the UK that was undoubtedly rationalist/ heroic in style, even though incrementalist/humdrum alternatives were available. It did so knowing full well that conflict would result and that a political battle would follow. Its choice was conditioned by a belief that a reorganised industry was the only way to solve the UK's long-term water problem. It decided, in the words of a senior civil servant involved, 'to attempt the impossible'.

On the other hand, the alternative 'value' is that the policy process is primarily concerned not with problem-solving in this rather technical, managerial sense but with minimising conflict and disagreement. If this is the primary objective then the incrementalist/ humdrum style of policy-making is appropriate and the process of accommodation, etc., is of paramount importance. In other words, the process *should* devise policies that maximise agreement, because that is the overriding goal of the political system. So ultimately we arrive at a situation where quite fundamental value choices determine the group/government relationships – namely, do we want a type of society in which governments are held responsible for a wide range of societal affairs and do we want a policy system designed to maximise agreement? Much of the argument in this book has been to the effect that Britain at least, and probably nearly all the Western societies, have 'decided' (without really deciding) that the answer to both questions is yes. But of course it might be argued that the choice between 'accommodation' and 'rational problem-solving' does *not* have to be made. Given sufficient political skill, the groups can be brought, through their incorporation in the policy process, to accept 'rational' solutions. The process of accommodation, in other words, can be an educative process. By looking at 'the problem' collectively, all participants may see the reality and the possibilities for choice. This, of course, is the essence of the 'Sector Working Parties' in the UK. The belief is that a tripartist approach to industrial strategy will expose the nature of the problem for all participants to see and that as they all look over the edge of the cliff they will all accept a solution designed to avoid falling over it.

Thus it may be possible to combine a high degree of group integration yet produce 'rational' policies. But to do so demands considerable political skills on the part of the participants – and probably a greater willingness to sacrifice short-term for long-term benefits.

GOVERNMENTS SHOULD GOVERN?

As governments seem to be drawn closer to the group system as a means of determining public policy outcomes, observers have become concerned that our traditional notions of democratic representative government seem to have been abandoned. If our book has achieved anything, we hope it has at least convinced the reader that for, say, Britain (though we believe it is true for virtually all Western democracies) the traditional model of Cabinet and parliamentary government is a travesty of reality. The job of the political researcher would be simple if the policy process was like this. The reality is much more murky, far more complex. Politics, in a sense, has gone underground.

But is there an alternative to the type of governmental process that we have outlined in this book. Theodore Lowi, too, sees at least the bad effects of pluralism as being avoidable. He considers that pluralism is 'not a natural phenomenon but in large part the result of careful and deliberate arrangements made for groups'.[43] No doubt there are means of increasing the strength of the government and increasing the influence of public opinion in the wider sense (for example Lowi, in a long list of suggested reforms, suggests an 'independent polling organisation that can operate as a kind of Tennessee Valley Authority of public opinion'), but we would doubt the ability of governments to roll back the tide of group involvement in policy-making. Governments have perhaps forgotten the advantages they do have, but in an advanced technological society there are bound to be severe practical constraints on governmental authority. We should therefore beware of any notions that we can return to a 'purer' age. Governments have always struck bargains with barons.

Notes and References

Where a short form of reference is given (author and date), fuller details can be found in the relevant chapter section of the Bibliography.

CHAPTER 1   GROUP THEORY AND INCREMENTALISM

1 Bentley (1967) p. 269.
2 Ibid., pp. 208–9.
3 Latham (1965) pp. 35–6.
4 See also Leo Panitch *Social Democracy and Industrial Militancy 1945–67* London, Cambridge University Press, 1976.
5 See Hagan (1958) p. 48.
6 For a fuller discussion see, 'Killing a Commitment: The Cabinet v the Children' *New Society* 17 June 1976, and *The Great Child Benefit Robbery*, Child Benefit Campaign, April 1977.
7 See *The Observer*, 28 August 1977, p. 16.
8 S. E. Finer, 'The Political Power of Organized Labour' *Government and Opposition* Vol. 8, No. 4, Autumn 1973.
9 See King (1975) p. 290.
10 P. H. Odegard, 'A Group Basis of Politics: A New Name for an Ancient Myth' *Western Political Quarterly* Vol. 11, September 1958, p. 701.
11 See W. J. M. Mackenzie, 'Pressure Groups in British Government' *British Journal of Sociology* Vol. 3, No. 2, 1955, pp. 133–48.
12 Truman (1971) p. 502.
13 Ibid., p. 510.
14 Ibid., p. 513.
15 See R. T. McKenzie (quoting S. J. Eldersveld), 'Parties, Pressure Groups and the Political Process' in R. Kimber and J. J. Richardson (eds) *Pressure Groups in Britain* London, J. M. Dent, 1974, p. 285.
16 Finer, op. cit., p. 405.
17 King (1975) p. 295.
18 Latham (1965) p. 35.
19 See Gordon Tullock *The Vote Motive* Chapter IV, 'Bureaucracy', Hobart Paper No. 9, London, Institute of Economic Affairs, 1976.
20 Odegard, op. cit., p. 695.
21 See Eckstein (1963).
22 H. E. Barnes *An Introduction to the History of Sociology* Chicago, Chicago University Press, 1948, p. 192.
23 See Kimber and Richardson, op. cit., p. 3.
24 S. E. Finer *Anonymous Empire* 2nd ed., London, Pall Mall, 1966, p. 3.
25 See A. Potter *Organized Groups in British National Politics* London, Faber, 1961, pp. 47–60 and 119–26.

26 Stein Rokkan, 'Numerical Democracy and Corporate Pluralism' in R. A. Dahl *Political Oppositions in Western Democracies* New Haven, Conn., Yale University Press, 1966, p. 107.

27 For a full account see Simon (1976).

28 C. Lindblom *The Policy-Making Process* Englewood Cliffs, N.J., Prentice Hall, 1968, p. 12. In the main, the present account of Lindblom's work is drawn from the frequently reprinted 'The Science of Muddling Through' (1959).

29 H. Simon, *Administrative Behavior*, 2nd ed. New York, Free Press, 1957, pp. 62–6.

30 Ibid., p. 67.

31 More extensive consideration of rational and incremental ideas are given in Peter Self (1975) and (1977).

32 Lindblom (1959) p. 81.

33 See Lindblom (1955).

34 Lindblom (1959) p. 55.

35 Lindblom (1965) pp. 12–17.

36 Ibid., p. 13.

CHAPTER 2   CENTRAL POLICY-MAKING

1 See, amongst others, Crossman (1972; 1975–7); Headey (1974); Heclo and Wildavsky (1974); Jock Bruce-Gardyne and Nigel Lawson *The Power Game*, London, Macmillan, 1976.

2 Lee (1974).

3 Andrew Dunsire, 'Administrative Doctrine and Administrative Change' *Public Administration Bulletin* No. 15, December 1973, p. 39.

4 *Sunday Times*, 10 June 1973, p. 17.

5 Crossman (1975), p. 275. (His comment on Crosland is in fact reversed on p. 433.)

6 Crossman (1977) p. 172.

7 Quoted by Heclo and Wildavsky (1974) p. 136.

8 Quoted in Barber (1977) p. 52.

9 Bruce-Gardyne and Lawson, op. cit., p. 158.

10 Crossman (1975) p. 69.

11 See also ibid., p. 189.

12 Bruce-Gardyne and Lawson, op. cit., p. 165.

13 Quoted in M. Kogan (ed.) *The Politics of Education* London, Penguin Education Special, 1971, p. 129.

14 Quoted in A. Potter *Organized Groups in British National Politics* London, Faber, 1961, p. 215.

15 Crossman (1977) p. 926.

16 See Heclo and Wildavsky (1974) for a full account of the emergence of PESC.

17 Crossman (1976) p. 131.

18 Heclo and Wildavsky (1974) p. 205.

19 See Heclo and Wildavsky (1974); Godley (1976); Pollitt (1977); Wright (1977).

20 Bruce-Gardyne and Lawson, op. cit.

21 Sir R. Clarke, 'Parliament and Public Expenditure' *Political Quarterly* Vol. 44, No. 2, 1973.

22 See Bruce-Gardyne and Lawson, op. cit., p. 26.

23 Heclo and Wildavsky (1974) pp. 136–7.

24 Quoted in M. Spiers *Techniques and Public Administration* London, Fontana 1975, p. 85.

25 Quoted in M. Kogan (ed.) *The Politics of Education*, op. cit., p. 167.
26 Clarke (1971) p. 43.
27 Ibid., p. 43.
28 Ibid., p. 45.
29 See Heclo and Wildavsky (1974) p. 279.
30 Ibid., pp. 264–303.
31 Ibid., p. 24.
32 J. E. S. Hayward, 'National Aptitudes for Planning in Britain, France and Italy' *Government and Opposition* Vol. 9, No. 4, Autumn 1974, pp. 398–9.

CHAPTER 3   THE POLICY MACHINERY

1 For a discussion of this criticism see A. King, 'Modes of Executive–Legislative Relations: Great Britain, France and West Germany' *Legislative Studies Quarterly* No. 1, 1976. The 'Post-Parliamentary' term is used therein.
2 See D. Greenwood, 'Defence and National Priorities since 1945' in J. Baylis (ed.) *British Defence Policy in a Changing World* London, Croom Helm, 1977.
3 H. Heclo and A. Wildavsky *Private Government of Public Money* London, Macmillan, 1974, p. 22.
4 N. Johnson (1977) pp. 63–79.
5 Julian Critchly, MP, *The Times* 14 April 1978; see also W. Robson, 'The Constraints on British Government' *Political Quarterly* Vol. 44, 1973.
6 See R. Crossman *The Diaries of a Cabinet Minister* Vol. I, London, Hamilton and Cape, 1975, pp. 101, 168, 175.
7 For a US view see G. McConnell (1970) p. 7.
8 S. Beer, 'The British Legislature and the 'Problem of Mobilizing Consent' in B. Crick (ed.) *Essays in Reform* London, Oxford University Press, 1967, p. 85.
9 P. Sheriff, 'Outsiders in a Closed Career: the Example of the British Civil Service' *Public Administration* Vol. 50, 1972.
10 See Johnstone (1975).
11 Quoted in Bruce-Gardyne and Lawson (1976) p. 178.
12 D. Berry et al., 'Neddy – an Organizational metamorphosis' *Journal of Management Studies*, Vol. 11, February 1974.
13 W. Grant and D. Marsh, 'Tripartism: Reality or Myth' *Government and Opposition*, Vol. 12, No. 2, 1977.
14 While one hesitates to claim that there is consensus between industry and unions, Jack Jones' Dimbleby Lecture of 1977 demonstrated a recognition that there are mutual benefits in improved relationships. His theme was 'arbitration' instead of 'confrontation'. *The Listener* 8 December 1977.
15 Granada Television, *The State of the Nation*, p. 191.
16 Bruce-Gardyne & Lawson (1976) p. 179.
17 K. Newton *Second City Politics* Oxford, The Clarendon Press, 1976.
18 Anthony Barker and Michael Keating, 'Public Spirits: Amenity Societies and Others' in C. Crouch (ed.) *British Political Sociology Yearbook*, London, Croom Helm, 1977.
19 Kogan (1971) p. 44.
20 Ibid., p. 45.
21 J. B. Christoph, 'High Civil Servants and the Politics of Consensualism in Great Britain' in M. Dogan (ed.), *The Mandarins of Western Europe* New York, Wiley, 1975.
22 J. La Palombara (1964) p. 7.

23 E. Suleiman, *Politics, Power and Bureaucracy in France* Princeton, Princeton University Press, 1974.
24 J. J. Richardson, A. G. Jordan and R. H. Kimber, 'Lobbying, Administrative Reform and Policy Styles: The Case of Land Drainage' *Political Studies* Vol. 26, No. 1, March 1978.
25 D. N. Chester and F. M. G. Willson *The Organisation of British Central Government* London, Allen & Unwin, 1968, p. 17.
26 See W. J. M. Mackenzie, Harry Hanson Memorial Lecture, University of Leeds, March 1976, 'Public and Private Enterprise: a new phase'.
27 See Grant Jordan, 'Hiving-Off and Departmental Agencies' *Public Administration Bulletin* No. 21, August 1976.
28 Hood (1978) p. 32.
29 G. Wilson *Special Interests and Policy-Making* London, Wiley, 1977, p. 112.
30 Bruce L. R. Smith, 'The Public Use of the Private Sector' in *The New Political Economy* London, Macmillan, 1975, p. 1.
31 Reported upon in detail in Hague et al. (1975) pp. 333–5.
32 For a comparative view see N. Johnson *The Government of Western Germany* London, Pergamon, 1973 quoted in C. Hood, 'So you think you know what government departments are …?' *Public Administration Bulletin* No. 27, August 1978, p. 20.
33 *Hansard*, 6 February 1978.
34 In A. H. Hanson and B. Crick *The Commons in Transition* London, Fontana, 1970, pp. 91–2. Cited by W. J. M. Mackenzie, Harry Hanson Memorial Lecture, op. cit.
35 See also R. B. Kvavik *Interest Groups in Norwegian Politics* Oslo, Universitets-forlaget, 1976, p. 88.
36 P. Sheriff, op. cit.
37 *Municipal Review*, January 1976, No. 553, p. 283.
38 Crossman *The Diaries* Vol. III, 1977, pp. 732 and 745.
39 M. J. Barnett *The Politics of Legislation* London, Weidenfeld and Nicholson, 1969.
40 *The Observer* 12 September 1976.
41 See Chapman (1973).
42 See Rhodes (1975).
43 Cartwright (1975).
44 M. Kogan, 'The Plowden Committee' in Chapman (1973) p. 81.
45 Kogan and Packwood (1974).
46 A. G. Jordan and J. J. Richardson, 'Outside Committees and Policy-Making: The Central Advisory Water Committee' *Public Administration Bulletin* No. 24, August 1977.
47 See P. Giddings, 'Parliament, Boards and Autonomy: The Case of Agricultural Marketing Boards' *Public Administration* Vol. 53, 1975, p. 384.
48 See 'The Minister for Committee Jobs' *Guardian* 4 January 1978, based on a parliamentary answer of 22 November 1977, *Hansard*, Cols. 645–8.

CHAPTER 4   THE EMERGENCE OF ISSUES AND POLICIES

1 Rose (1976) p. 274.
2 Ibid., p. 262.
3 Schattschneider (1960).
4 Ibid., p. 20.

5   Ibid., p. 35.
6   Ibid., p. 71.
7   Ibid., p. 73.
8   Ibid.
9   Minutes, *Child Poverty Action Group*, 23 June 1972.
10 For a valuable analysis of the work of the CPAG, see M. McCarthy, *The Child Poverty Action Group*, Trent Polytechnic.
11 Jack L. Walker, 'Setting the Agenda in the US Senate: A Theory of Problem Selection' *British Journal of Political Science* Vol. 7, No. 4, 1977, p. 445.
12 See P. Bachrach and M. Baratz, 'The Two Faces of Power' *American Political Science Review* Vol. 56, No. 4, December 1962, pp. 947–52; Bachrach and Baratz (1970); K. Newton, 'Democracy, Community Power and Non-Decision Making' *Political Studies* Vol. 20, No. 4, December 1972, pp. 484–7.
    For a more sophisticated development of the Bachrach and Baratz concept, see S. Lukes *Power. A Radical View* London, Macmillan Studies in Sociology, 1974, where he develops a 'three-dimensional view' of power.
    For an interesting discussion of power in terms of contribution to outcomes (intended and unintended) see P. Georgiou, 'The Concept of Power: A Critique and an Alternative' *The Australian Journal of Politics and History* Vol. 23, No. 2, August 1977.
13 Bachrach and Baratz (1970) p. 7.
14 Ibid., p. 18.
15 Ibid., p. 57.
16 Crenson (1971).
17 Ibid., p. 36.
18 Ibid., pp. 35–82.
19 Ibid., p. 78.
20 Ibid., p. 80.
21 Ibid., p. 178.
22 S. E. Finer, 'The Political Power of Organized Labour' *Government and Opposition* Vol. 8, No. 4, October 1973, p. 397.
23 Ibid.
24 *The Times* 6 December 1977.
25 J. B. Sanderson, 'The National Smoke Abatement Society and the Clean Air Act (1956)', reprinted in R. Kimber and J. J. Richardson *Campaigning for the Environment* London, Routledge and Kegan Paul, 1974, p. 29.
26 Ibid., p. 30.
27 Ibid., p. 33.
28 Finer, op. cit., p. 393.
29 *The Times* 11 January 1978.
30 The following account is based on R. Kimber, et al., 'The Deposit of Poisonous Waste Act 1972: A Case of Government by Reaction?' *Public Law*, Autumn 1974, pp. 148–219.
31 In M. Kogan (ed.) *The Politics of Education* London, Penguin Education Special, 1971, p. 109.
32 See S. E. Finer *Anonymous Empire* 2nd ed., London, Pall Mall, 1966, p. 83.
33 R. Gregory, 'Conservation, Planning and Politics: Some Aspects of the Contemporary British Scene' *International Journal of Environmental Studies* Vol. 4, 1972, pp. 33–9.
34 Ibid., p. 38.
35 A. Downs (1973).
36 *The Times* 24 January 1978.
37 Ibid.

38   A. Downs *Inside Bureaucracy* Boston, Little Brown, 1967, p. 212.
39   R. Crossman *The Diaries of a Cabinet Minister* London, Hamilton and Cape, Vol. III, 1977, p. 125.
40   Kogan, op. cit., p. 29.
41   18 December 1969, quoted by Kogan, ibid.
42   Kogan, ibid., p. 138.
43   Dame Evelyn Sharp claims that Crossman could not get used to thousands of planning decisions being taken in his name by others: 'Every now and again he would explode and say, "It says here the Minister has approved ... I not only didn't approve, I wouldn't have approved"' *Sunday Times* October 1975.
44   Crossman *The Diaries* op. cit., Vol. I, 1975, p. 86.
45   C. J. Train, 'The Development of Criminal Policy Planning in The Home Office' *Public Administration* Vol. 55, 1977.
46   R. H. S. Crossman *Inside View* London, Jonathan Cape, 1972.
47   Ibid., p. 15.
48   See Bruce-Gardyne's interview with Sir Anthony Part in *The Director*, Vol. 27, 1975.
49   See J. Haines, *The Politics of Power* London, Coronet, 1977, p. 54.
50   J. Bruce-Gardyne and N. Lawson *The Power Game* London, Macmillan, 1976.

CHAPTER 5   THE PROCESSING OF ISSUES

1   This heading is borrowed from J. Bruce-Gardyne and N. Lawson *The Power Game* London, Macmillan, 1976, where, by a slip of the pen, they misquoted the title of Heclo and Wildavsky's *The Private Government of Public Money* as *The Private Management of Public Business* – in a sense a rather more apt title!
2   H. Heclo and A. Wildavsky *The Private Government of Public Money* London, Macmillan, 1974.
3   M. Kogan, *Education Policy-Making: A Study of Interest Groups* London, Allen and Unwin, 1975, p. 75.
4   J. Dearlove *The Politics of Policy in Local Government* London, Cambridge University Press, 1973, p. 168.
5   W. Grant 'Insider Groups, Outsider Groups and Interest Group Strategies in Britain', unpublished paper, 1977, p. 16. See also B. G. Peters, 'Insiders and Outsiders' *Administration and Society* Vol. 9, No. 2, 1977.
6   T. Lowi, 'American Business Public Policy' *World Politics* July 1964. See also R. H. Salisbury, 'The Analysis of Public Policy' in A. Ranney (ed.) *Political Science and Public Policy* Chicago, Markham, 1968.
7   A. Strauss et al. (1976). James Barber is also drawn to this idea in *Who Makes British Foreign Policy* Bletchley, Open University Press, 1976.
8   Quoted by Strauss et al. (1976) p. 103.
9   Heclo and Wildavsky, op. cit., p. xv.
10   J. P. Olsen *Organisational Participation in Government* University of Bergen, 1977.
11   March and Simon (1958).
12   Lijphart (1968).
13   From A. D. Robinson *Dutch Organized Agriculture in International Politics* The Hague, Nijhoff, 1961, p. 37.
14   See W. Grant and D. Marsh *The CBI* London, Hodder and Stoughton, 1977.
15   For a discussion of the related concepts of network and linkage in public

administration see J. Friend and P. S. Spink, 'Networks in Public Administration' *Linkage* Vol. 3, July 1978.

16 CPRS (1977) p. 21.
17 See W. Robson, 'The Central Domination of Local Government' *Political Quarterly* Vol. 4, No. 1, 1933.
18 See, e.g., N. Boaden *Urban Policy-Making* Cambridge, Cambridge University Press, 1971.
19 See Lord Redcliffe-Maud and B. Wood *English Local Government Reformed* London, Oxford University Press, 1974, p. 121.
20 The CCLGF machinery is described more fully in T. H. Caulcott, 'The Consultative Council on Local Government Finance' *Telescope* November 1977.
21 For example P. Self and H. Storing (1962) and G. K. Wilson (1977). See also P. Self and H. Storing, 'The Farmer and the State' in R. Kimber and J. J. Richardson (eds) *Pressure Groups in Britain* London, J. M. Dent, 1974 with EEC entry, an 'Annual Review' replaces the 'Price Review'.
22 'The Farmer and the State', op. cit., p. 61.
23 See Wilson (1977) p. 43.
24 Ibid., p. 37.
25 Ibid., p. 38.
26 Ibid., p. 45.
27 Ibid.
28 See W. Grant (1978).

CHAPTER 6   LEGISLATION, DECISIONS AND THE ROLE OF GROUPS

1 For details see P. Jenkins *The Battle of Downing Street* London, Charles Knight, 1970.
2 G. K. Wilson *Special Interests and Policy-making* London, Wiley, 1977, p. 170.
3 See *The Times* 9 March 1978 (our emphasis).
4 P. Self, 'Are We Worse Governed?' *New Society* 19 May 1977, p. 334.
5 Ibid., p. 332.
6 Ibid.
7 S. A. Walkland and M. Ryle (1977) p. 239.
8 Ibid., p. 241.
9 Ibid., p. 244.
10 J. A. G. Griffith (1974) p. 197.
11 Ibid.
12 Ibid., p. 203.
13 Ibid., p. 207.
14 Jenkins, op. cit., p. 153.
15 For details see R. H. Kimber and J. J. Richardson, *Campaigning for the Environment*, London, Routledge and Kegan Paul, 1974, pp. 165–211.
16 For a discussion of all-party committees see J. J. Richardson and R. H. Kimber, 'The Role of All-Party Committees in the House of Commons' *Parliamentary Affairs* Autumn 1972.
17 S. E. Finer *Anonymous Empire* 2nd ed., London, Pall Mall, 1966, p. 93.
18 See K. Hindell and M. Simms, 'How the Abortion Lobby Worked' in R. H. Kimber and J. J. Richardson (eds) *Pressure Groups in Britain* London, Dent, 1974, p. 161.
19 Ibid., p. 163.
20 See Kimber and Richardson, *Campaigning for the Environment* op. cit., p. 142.

21 See the 14th and 15th sittings of the standing committee on 3 April 1973, cols. 693–768.
22 Finer, op. cit., p. 75.
23 See B. Hogwood, 'The Politics of Industrial Change: Government Involvement in the UK Shipbuilding Industry 1959–73', PhD thesis, University of Keele, 1977, p. 305.
24 Brian Smith *Policy-Making in British Government* London, Martin Robertson, 1976, p. 84.

CHAPTER 7   GROUPS AND THE IMPLEMENTATION PROCESS

 1 Hood (1976) p. 6.
 2 Ibid., p. 9.
 3 Ibid., p. 10.
 4 See Leslie Chapman *Your Disobedient Servants* London, Chatto and Windus, 1978.
 5 G. Tullock *The Vote Motive* Hobart Paper No. 9, London, Institute of Economic Affairs, 1976, pp. 135–6.
 6 Pressman and Wildavsky (1973) p. xvi.
 7 Ibid., p. 109.
 8 A. King, 'Overload: Problems of Governing in the 1970's' *Political Studies* Vol. 23, Nos. 2–3, June/September 1975, p. 290.
 9 Hood (1976) p. 190.
10 *The Times* 22 November 1977.
11 G. W. Jones, 'The Eclipse of Fulton' *New Society* 17 August 1972.
12 See J. J. Richardson *The Policy-Making Process* London, Routledge and Kegan Paul, 1969, p. 65.
13 A. Shonfield *Modern Capitalism* London, Oxford University Press, 1965, p. 94.
14 For a full discussion see J. J. Richardson, A. G. Jordan and R. H. Kimber, 'Lobbying, Administrative Reform and Policy Styles: The Case of Land Drainage' *Political Studies* Vol. 26, No. 1, March 1978, pp. 47–64.
15 S. E. Finer *Anonymous Empire* 2nd ed., London, Pall Mall, 1966, p. 24.
16 J. W. Grove *Government and Industry in Britain* London, Longmans, 1962, p. 56.
17 Ibid., p. 61.
18 See 'More state aid for voluntary organizations urged', *The Times* 23 November 1977.
19 *The Times* 16 November 1977.
20 *50 Million Volunteers* London, HMSO, 1972, p. 27.
21 Ibid., p. 29.
22 For a full account of the work of CTNW, see R. H. Kimber and J. J. Richardson, 'The Integration of Groups in the Policy Process: A Case Study' *Local Government Studies* April 1977, pp. 31–47.
23 W. Grant and D. Marsh *The CBI* London, Hodder and Stoughton, 1977, p. 188.
24 Ibid., p. 191.
25 Ibid., p. 192.
26 Ibid., p. 196.
27 See Treasury *Economic Progress Report* No. 96, March 1978, p. 4.
28 Ibid., p. 6.
29 See *The Times* 2 February 1978.
30 Pressman and Wildavsky (1973) p. 143.

CHAPTER 8   PRESSURE GROUPS AND THE POLITICAL SYSTEM

1   Although our treatment is deliberately broad, we do not pursue all connections that seem relevant – such as 'post-industrial' writings or the 'end of ideology' debate.
2   Quoted in R. T. McKenzie, 'Parties, Pressure Groups and the Political Process' *Political Quarterly* Vol. 29, 1958.
3   Eckstein (1960).
4   S. Beer, 'Pressure Groups and Parties in Britain' *American Political Science Review* Vol. 50, No. 1, 1956, p. 7.
5   Quoted in R. T. McKenzie, op. cit.
6   F. Stacey *The Government of Modern Britain* Oxford, Clarendon Press, 1965.
7   See *Modern British Politics* London, Faber, 2nd ed., 1966; 'The Representation of Interests in British Government' *American Political Science Review* Vol. 51, No. 3, 1957; 'Pressure Groups and Parties in Britain' op. cit.
8   'Pressure Groups and Parties', p. 7.
9   *Modern British Politics*, Ch. XII.
10 R. Dahl *Pluralistic Democracy in the United States* Chicago, Rand McNally, 1967, p. 325. It is, of course, too simple to label Beer as a pluralist, but Chapter XIII of *Modern British Politics* can be seen as an important extension of pluralist thought.
11 T. J. Lowi *The End of Liberalism* New York, Norton, 1969, p. x.
12 Ibid., p. 8.
13 See P. Selznick *TVA and the Grass Roots* Berkeley, University of California Press, 1946; M. Bernstein *Regulating Business by Independent Commission* Princeton, Princeton University Press, 1955.
14 London, Oxford University Press.
15 N. Harris *Competition and the Corporate Economy Theory* London, Methuen, 1972.
16 R. A. Pahl and J. Winkler, 'The Coming Corporatism' *New Society* 10 October 1974.
17 J. Winkler, 'Keynes and the Coming Corporatism' *The Spectator* 8 January 1977, p. 15.
18 Schmitter (1975) p. 9.
19 H. Eckstein *Division and Cohesion in a Democracy: A Study of Norway* Princeton, Princeton University Press, 1966; S. Rokkan, 'Numerical Democracy and Corporate Pluralism' in R. Dahl (ed.) *Political Oppositions in Western Democracies* New Haven and London, Yale University Press, 1966.
20 Op. cit., p. 106.
21 Ibid., p. 107.
22 J. P. Olsen *Organisational Participation in Government*, University of Bergen, 1977.
23 R. B. Kvavik *Interest Groups in Norwegian Politics* Oslo, Universitetsforlaget, 1976, p. 15.
24 Ibid., p. 123.
25 Thom Christensen and Rolf Rønning, 'Organisational Participation in Governmental Politics', Paper prepared for European Consortium for Political Reseach Workship on Interest Group Strategy, 1977.
26 N. Elvander, 'Interest Groups in Sweden' *The Annals*, May 1974.
27 For discussion of Germany see J. Wolfe, 'Corporatism in German Political Life' in M. Heisler. (ed.) *Politics in Europe* New York, David MacKay, 1974.
28 E. Suleiman *Politics, Power and Bureaucracy in France* Princeton, Princeton University Press, 1974, p. 230.

29 Quoted in Leon Dion, 'The Politics of Consultation' *Government and Opposition* Vol. 8, No. 3, 1973.
30 Op. cit., p. 329.
31 Ibid., p. 330.
32 Ibid., p. 344.
33 A. L. Lijphart *Democracy in Plural Societies* New Haven and London, Yale University Press, 1977.
34 See Val R. Lorwin, 'Segmented Pluralism' *Comparative Politics* Vol. 3, No. 2, 1971; R. P. Stiefbold, 'Segmented Pluralism and Consociational Democracy in Austria: Problems of Political Stability and Change' in Heisler *Politics in Europe* op. cit.; H. Daadler and G. A. Irwin, 'Interests and Institutions in the Netherlands' *The Annals* May 1974.
35 Daadler and Irwin, op. cit., p. 62.
36 Kvavik, op. cit., p. 11.
37 T. Ishida, 'Interest Groups under a Semipermanent Government Party: The Case of Japan' *The Annals* May 1974, p. 1.
38 Elvander, op. cit., p. 27.
39 Daadler and Irwin, op. cit., p. 58.
40 Beer, 'Pressure Groups and Parties in Britain', op. cit., p. 3.
41 Quoted in Heisler, op. cit., p. 50.
42 For an attempt at such a model see M. O. Heisler and R. B. Kvavik, 'Patterns of European Politics: The "European Polity" Model' in Heisler *Politics in Europe* op. cit., pp. 27–89.

CHAPTER 9   COSTS, BENEFITS AND THE DEVELOPMENT OF THE GROUP SYSTEM

1   T. Caulcott in Centre for Studies in Social Policy *The Corporate State – Reality or Myth* London, CSSP, 1976, p. 134.
2   S. E. Finer *Anonymous Empire* 2nd ed., London, Pall Mall, 1966, p. 56.
3   R. T. Mckenzie in R. Kimber and J. J. Richardson *Pressure Groups in Britain* London, Dent, 1974, p. 286.
4   Quoted in M. Kogan (ed.) *The Politics of Education*, London, Penguin, 1971, p. 90.
5   J. E. S. Hayward (1974).
6   Ibid., pp. 405 and 407.
7   A. Shonfield *Modern Capitalism* London, Oxford University Press, 1965, p. 94.
8   Hayward (1974) p. 399.
9   Johan P. Olsen, 'Public Policy-Making and Theories of Organisational Choice' *Scandinavian Political Studies* Vol. 7, 1972, p. 2.
10 Ibid.
11 Ibid., pp. 22–3.
12 Ibid., p. 11.
13 P. Gundelach *Grass Roots Organizations: Can they be subversive?* Grenoble, European Consortium for Political Research, 1978, p. 7.
14 B. Jacobs *Local Level Interest Group Activity* Research Paper, University of Keele, 1978.
15 Olsen, op. cit., pp. 17–19.
16 Ibid., p. 69.
17 Ibid., p. 71.
18 Ibid.

19 See W. F. Averyt *Agropolitics in the European Community* New York, Praeger, 1977, p. 3.
20 Ibid., p. 78.
21 See 'Whitehall Denies Trend towards Corporatism' *The Times* 10 January 1978.
22 See 'Government Limits' *The Times* 15 May 1978, p. 14.
23 'In a Nationalised Piranha Bowl' *The Times* 15 May 1978, p. 16.
24 Sir Ronald McIntosh, quoted in *The Times* 29 December 1977.
25 See *The Times Business News* 12 May 1978.
26 See 'Pulling the Pressure Groups Together' *The Times* 21 February 1978.
27 See V. Bogdanor, 'A House of Industry'. in CSSP *The Corporate State* op. cit.
28 Ibid., pp. 154 and 155.
29 G. Ionescu (1975).
30 Ibid., p. 213.
31 Olsen, op. cit., p. 49.
32 See A. Lijphart *The Politics of Accommodation* Berkeley, University of California Press, 1968.
33 Hans Slomp *Functional Political Participation in Dutch Liberal Corporatism* Grenoble, European Consortium for Political Research, 1978, p. 12.
34 J. M. Wiltse *John C. Calhoun, Sectionalist 1840–1850* New York, Bobbs-Merrill, 1951, p. 417.
35 Quoted by Wiltse, Ibid.
36 Ibid.
37 Ibid., p. 419.
38 S. E. Finer in CSSP *The Corporate State* op. cit., p. 141.
39 H. Eckstein *Division and Cohesion in Democracy: A Study of Norway* Princeton, Princeton University Press, 1966, p. 191.
40 O. Ruin, 'Participatory Democracy and Corporativism' *Scandinavian Political Studies* Vol. 9, 1974, p. 178.
41 Ibid.
42 See J. E. S. Hayward, 'Institutional Inertia and Political Impetus in France and Britain' *European Journal of Political Research* Vol. 4, 1976, pp. 341–359.
43 T. Lowi, 'Interest Groups and the Consent to Govern: Getting the People Out, For What?' *The Annals* May 1974, p. 100.

Select Bibliography

This bibliography is not comprehensive but it does indicate the kind of works that support (and in some cases dissent from) our claims. The various sources are grouped following the pattern of our book – but clearly certain important sources are relevant throughout.

CHAPTER 1

Group Theory

BENTLEY, A. F. (1967) *The Process of Government* (ed. P. Odegard) Harvard, Belknap Press.

ECKSTEIN, H. (1963) 'Group Theory and the Comparative Study of Interest Groups' in H. Eckstein and D. Apter (eds.) *Comparative Politics* London, Free Press of Glencoe.

GOLEMBIEWSKI, R. T. (1960) The Groups Basis of Politics: Notes on Analysis and Development' *American Political Science Review* Vol. 54, No. 4.

HAGAN, C. B. (1958) 'The Group in Political Science' in R. Young (ed.) *Approaches to the Study of Politics* London, Atlantic Books.

HERRING, E. P. (1929) *Group Representation Before Congress*, Baltimore, Johns Hopkins Press.

LATHAM, E. (1965) *The Group Basis of Politics* New York, Octagon Books.

TRUMAN, D. (1971) *The Governmental Process* New York, Knopf, 2nd edition.

'Overload'

BRITTAN, S. (1977) *The Economic Consequences of Democracy* London, Temple Smith.

DOUGLAS, J. (1976) 'The Overloaded Crown' *British Journal of Political Science* Vol. 6, No. 4.

KING, A., (1975) 'Overload: Problems of Governing in the 1970's' *Political Studies* Vol. 23, Nos. 2–3, June/September.

Policy-making models

BAILEY, J. J. and O'CONNOR, R. J. (1975) 'Operationalising Incrementalism: Measuring the Muddles' *Public Administration Review* Vol. 35, January/February.

DROR, Y. (1968) *Public Policy Making Re-examined* San Francisco, Chandler.

DROR, Y. (1964) 'Muddling Through – "Science" or Inertia' *Public Administration Review* Vol. 24, September.

LINDBLOM, C. E. (1965) *The Intelligence of Democracy* New York, Free Press.

LINDBLOM, C. E. (1959) 'The Science of Muddling Through' *Public Administration Review*, Vol. 19, Spring.

OLSEN, J. P. (1972) 'Public Policy-Making and Theories of Organisational Choice' *Scandinavian Political Studies* Vol. 7. (garbage-can model)

SELF, P. (1975) *Econocrats and the Policy Process* London, Macmillan.

SELF, P. (1977) *Administration Theories and Politics* London, Allen and Unwin, 2nd edition.

SIMON, H. (1976) *Administrative Behavior* New York, Free Press, 3rd edition.

CHAPTER 2

Central Policy-Making

BARBER, J. P. (1977) *Who Makes British Foreign Policy* Milton Keynes, The Open University.

CROSSMAN, R. (1972) *Inside View* London, Cape.

CROSSMAN, R. (1975–7) *The Diaries of a Cabinet Minister* Vols I–III, London, Hamish Hamilton and Cape.

DAADLER, H. (1964) *Cabinet Reform in Britain 1914–1963* London, Oxford University Press.

HEADEY, B. (1974) *British Cabinet Ministers* London, Allen and Unwin.

LEE, J. M. (1974) 'Central Capability and Established Practice' in B. Chapman and A. Potter (eds) *WJMM: Political Questions* Manchester, Manchester University Press.

MACKINTOSH, J. P. (1977) *The British Cabinet* London, Stevens and Sons, 3rd edition.

Departmental pluralism/bureaucratic competition

DOGAN, M. and ROSE, R. (1971) *The Mandarins of Western Europe* London, Macmillan.

DOWNS, A. (1967) *Inside Bureaucracy* Boston, Little Brown.

MELTSNER, A. J. (1976) *Policy Analysts in the Bureaucracy* London, University of California Press.

NISKANEN, W. A. (1971) *Bureaucracy and Representative Government* Chicago, Aldine-Atherton.

TULLOCK, G. (1976) *The Vote Motive*, Hobart Paper No. 9, London, Institute of Economic Affairs.

PESC and PAR

CLARKE, Sir R. (1971) *New Trends in Government* Civil Service College Studies No. 1, London, HMSO.

EAST, R. J. (1973) 'Improving Government Expenditure Decisions through Programme Analysis and Review' *Long Range Planning*, Vol. 6, No. 1.

GODLEY, W. (1976) 'The Measurement and Control of Public Expenditure' *Economic Policy Review*, No. 2.

GOLDMAN, Sir S. (1973) *The Developing System of Public Expenditure Control*, Civil Service College Studies No. 2, London, HMSO.

HECLO, H. and WILDAVSKY, A. (1974) *The Private Government of Public Money* London and Basingstoke, Macmillan.

POLLIT, C. (1977) 'The Public Expenditure Survey 1961–72' *Public Administration* Vol. 55, Summer.

WRIGHT, M. (1977) 'Public Expenditure in Britain: The Crisis of Control' *Public Administration* Vol. 55, Summer.

CHAPTER 3

Discussions of the British policy machinery

BEER, S. (1966) *Modern British Politics* London, Faber, 2nd edition.
HALL, P., LAND, H., PARKER, R. and WEBB, A. (1975) *Change, Choice and Conflict in Social Policy* London, Heinemann.
JOHNSON, N. (1977) *In Search of the Constitution* Oxford, Pergamon Press.
ROSE, R. (1976) *The Problem of Party Government* Harmondsworth, Pelican.
SMITH, B. (1976) *Policy-Making in British Government* London, Martin Robertson.

Consultation: examples of British policy-making

BARNETT, M. J. (1969) *The Politics of Legislation: The Rent Act 1957* London, Weidenfeld and Nicolson.
BRUCE-GARDYNE, J. and LAWSON, N. (1976) *The Power Game* London, Macmillan.
GRANT, W. and MARSH, D. (1977) *The CBI* London, Hodder and Stoughton.
JOHNSTONE, D. (1975) *A Tax Shall be Charged*, Civil Service Studies No. 1, London, HMSO.
KOGAN, M. (ed.) (1971) *The Politics of Education* Penguin Education Special.
KOGAN, M. (1975) *Education Policy-Making* London, Allen and Unwin.
WOOD, B. (1976) *The Process of Local Government Reform* London, Allen and Unwin.

Group subgovernment/clientelism

LA PALOMBARA, J. (1964) *Interest Groups in Italian Politics*, Princeton, Princeton University Press.
LOWI, T. J. (1969) *The End of Liberalism* New York, Norton and Co.
MCCONNELL, G. (1970) *Private Power and American Democracy* New York, Vintage Books.
WILSON, G. K. (1977) 'Are Department Secretaries Really a President's Natural Enemies' *British Journal of Political Science*, Vol. 7, Pt. 3.

Pragmatic organisation and policy

GANZ, G. (1977) *Government and Industry* London, Professional Books.
HAGUE, D. C., MACKENZIE, W. J. M. and BARKER, A. (1975) *Public Policy and Private Interests*, London, Macmillan.
HOOD, C. C. (1974) 'Government by Other Means: The Grants Economy and the Contract State' in B. Chapman and A. Potter (eds) *WJMM Political Questions* Manchester, Manchester University Press.
HOOD, C. C. (1978) 'Keeping the Centre Small: Explanations of Agency Type' *Political Studies* Vol. 26, No. 1.

Committees

CARTWRIGHT, T. J. (1975) *Royal Commissions and Departmental Committees in Britain* London, Hodder and Stoughton.
CHAPMAN, R. (ed.) (1973) *The Role of Commissions in Policy Making* London, Unwin University Books.
GIDDINGS, P. (1974) *Marketing Boards and Ministers* Westmead, Saxon House.
KOGAN, M. and PACKWOOD, T. (1974) *Advisory Councils and Committees in Education* London, Routledge.
RHODES, G. (1975) *Committees of Inquiry*, London, Allen and Unwin.

CHAPTER 4

The emergenge of issues

BACHRACH, P. and BARATZ, M. S. (1970) *Power and Poverty: Theory and Practice* New York, Oxford University Press.
COBB, R. W. and ELDER, C. (1975) *Participation in American Politics: The Dynamics of Agenda Building* Baltimore, Johns Hopkins University Press.
CRENSON, M. (1971) *The Un-Politics of Air Pollution* Baltimore, Johns Hopkins Press.
DOWNS, A. (1973) 'Up and Down with Ecology' in J. Bains *Environmental Decay* Boston, Little Brown.
SCHATTSCHNEIDER, E. E. (1960) *The Semi-Sovereign People: A Realist's View of Democracy in America* New York, Holt.
ROSE, R. (1976) 'On the Priorities of Government: A Developmental Analysis of Public Policies' *European Journal of Political Research* Vol. 4, 1976.

CHAPTER 5

The negotiated order – the rules of the game

BRIAN, BARRY (1975) Review Article 'Political Accommodation and Consociational Democracy' *British Journal of Political Science* Vol. 5, Part 4.
LIJPHART, A. L. (1968) *The Politics of Accommodation, Pluralism and Democracy in the Netherlands* Berkeley and Los Angeles, University of California Press.
MARCH, J. and SIMON, H. (1958) *Organisations* New York and London, Wiley.
STRAUSS, A., SCHATZMAN, L., EHRLICH, D., BUCHER, R. and ABSHIN, S. (1976) 'The Hospital and its Negotiated Order' (1963) reprinted in F. Castles et al. (eds) *Decisions, Organisations, and Society*, Penguin in association with the Open University Press, 2nd edition.
STRAUSS, A. (1978) *Negotiations Values, Contexts, Processes and Social Order* London, Jossey-Bass.

The local government examples

BOADEN, N. (1971) *Urban Policy-Making* Cambridge, Cambridge University Press.
CENTRAL POLICY REVIEW STAFF (1977) *Relations between Central Government and Local Authorities* London, HMSO.
'LAYFIELD' (1976) *Report of the Committee of Enquiry on Local Government Finance* London, HMSO, Cmnd. 6453.
RHODES, R. A. W. (1976) 'Central–Local Relations' in Layfield Report, London, HMSO, Cmnd. 6453, Appendix 6.

The agriculture case

AVERYT, W. F. (1977) *Agropolitics in the European Community* New York and London, Praeger.
GRANT, W. (1978) 'Industrialists and Farmers: British Interests and the European Community' *West European Politics* Vol. 1, No. 1.
SELF, P. and STORING, H. (1962) *The State and the Farmer* London, Allen and Unwin.
WILSON, G. K. (1977) *Special Interests and Policy Making* London, Wiley.

CHAPTER 6

Legislation

GRIFFITH, J. A. G. (1974) *Parliamentary Scrutiny of Government Bills* London, Allen and Unwin.

WALKLAND, S. and RYLE, M. (1977) *The Commons in the 1970s* London, Fontana.
WALKLAND, S. (1968) *The Legislative Process in Great Britain* London, Allen and Unwin.

CHAPTER 7

Implementation

DUNSIRE, A. (1979) *Implementation in a Bureaucracy* and *Control in a Bureaucracy* London, Martin Robertson.
HOOD, C. C. (1976) *The Limits of Administration* London, Wiley.
PRESSMAN, J. L. and WILDAVSKY, A. (1973) *Implementation* Berkeley, University of California Press.
WEISS, C. H. (1972) *Evaluation Research* Englewood Cliffs, Prentice Hall.

CHAPTER 8

British pluralists

ECKSTEIN, H. (1960) *Pressure Groups Politics: The Case of the British Medical Association* London, Allen and Unwin.
FINER, S. (1958) *Anonymous Empire* London, Pall Mall.
STEWART, J. D. (1958) *British Pressure Groups* Oxford, Clarendon Press.
WILSON, H. H. (1961) *Pressure Groups: The Campaign for Commercial Television in England* London, Seeker and Warburgh.

American post-pluralists

GREENBERG, E. S. (1974) *Serving the Few: Corporate Capitalism and the Bias of Government Policy* New York, Wiley.
MILLER, A. S. (1976) *The Modern Corporate State* London, Greenwood Press.
MINTZ, M. and COHEN, J. S. (1971) *America Inc.* New York, The Dial Press.
ZEIGLER, L. H. and DYE, T. (1975) *The Irony of Democracy* 3rd edition, Belmont, Duxbury Press.

British corporate state

CENTRE FOR STUDIES IN SOCIAL POLICY (1976) *The Corporate State – Reality or Myth? A Symposium*, London, CSSP.
CROUCH, C. (1977) *Class Conflict and the Industrial Relations Crisis* New York, Humanities Press.
SCHMITTER, P. C. (1975) *Corporatism and Public Policy in Authoritarian Portugal* London and Beverly Hills, Sage Contemporary Political Sociology Series, Vol. 1.
WILENSKY, H. L. (1976) *The New Corporatism, Centralisation and the Welfare State* London and Beverly Hills, Sage Contemporary Political Sociology Series, Vol. 2.
WINKLER, J. T. (1975) 'Law, Society and Economy: The 1975 Industry Act' *British Journal of Law and Society* Vol. 2, No. 2.
WINKLER, J. T. (1976) 'Corporatism' *European Journal of Sociology* Vol. 1, No. 1.

CHAPTER 9

Costs, Benefits and Development of the Group System

DION, L. (1973) 'The Politics of Consultation' *Government and Opposition* Vol. 8, No. 3.
HAYWARD, J. E. S. (1974) 'National Aptitudes for Planning in Britain, France and Italy' *Government and Opposition* Vol. 9, No. 4.

IONESCU, G. (1977) *Centripetal Politics: Government and the New Centres of Power* London, Hart-Davis.

OLSEN, J. P. (1977) *Organisational Participation in Government* University of Bergen.

OLSEN, M. (1967) *The Logic of Collective Action* Cambridge, Mass., Harvard University Press.

PETERS, B. G. (1977) 'Insiders and Outsiders: The Politics of Pressure Groups Influence on Bureaucracy' *Administration and Society* Vol. 9, No. 2.

PETERS, B. G. (1978) *The Politics of Bureaucracy: A Comparative Perspective* London, Longmans.

SMITH, T. (1972) *Anti-Politics: Consensus, Reform and Protest* London, C. Knight.

WOOTON, G. (1978) *Pressure Politics in Contemporary Britain* Lexington, Lexington Books.

Index

Abortion Law Reform Association (ALRA), 11, 17, 126, 135
'Accommodation', 40, 103–105, 158, 159, 172, 188, 191
Agenda setting, *see* issue emergence
Agriculture, 99, 113–115, 150, 182

Bachrach, P. (and Baratz, M. S.), 81, 83
Baratz, M. S., *see* Bachrach, P.
Beer, S., 45, 158, 159
Bentley, A. F., 3, 4, 8, 17, 24, 189
Boyle, E. Sir, 30, 89, 94, 173
British Medical Association (BMA), 15, 17
Bruce-Gardyne, J., (and Lawson, N.), 25n, 27n, 28n, 33n, 53, 95, 96

Castle, B., 26, 31
Central Policy Review Staff (CPRS), 36, 37, 106, 119
Child Poverty Action Group (CPAG), 7n, 80
Civic Trust, 6, 67, 127
Classification
 sectional/promotional groups, 17
 legitimised/non-legitimised, 99
 helpful/unhelpful, 99
 insider/outsider, 99
Clarke, R. Sir, 33n, 37–39
Clean Air Act 1956, 85, 86
Clientelism, 30, 31, 55–57
Common Cause, 8
Confederation of British Industry, (CBI), 10, 13, 17, 51–53, 121, 149, 151, 177, 180
Conservative Party
 and business experience, 65
 and devolution, 17
 and economic planning, 92
 and incomes policy, 151, 183
 and industrial relations, 4, 143

and restrictive trade practices, 144
and road haulage, 92, 134
and tripartism, 50
Consultation, 6, 44–53, 57, 83, 98, 107, 109, 127, 133, 174, 180
Corporatism, 161–163
Cristoph, J. B., 55
Crosland, C. A. R., 26, 36
Crossman, R. H. S., 25n, 26, 28, 30, 32, 43, 66, 93–95
Crenson, M., 81, 82

Dearlove, J., 99
Departmental pluralism, 28
Deposit of Poisonous Waste Act, 87–88, 147
Downs, A.,
 and issue emergence, 90–91
 and policy space, 93

Eckstein, H., 15, 158
Education issue, 30, 54, 72, 89, 141, 173
Environmental Issue, 5, 6, 11, 77, 83, 86, 88–91, 142, 182
Finer, S., 7, 14, 84, 86, 93, 125, 146, 186
Formulation (of policies), 4, 136
Friends of the Earth, 83, 86

Grant, W., 99
Grant, W. and Marsh, D., 50, 152
Gregory, R., 89
Griffith, J. A. G., 122–124
Group theory, 3, 18
Group Subgovernment, 53–55

Harris, N., 161
Hayward, J. F. S., 40, 175, 189, 190
Heclo, H. and Wildavsky, A., 25n, 32–34, 39, 42, 98, 99, 101, 105
Herring, E. P., 24, 159
Hood, C., 58, 60n, 137, 138

Implementation (of policies), 137–153, 176
Incrementalism, 18–24, 29, 35, 36, 40, 189
  partisan mutual adjustment, 22
  successive limited comparisons, 21, 22
Issue emergence, 77–96

Johnstone, D., 45–46

King, A., 7, 14, 140
Kogan, M., 54, 72, 89, 99
Kvavik, R. B., 164, 165

Labour Party
  and blood sports, 17
  and Cabinet Government, 26
  and Child Benefit Bill, 6, 7
  and housing, 136, 143
  and incomes policy, 4, 59
  and industrial relations, 5, 91, 119
  and nationalisation, 91, 135
La Palombara, J., 55
Latham, E., 4, 10, 15, 16, 24
Lawson, N., *see* Bruce-Gardyne, J.
Lijphart, A. L., 40, 103–5, 168
Lowi, T., 100, 160, 191
Lindblom, C. E., 19–24
Local Government, 65, 105–113, 108, 109, 116, 121, 143

McKenzie, R. T., 13n, 173
MacKenzie, W. J. M., 8, 61n

National Coal Board (NCB), 11, 119
National Economic Development Organisation (NEDO), 49–51, 141, 152, 183, 184, 191
National Farmers' Union (NFU), 10, 15, 48, 113–115, 120, 150, 173
'Negotiated Order', 101–103, 158

Odegard, P., 7, 15
Olsen, J. P., 164, 177–179, 185

Pahl, R. A. and Winkler, J., 161, 162
Parliament, 41, 42, 17, 52, 83, 88, 117, 118, 136, 184, 185

Plowden Committee, 29
Policy Cabinet, 27, 36
Policy Communities, 44, 73, 74, 174
Pressman, J. L. and Wildavsky, A., 139, 152
Programme Analysis and Review (PAC), 36–39
Public Expenditure Survey Committee, 31–35, 36, 37, 52
Public Citizen, 7

'Rational' decision making, 19–21
Retail Price Maintenance, 95, 96
Rokkan, S., 18, 164, 186
Rose, R., 78

Schattschneider, E. E., 79, 80
Schmitter, P., 163, 166
Self, P., 21n, 121
Shonfield, A., 161
Simon, H., 18–24
  behaviour alternative model, 20, 22
  satisficing, 21
Society for the Protection of the Unborn Child (SPUC), 11
Strauss *et al.*, 101–103
Suleiman, E., 167, 168

Thatcher, M., 27, 183
Thorneycroft, Peter, 27
Trades Union Congress (TUC), 4, 7, 12, 13, 17, 51, 89, 121, 179, 180, 183
Transport 2000, 9, 180
Tripartism, 48–53, 166, 175, 183, 191
Truman, D., 8–14, 24

Walker, P., 31
Walkland, S., 121, 122
Water example, 31, 46–48, 54, 56, 94, 109–113, 128–134, 145, 146, 190
Wildavsky, A., *see* Heclo and Wildavsky, *see* Pressman and Wildavsky
Wilson, G. K., 59, 114, 115
Wing Airport Resistance Association, 9, 124, 125, 134
Winkler, J., *see* R. A. Pahl